INNOVATING
ANALYTICS

INNOVATING ANALYTICS

**WORD of MOUTH INDEX—
HOW THE NEXT GENERATION
of NET PROMOTER
CAN INCREASE SALES
and DRIVE BUSINESS RESULTS**

LARRY FREED

WILEY

Published by John Wiley & Sons, Inc., Hoboken, New Jersey.
Published simultaneously in Canada.

For general information about our other products and services, please contact our Customer Care Department within the United States at (800) 762-2974, outside the United States at (317) 572-3993 or fax (317) 572-4002.

Wiley publishes in a variety of print and electronic formats and by print-on-demand. Some material included with standard print versions of this book may not be included in e-books or in print-on-demand. If this book refers to media such as a CD or DVD that is not included in the version you purchased, you may download this material at http://booksupport.wiley.com. For more information about Wiley products, visit www.wiley.com.

Library of Congress Cataloging-in-Publication Data:

Freed, Larry.
    Innovating analytics : word of mouth index—how the next generation of net promoter can increase sales and drive business results / Larry Freed.
       pages cm
    Includes index.
       ISBN 978-1-118-77948-4 (cloth); ISBN 978-1-118-77949-1 (ebk);
    ISBN 978-1-118-77950-7 (ebk)
       1. Consumer satisfaction. 2. Marketing research—Statistical methods. 3. Word-of-mouth-advertising. 4. Internet marketing. I. Title.
    HF5415.335.F74   2014
    658.8'72—dc23
                                                                        2013025416

Printed in the United States of America
10 9 8 7 6 5 4 3 2 1

Contents

Introduction

In 2006, Pulitzer Prize winner Thomas Friedman of the *New York Times* wrote an international best seller titled *The World Is Flat* in which he analyzed the accelerating pace of globalization. The title encapsulated the idea that the world had increasingly become a level playing field in terms of commerce: new companies could rise to prominence in the blink of an eye and could fail as quickly. The title also described the shift required by countries, companies, and individuals to remain competitive in a global market where historic advantages were becoming increasingly irrelevant.

Friedman outlined 10 flatteners of the world, including the fall of the Berlin Wall, the development of Netscape, and the rise of search engines like Google. The tenth flattener was the most potent of them all: the "steroids," which involved digital, virtual, mobile, and personal. Friedman showed that all analog content and processes (from entertainment, to photography, to word processing) were being digitized and therefore they could be shaped, manipulated, and transmitted. The virtual could be performed at high speed with total ease, the mobile could be executed anywhere and anytime, and the personal could be performed by anyone—ergo more and more flatteners, such as the iPhone and iPad, Twitter, Facebook, Yelp, and on and on.

These steroids have greatly influenced the field that I study, the customer experience. To adjust Friedman's metaphor to this area, I would describe it as *The World Has Turned Upside Down*. There has been a dramatic shift in the relationship between companies and customers. In the twenty-first century, customers have vast amounts of information at their disposal, they have the ability to switch from one product and service to another with incredible ease, and they can broadcast their pleasure or unhappiness to thousands if not millions of others. Where consumers have freedom of choice, the companies they do business with and are loyal to will be determined by how satisfied they are with the customer experience.

In such a world, how does a CEO, manager, or entrepreneur begin to sort out what defines and drives a good customer experience and how it can be measured and made actionable?

Every smart company and every smart manager knows that an excellent customer experience always has been and should be a business goal. But without a concrete metric, customer experience efforts in the past were often nonspecific and lacking in meaning and direction. The starting point is understanding that customer satisfaction is the right measurement system to gauge the customer experience.

That is how I saw customer satisfaction when I was the vice president of e-business at Compuware, the information technology company, and when I worked in other roles at financial institutions, including chief technology officer for Bank One. Customer satisfaction efforts tended to end up like other initiatives, like TQM (total quality management), Five 9s (reliability to 99.999%), Zero Defects (striving for no quality defects), BPR (business process reengineering), and even Six Sigma (a Motorola-developed strategy utilizing quality methods and statistical analysis). Many programs sounded great, looked great, got people excited, and sometimes even added a little value, but very rarely could you quantify the impact on a company's bottom line. The average satisfaction program went the way of the dinosaur after a few months.

Similarly, traditional satisfaction studies in the past were short-lived and ineffective. Data and action plans were shared in follow-up meetings and quickly forgotten. The one exception to this morass of misinformation and forgotten efforts over the past two decades was the American Customer Satisfaction Index (ACSI) that Dr. Claes Fornell and his colleagues at the University of Michigan created. The ACSI is a macroeconomic indicator that economists use to predict gross domestic product and consumer spending at the macroeconomic and microeconomic levels. The ACSI releases customer satisfaction scores for hundreds of individual companies each year.

Established in 2001, ForeSee built on this scientific, academic work by Dr. Fornell and his partners. By taking the scientific approach of the ACSI and constructing a practical business approach on its foundation, my colleagues and I knew that properly measuring satisfaction with the customer experience could actually predict the *future* of a business and help companies decide where to *focus* their improvement efforts in order to optimize their investments and maximize their returns. More than twenty years of research gave us confidence that an effective customer satisfaction methodology could:

- Measure what we can't see with our own eyes (e.g., customer attitudes and expectations).
- Put nonobservables into a cause-and-effect system.
- Separate the relevant from the trivial (smart companies need to know the difference between what people complain about loudest and what actually impacts their likely future behaviors, which are often very different things).
- Generalize from a small sample to a target population (a methodology that allows a smaller sample size while still maintaining statistical significance at a high confidence interval, saving companies millions of dollars).
- Use customer satisfaction to measure the customer experience and accurately and reliably predict financial success and other desired outcomes.

Over the past decade since our founding, we have developed proprietary customer experience measurement technologies and a methodology to understand today's powerful consumers, who have so many choices available to them.

What we've cultivated is an analytical approach that allows managers, executives, and companies to connect customer experience to the bottom line and optimize the efforts to achieve customer satisfaction.

In the last decade, customer satisfaction is no longer the warm and fuzzy program worthy of a few inspirational posters in a lobby that it was in the 1980s and 1990s. Instead it is now an incredibly powerful management tool, an actionable metric that objectively could quantify the direct impact the customer experience has on a company's bottom line. The customer experience, when measured correctly, shows that a satisfied customer is a long-term, loyal, and profitable customer who is likely to recommend your business to others. Such future customer behaviors are critical to the success of any business.

If you know how well the customer experience is satisfying your customers and you know how to increase their satisfaction, you can then increase sales, return visits, recommendations, loyalty, and brand engagement across all channels. More reliable and more useful data lead to better decisions and better results.

As for ForeSee, what started in 2001 as a scientific, robust, incredibly sophisticated technology used to measure online customer satisfaction continues to expand: deeper into the online customer experience analytics and broader into other channels of customer experience analytics (such as call centers, stores, mobile sites and apps across every kind of device, kiosks, and social media channels).

In this book, I introduce a powerful new metric we developed at ForeSee called Word-of-Mouth Index (WoMI), which incorporates and builds on a widespread metric of customer loyalty and customer satisfaction called Net Promoter Score (NPS). NPS has many strengths but just as many weaknesses and has outlived its usefulness as a metric. This book is also about the need for a comprehensive customer experience measurement ecosystem in addition to WoMI to accurately assess and improve the other elements of customer experience. This is a time of great change and great opportunity. The companies that use the right tools and make the right assessments of how to satisfy their customers will be the ones that will enjoy a substantial competitive advantage and, ultimately, success. Your customers have high expectations and the power to get those expectations met—from you, or from your competitor. It is your job to meet these expectations, and it is our job to help you meet them. It is a job I look forward to every day.

Chapter 1

Customer Experience 2.0

In the fall of 2011, ForeSee played host to a few hundred clients who came to our hometown of Ann Arbor, Michigan, for our annual user summit. The week of our user summit is always such a great time to interact with our clients and hear their opinions, not only about what we're doing but also about the customer experience industry in general. Among many other topics up for discussion over the three days, I was planning to introduce WoMI, or the Word of Mouth Index, which my company, ForeSee, designed to substantially build on the value of the Net Promoter Score (NPS). At that point, we'd already conducted research to test the fundamental concepts behind WoMI and were ready to invite our clients to join in for the second round of testing.

I didn't have long to wait to start hearing attendees' opinions. In the lobby, on my way to grab an early breakfast in the University of Michigan's Executive Education Center, I passed one of our clients on his way back from the exercise room. (I wish I could say I ran into him *in* the hotel gym, but I can barely make time to eat during our summit, much less exercise!)

As we crossed paths, he caught my eye and bellowed, "Hey, I hear you're gonna tell us tomorrow all about why you hate NPS! Let me tell you something. You're way off base. I love it."

I smiled, not quite prepared for a confrontation at 7:24 in the morning, and replied, "Well, you've got me wrong. I don't *hate* NPS, although in the past I've had critical things to say about it. But I've come to recognize some of its strengths. Why do you like it so much?"

John was a CEO at a multichannel retailer. It was his first year at our summit, though his staff had attended every year the company had been a client. As the company struggled to make sense of how various customer touch points interacted with each other and impacted the overall customer experience with its brand, John had come to sit in on some of the higher-level strategic sessions at our summit. I'd been told he was looking forward to hearing our take on NPS, which he enthusiastically endorsed in investor and analyst calls as a critical metric for his company. John explained that he loved the simplicity of one question.

"All you need to do is ask, 'Would you recommend us to a friend or colleague?'" he said. "Then you just find out your score and whether your customers are detractors, passives, or promoters. Of course you know all this. But what I really like is that it helped me line up my entire organization to focus on the customer experience. I know you say the margins of error are high, but who cares? It's a single number, and it's directionally accurate. It doesn't need to be exact." He shrugged. "So how can you be so against it?"

Normally, I'm the first guy in line for a rousing debate about NPS, but I had exactly six minutes to get a bagel before I had to be at my first pre-summit morning meeting. I sidestepped an answer by politely laughing and saying that if he would attend my presentation the next day, he would hear my concerns about NPS. And he would hear how WoMI was a next-generation approach for companies who wanted to take their measurement of word of mouth to another level. John agreed to listen, and I agreed to further discuss my ideas with him after my talk.

My next opportunity to meet attendees and listen to their concerns came later that same morning between sessions during a snack break in the atrium. I ran into Anna, a vice president of customer experience at a packaged-goods company who was not as glowing as John was about NPS. Anna admired certain features of NPS, particularly its seeming simplicity, but was having trouble making it actionable in her company.

"It's great to have this one number," Anna said, "but what do I *do* about it? So I know that some of my customers are detractors, but how do I turn them into promoters? And are detractors really out there bad-mouthing us, or are they just the kind of people who never recommend anything?"

I nodded in agreement since I had heard these concerns many times before and, in fact, had substantial research that I intended to present the next day that confirmed Anna's suspicions that you can't accurately measure or predict detractor behavior by asking only how likely someone is to recommend something. Like John, I told Anna I would be glad to discuss her situation with her after my talk.

As I listened to the speakers on the first day, I was reminded that both John's and Anna's opinions had to be viewed in the context of how far and fast the fields of customer satisfaction and customer experience had come in only a few years. Providing a good customer experience had transformed from an ancient, always acknowledged but soft goal of every company. The growth in the use of websites and mobile apps allowed companies to track just about every action a consumer would take and where analytics were making it scientifically measurable. In my mind, the major competitive advantage that companies have in an era where innovation in products and services is increasingly difficult to achieve is providing a superior customer experience. As I shared in my first book, *Managing Forward*, when you collect and calculate customer experience data the right way, it is possible to predict with a surprising degree of accuracy a company's future success or failure.

The data revolution in business is evident in many other fields. Take baseball and politics.

If you have read Michael Lewis's book *Moneyball* or seen the movie based on it, you are already familiar with the impact of the new stats (or Sabermetrics) on America's pastime. From the game's earliest days, the numbers that counted in assessing a hitter were batting average, a simple compilation of the number of hits per times at bat; home runs, a total; and runs batted in, where anything over 100 was considered Hall of Fame level. A .300 hitter, three hits every 10 times up, was the rarest of talents and eagerly sought after by every major league team.

That all changed when Billy Beane became the general manager of the Oakland Athletics. With a very limited budget by baseball terms and forced to play against teams such as the New York Yankees and the Boston Red Sox, whose payrolls could approach and exceed $200 million, Beane had been drawn to the analytical work first done by a baseball fan named Bill James in the late 1970s and 1980s for new ways to gain a competitive advantage. Within a few years, James's groundbreaking analysis had begun to claim believers among a few baseball executives.

One of James's major arguments was that on-base percentage, the amount of times a player reaches base by either a walk or a hit, was actually a much greater factor for predicting team success than batting average. Put simply, the more runners who make it to base, the greater the likelihood a team will score runs—and runs win games. Beane adopted the Sabermetrics approach and has constantly produced winning teams and play-off contenders for many years. The analytics developed by James have now been refined by others in baseball and have become increasingly sophisticated. Analytics have spread to other sports, as any follower of ESPN like me can attest, and to the arguments fans use as they voice their opinions on sports talk shows. Even MIT now hosts a sports analytics conference every year.

A similar revolution has occurred in politics. In the 2012 presidential election, the Obama campaign focused on analytics to drive decisions about messaging and marketing. Each night in the final stretch of the race, Obama's analytics team ran 66,000 simulations through its computers to have a fresh perspective on the battleground states. The real-time data then drove decisions on how to spend money and make it count. "We were going to demand data on everything; we were going to measure everything," Jim Messina, Obama's campaign manager, said. Whether optimizing e-mails, building polling models, developing a communications strategy, or creating a social media army, analytics gave the Obama campaign an edge over that of its competitor, Mitt Romney, in an incredibly tight race for the popular vote.

The predictive power of analytics in politics was shown in even sharper relief by the prognostications of the *New York Times*'s Nate Silver. A big fan of Sabermetrics, Silver correctly predicted the election results of *every single* state, including the overall Electoral College totals. It was a dazzling display of the new analytics, trumping the observations of former Republican presidential advisor Karl Rove and the more traditional analytics of the Gallup organization, both of which predicted the election for Romney.

Analytics are a moving target; where you sit in time determines your sense of their power and utility. In the 1950s, New York Yankees manager Casey Stengel found that RBIs were a meaningful and useful stat; in the 1990s and 2000s, for Yankee skipper Joe Torre—not so much. When Boss Tweed was counting votes at the beginning of the twentieth century, all he needed was a pad and a pencil; for David Axelrod, Obama's chief advisor in the past two elections, his BlackBerry was capable of absorbing all the data flying at him.

So it was not surprising that John and Anna had different takes on NPS: John, the head of a company, looked for ways to simplify an already overcrowded score sheet of Key Performance Indicators (KPIs); Anna, a vice president, tried to find approaches to implement a concept she didn't quite have total faith in while still moving the needle on actually improving the customer experience. Thus it came as no surprise to me when that evening, at my favorite event of the summit (a huge party in the University of Michigan football stadium, aka the Big House, that has become an annual tradition), I was buttonholed by an analytics manager who had the exact feelings toward NPS that John had assumed I had—he really hated it.

Alex led a team of analysts at a Fortune 500 financial services giant who managed all the behavioral and attitudinal data coming in about the company's web and mobile channels. Alex was fuming about something I had long been aware of—that the whole idea of "the ultimate question" didn't make much sense.

"Just for starters," said Alex as we waited to order our first beers (Bell's Oberon of Michigan, of course), "NPS doesn't distinguish between positive and negative word of mouth, nor does it differentiate between passive and active word of mouth."

Downing a handful of peanuts, Alex launched into a full frontal attack on the NPS methodology, including the dangers of reducing a 10-point scale to a 3-point scale, which he contended greatly increased the margin of error and eliminated subtle but important differences in customer behavior.

I told Alex that I would be addressing his concerns the next day and giving my take on both the advantages and the disadvantages of NPS. I also told him that I would be introducing both a new metric that greatly enhanced NPS called WoMI, which would go a long way toward alleviating his concerns, and a more complex model of the Customer Experience Measurement Ecosystem.

Accelerated Darwinism

Despite my attempt to delay responding to Alex for a few hours, as I drank my Bell's Oberon I couldn't help expressing some of my next day's comments. I agreed with Alex that businesspeople today must have an in-depth understanding of their consumers because those customers have a lot more power now than when I was a young man—which, believe it or not, was not that long ago! Most consumers then dealt with local retailers who enjoyed a near monopoly. Whether it was a department store, a hardware store, or an appliance store, most were located within a short distance from where customers lived. The selection was limited, and customers were almost entirely dependent on salespeople to provide information about a product or service. On the other hand, the merchants often knew their customers well and understood what would satisfy them. They often lived in the same town, had children who went to the same schools, and belonged to the same local organizations.

Lack of choice existed across other areas as well. When I was growing up in Southfield, a suburb of Detroit, we had three network TV stations to choose from instead of the hundreds of channels available on cable systems today (not to mention Netflix and Hulu and other streaming services). Audiences for popular major network shows approached 40 million nationwide, an almost unimaginable number today. If I wanted to find out what was happening in the world, I had the *Detroit Free Press* or the *Detroit News* newspapers available instead of hundreds of online editions of print newspapers from cities all over the world, a dozen cable news channels such as CNN and Fox News, and websites such as the Daily Beast, the Huffington Post, or Yahoo! News that are updated with breaking news throughout the day. My banking choices were basically limited to those branches in my neighborhood. Chase, Bank of America, and Wells Fargo were unknown entities, restricted by law from coming into my state. And when my parents wanted to book a vacation, which was usually not that far away, they went to the local travel agent. Being able to jump on the computer and scan hundreds of different vacation offers and instantaneously get information about dozens of discounted hotel room rates was as futuristic as an episode of *Star Trek* or a novel by Ray Bradbury.

As I finished my brief discussion of the immediate past, Alex had the same glazed-over look on his face I used to get when I heard my grandfather talking about World War II or iceboxes: that's ancient history.

But this history is important to understand. Once, businesses had almost all of the power. When consumers walked through the door, they were almost captives. Businesses had the perennial real estate advantage (location, location, location) and almost all the information about products, services, and competitors.

Not anymore.

The balance of power—especially the balance of power in terms of information and choice—has dramatically shifted over time toward the consumer. This shift toward consumer power is a phenomenon I call Accelerated Darwinism—business survival of the fittest at breakneck speed.

Accelerated Darwinism is the result of a number of factors, but the communications and technological revolutions are, by far, the most important reasons behind the rapid pace of change and the shift in the balance of power between the consumer and business. It has resulted in the rise of what I call the Super Consumer.

Today's consumers have amazing, superhero-like capabilities. They can:

- Clone themselves by shopping in five stores at once through the use of multitabbed browsing or by utilizing multiple channels (shopping in a store while using an iPhone to browse other retailers).
- Speak with a very loud voice where potentially hundreds, thousands, and sometimes even more than that can hear them

express their feelings about their consumer experiences, good or bad, with any company by posting on Facebook and Twitter.

- Have incredible range of hearing where they can listen to friends' opinions on Facebook, Twitter, and e-mail and to millions of voices via social media rants and recommendations such as those on Yelp.
- Have genius-level intelligence, often possessing as much or even more knowledge than a company's employees by utilizing the web for customer-generated product reviews, detail specifications, and the competitive landscape.

Yesterday's shoppers for a television walked through a single store, glanced at a few different models, possibly asked a salesperson for help, and made a decision. Today's shoppers may do a little research online, cruise the aisles of a store to look at products in person, check online reviews with an iPhone, and then visit an online retailer to complete their shopping process—all the while comfortable and secure in the knowledge that if *this* website doesn't have what they need, they can sprint off to dozens of other online retailers with a few clicks. And if their experience was great (or was horrible), they are likely to tell others on Facebook or Twitter what their shopping experience was like.

Because the customer's voice is incredibly loud and because so many people can hear it, measuring the customer experience (and word-of-mouth) is a vastly more complicated phenomenon than it was even a few years ago, let alone what it was 20 years ago or for my parents and grandparents. The impact of the satisfaction with the customer experience is magnified by a factor of thousands and cannot be ignored anymore by businesses.

It is impossible for anyone to predict the new communication tools, much less which of those tools will capture popular imagination and be adopted by millions of users (Google glasses, anyone?). What we can guarantee is that any new tools will be broader and faster than the ones consumers use today. As a result, Super Consumers will share ideas and opinions with more people at a faster speed, and they will also listen to the opinions of many more people at a faster speed. This magnified voice of the customer will grow only louder. And the only way to keep up with these developments is to utilize increasingly sophisticated analytics to understand what customers want and allocate resources accordingly.

Alex nodded along—whether it was the force of my argument or the excellence of the local beer, I'm not sure. But when I finished, he asked, "So how do you recommend I deal with my problems with NPS?"

I smiled and said, "You'll just have to wait until tomorrow morning. But I have been having conversations like the one we just had for the past five years. Your concerns and issues are exactly what led my colleagues and me to work on developing WoMI. I am eager to hear what you and others think about what I say."

The next day, after my speech, I did talk with John, Anna, and Alex, and each seemed to have learned something and to be eager to understand more about WoMI and the Customer Experience Measurement Ecosystem. And each seemed to clearly understand my ideas on how to evolve NPS, which is the focus of the next two chapters.

Chapter 2

NPS—What It Is and What It Does Well

In the December 2003 issue of the *Harvard Business Review*, in an article titled "The One Number You Need to Grow," Frederick Reichheld proposed provocatively that there was a simple, practical way to categorize customers on the basis of their answer to a single question, which was phrased like this:

On a 0-to-10 scale, how likely is it that you would recommend us (or this product/service/brand) to a friend or colleague?

He then instructed companies to ask at least one follow-up question: *What is the primary reason for your score?*

Reichheld, who is director emeritus of the consulting firm Bain and Company and a Bain Fellow, argued in the article and later in a 2006 book titled *The Ultimate Question* that the 10-point scale allowed companies to take a quick measurement of customers' feelings and attitudes. The open-ended follow-up question enabled companies to "hear the reasons for these attitudes in the customers' own words."

On the basis of the answers, the idea is that a company can easily sort out customers who love it, those who hate it, and those who don't care for it one way or the other. It can then compile a simple, easily understandable score—a Net Promoter Score (NPS)—which shows how it is doing on customer relationships. The company can track that score week in and week out, in much the way a business tracks its financial performance.

Reichheld posited that when he and his colleagues at Bain studied the use of these questions, they found that customers fall into three well-defined groups. Each group of customers exhibited a distinct pattern of behaviors and attitudes. Each called for a different set of actions from a company in order to achieve customer satisfaction.

The three groups were as follows:

1. **Promoters.** These were people who responded with a 9 or 10 on the 0-to-10 scale. This numerical designation indicated that their lives had been enriched by the company. They behaved like loyal customers, usually making repeated purchases and supplying the company with a significant share of their spending. Promoters talked up the company to their friends and colleagues. They responded to surveys and provided constructive feedback and suggestions to the company. Reichheld labeled these people promoters because in their "energy and enthusiasm," that is exactly how they acted. He said, "Any company should want to maintain the promoters' enthusiasm, to learn economical ways to create even more customers who feel and act this way, and to provide recognition and rewards to the teams or individual employees who do so."

2. **Passives.** These were people who gave the company a 7 or 8 on the 0-to-10 scale. According to Reichheld, these customers "got what they paid for, nothing more." They were passively satisfied customers, not loyal ones, and they exhibited a set of attitudes that were "markedly different" from those of promoters. They made "few referrals, and when they made one, it was likely to be qualified and unenthusiastic." They easily could defect to a competitor either because of discounts that were offered or because of effective advertising appeals. Reichheld described these responders as passives because "they bring little energy to the company and cannot be counted on as long-term assets." A company's goal, he said, is to improve its services, products, or processes to the point where it can "delight" customers and turn some into promoters.

3. **Detractors.** These were responders who gave a company a rating of six or below. This score indicated that these customers' "lives have been diminished" by their dealings with

the company; they were "dissatisfied, disaffected, even dismayed" by how they had been treated. They bad-mouthed the company to their friends and colleagues. If they couldn't easily switch from a company because they had long-term contracts or no other competitors had suitable offers to make, they become complainers. These detractors repeatedly criticized the company and drove up costs, as employees had to respond to their concerns. According to Reichheld, companies faced with detractors had to "probe for the root cause of their disappointment, then apologize and determine ways to solve the problem." Reichheld recommended that if there was no economically rational solution to the detractors' complaints, then the company "must learn not to acquire this type of customer in the first place."

NPS was determined simply by subtracting the percentage of detractors from the percentage of promoters, a score that could theoretically range from –100 to +100 (see Figure 2.1).

Reichheld framed these differences in word-of-mouth behavior, within a description of what he considered success in business. He considered these customer distinctions of promoters, passives, and detractors a way of measuring "how well an organization treats the people whose lives it affects, how well it generates relationships worthy of loyalty." In short, having a high NPS should be a company's aspirational goal and was vital in making sure that a company

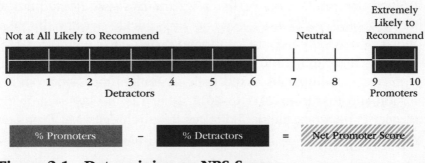

Figure 2.1 Determining an NPS Score

was generating good profits versus bad profits. For Reichheld, bad profits are those that are earned at the expense of customer relationships. He defined them as:

> *Whenever a customer feels misled, mistreated, ignored, or coerced. . . . Bad profits come from unfair or misleading pricing. Bad profits arise when companies shortchange customers . . . by delivering a lousy experience. Bad profits are about extracting value from customers, not creating value.*
>
> *Good profits are dramatically different. [They are] earned with customers' enthusiastic cooperation. A company earns good profits when it so delights its customers that they willingly come back for more—and not only that, they tell their friends and colleagues. . . .*

Companies that want to generate good profits can use NPS to listen to customers, fix the problems that lead to unhappiness or anger, and create experiences that lead to more and more delight. Reichheld contended that the very existence of the NPS score engaged every employee "in the quest to build a true customer focus into their daily operations and that they were meeting their customer relationship goals."

Since the publication of the *Harvard Business Review* article and the book *The Ultimate Question*, NPS quickly became the most popular and widely adopted customer experience metric for U.S. businesses. Research from the Temkin Group in 2012 shows that 83 percent of companies asked their customers the Net Promoter question and that from 2011 to 2012, NPS was the fastest growing customer experience metric. Forrester Research calls Net Promoter "wildly popular," and a 2011 article in *Inc.* magazine declared that

"Fortune 500 companies around the globe latch[ed] on to [NPS]. Today, companies such as Intuit and Southwest Airlines use the NPS methodology as a way to quantify their customer experience." Other companies quoted publicly endorsing the Net Promoter System include Charles Schwab, Apple retail stores, Ascension Health, and American Express.

Without a doubt, NPS has truly been helpful in some ways. It has brought more attention to the importance of the customer in growing a business (a focus I always appreciate and encourage). More resources have been allocated to focus on the customer experience. It has also brought more attention and focus to the power of positive word of mouth as a driver of growth. NPS has served as a rallying cry for executives focusing their employees on the importance of the customer, and sometimes that action alone makes a difference in the customer experience. NPS has been used as part of incentive bonus plans to keep the employees and management focused on the importance of the customer. NPS has also become a metric that executives have used to talk to Wall Street analysts about the customer focus of their company. Finally, it has framed a concept in a way that is easy and simple for companies to understand.

Those outcomes are all positive, or at least they can be positive. But as Anna and Alex indicated to me, there are also a number of problems with NPS, which is the focus of the next chapter.

Chapter 3

NPS—Fundamentally Flawed

It is easy to assume that anything called a metric has real validity—especially if that metric receives widespread corporate and media attention, despite having a number of flaws, some of which are immediately apparent and some of which become more visible as it becomes more widespread. But just because people call it a metric doesn't mean it is accurate, reliable, precise, credible, predictive, or actionable.

The appeal of tracking a simple, single metric is understandable. In many ways I understand where John, the CEO I talked to at our user summit, is coming from when he said he loves how easy it is and doesn't really care if it's exact, as long as it is directionally accurate.

It *does* sound simple. It *does* sound easy. The idea behind the Net Promoter concept makes sense. Word of mouth, whether positive, negative, or nonexistent, is a crucial business metric and should absolutely be measured. But as a management tool, NPS just does not work.

How do I know? Overwhelming evidence.

Since 2001, ForeSee has collected over 100 million online customer satisfaction surveys that measure "likelihood to recommend." In fact, our research on word-of-mouth recommendations precedes the introduction of the NPS concept. We also do dozens of original research projects every year studying the customer experience with top retailers, financial institutions, government agencies, auto companies, nonprofits, and more. These surveys have long included additional questions that have allowed us to measure just how accurate, precise, actionable, and predictive NPS really is. In addition, we work with top economists at the University of Michigan and other universities who have helped us evaluate the science and statistics behind the Net Promoter claims.

Here are a few of the problems we have found with NPS. Keep these issues in mind as you evaluate your own measurement tools.

Accuracy

At first glance, a scale of 0 to 10 appears to provide a great deal of accuracy and precision. (Accuracy is to what degree you are correct; precision is to what degree you are exact—more on the difference between these terms in Chapter 6.) But upon closer inspection, NPS actually uses a three-point scale—what I like to call a three-point unbalanced scale. This was one of Alex's concerns with NPS. Since values from 0 to 6 are detractors, 7 and 8 are passives, and 9 and 10 are promoters, the scale does not use 11 points. The scale uses three points.

Using the NPS calculation does not result in scores that fall between 0 and 10. There are only three results: detractors, passives, and promoters. The scale is unbalanced. In the real world, the difference between a 4 and a 5 is the same as the difference between a 6 and a 7; each is different by one. Under the NPS scale, that is no longer true. There is *no* difference between a 4 and a 5, since both are considered to be detractors, but there *is* a difference between a 6 and a 7 because a 6 is a detractor and a 7 is a passive.

The scale is unbalanced because the groupings arbitrarily combine real differences into general categories.

Margin of Error

As a result of the scale used by NPS, the margin of error almost always falls well outside the range of statistical confidence. We evaluated published NPS benchmarks and calculated the margin of error. In most cases, 60 to 80 percent of the published results were statistically the same and fell within the margin of error.

In simpler terms, even though two different NPS scores may have been reported as a 40 and a 50, when we applied the rules of statistics, the numbers were, in fact, not statistically different. That's a pretty big range. If your NPS score is a 40 and your closest competitor is a 50, are they better than you? Are you the same? Are you actually better than them? You have no way of knowing.

When we calculate overall customer satisfaction scores for the 100 top-grossing online retailers, on the basis of our sample size we find that the margin of error for a customer satisfaction score is +/−2.6 points. When we assess NPS (using the same sample size and confidence level), we find a +/−10-point margin of error.

Essentially, an NPS of 12.5 could actually be anywhere from 2.5 to 22.5, a range so large that it is basically useless.

Oversimplification

Reducing a 10-point scale to a 3-point scale not only greatly increases the margin of error but also eliminates subtle but important differences in customer behavior.

The results from the ForeSee Online Retail Satisfaction Index show that people who rate their likelihood to recommend as a 6 are 10 times more likely to buy *offline* than people who score themselves as a 1. More impressively, the 6s are 14 times more likely to purchase next time they're in the market for a similar product and a colossal 30 times more likely to buy *online* than the ones. Lumping 1s and 6s together causes a manager to lose the ability to differentiate between customers with disparate buying behaviors.

It gets worse. When we looked at the respondents considered to be promoters (people who scored themselves as 9 or 10 on the Net Promoter Scale), we found that people who rated their likelihood to recommend as a 10 were 57 percent more likely to purchase than those who rated themselves as a 9. The 10s were also 56 percent more likely to make a purchase with the same retailer the next time they shopped for similar merchandise.

So why do people fall for the rating "bucket" trap? Well, when you evaluate the promoters they are more likely to purchase than the passives, which are more likely to purchase than the detractors. That looks like compelling evidence to a casual observer. To an untrained eye you would conclude that it is proof that NPS is a good leading indicator. However, when you evaluate according to the scale that was specified you can see the oversimplification and lack of accuracy introduced by the bucket approach is significant and can lead to the wrong conclusions, bad decision making, misguided action plans, and improperly allocated bonuses. Create ratings buckets and toss out results differentiation, and you are left with no real way to interpret and act on subtleties in customer attitudes and behaviors— attitudes and behaviors that can have a direct and tangible impact on revenues and profitability.

Detractors Don't *Always* Detract, and Promoters Don't *Always* Promote

Following a hunch, we added two additional questions to our surveys to see whether the Net Promoter concept accurately reflects the customer behavior it claims to measure.

Our initial assumption was that people decide to recommend or not recommend a product or company for a number of different reasons. Some recommend only items that make them feel trendy, such as the latest smartphone. Some will recommend only items that reflect well on them. Others will not recommend a product or service, regardless of how much they love it. They won't recommend because the product or company lacks prestige or is the discount alternative. There are just certain personality types who never recommend anything. They never have a positive word about anyone or anything. They would even be silent about the doctor who performed their successful heart surgery! In very competitive environments such as the B2B market or in a collector's category, some people won't recommend a product or company because they may feel they lose their competitive edge.

And some products no one will recommend because those products are too personal. Can you imagine recommending your favorite brand of toilet paper or toothpaste to a friend? It is not likely even though you may be extremely loyal to that brand. Or a McDonald's

Quarter Pounder with Cheese unless you are John Travolta in the movie *Pulp Fiction*? Or your favorite bank or utility company? We expect those companies to consistently cash our checks and keep our lights on. We may be very satisfied and very loyal, but most people are not going to recommend their power company to a friend. In many cases NPS is not a good proxy for loyalty or satisfaction. Promoters can be a good representation of positive word of mouth, but jumping to the assumption that it is a proxy for other metrics is a very dangerous and often wrong assumption.

In addition, NPS does not at all measure how likely a consumer is to say something negative. It purports to measure only a customer's likelihood of saying something positive. Is it safe to assume if someone is not likely to recommend a company or product that they are going to be a detractor? We didn't think so and we set out to investigate and find the answer.

When we ran the next ForeSee Online Retail Satisfaction Index (and as we have done ever since), we asked three questions, including the Net Promoter question:

1. How likely are you to recommend this website to someone else? (the Net Promoter question)

2. How likely would you be to communicate your experience with this website to other people?

3. Assuming you communicated your experiences with this website to others, how favorable would your comments be?

When we evaluated the Net Promoter question, we found that 40 percent of the survey respondents were considered promoters, 33 percent were passives, and 27 percent were detractors. (Not only were 27 percent detractors but also Net Promoter considers those people to be a source of bad profit.) Had we simply stopped at this point, we would have assigned an NPS score of 13: 40 percent promoters – 27 percent detractors = NPS of 13.

Then we evaluated results for the two additional questions we asked and found that the Net Promoter metric misrepresented detractors by a wide margin. Worst of all, NPS overstated detractors by a factor of 27. The NPS question labeled 27 percent of our 20,700 survey respondents as detractors, but only 1 percent of the 20,700 people surveyed said they would be likely to communicate a bad experience.

That is what statisticians call, in technical terms, a really big difference.

How can people who do not even talk to others about your products or services become detractors and the source of bad profits?

In my mind, they can't.

In another study for another client, we looked at so-called detractors to determine whether any loyal customers were found in that bucket. We determined that while 32 percent were labeled detractors by NPS, more than 60 percent of those so-called detractors were, in fact, very loyal customers. They had paid for the service provided for at least two years and were very likely to continue to pay for that service in the future. They weren't very likely to shout about it from the rooftops, but they certainly weren't bashing the company to anyone either.

Misrepresentations of the numbers of detractors and passives—if you even believe in those general categories—are caused by a basic flawed assumption: that the likelihood to recommend can measure both positive word of mouth *and* negative word of mouth. It can't.

You simply cannot assume that a person who is not likely to recommend will actively generate negative word of mouth. Likelihood to recommend can measure only positive word of mouth. That's why detractors are significantly overstated by NPS.

Don't stop with asking one question and following up with people who have been misidentified as brand detractors. Take it one step further. If you really want to eliminate what Reichheld calls "bad profits," identify the people genuinely dissatisfied with your products and services, and those who will generate negative word of mouth as a result. Find out why by using customer experience analytics, and take direct actions that will result in increased satisfaction and a better customer experience.

And while you're at it, work hard to convert passives into promoters. Find concrete ways to convert good customers into long-term, loyal customers by better meeting their needs and expectations. This is all very achievable when a business is asking the right questions and analyzing the results in the right way.

Where's the Growth?

If NPS accurately measured satisfaction, then it could predict future growth. Researchers at the University of Michigan have scientifically proven over nearly three decades that, when measured correctly, customer satisfaction *is* a predictor of company financial performance, stock prices, and other future behaviors, such as word of mouth and likelihood to purchase again.

But the Net Promoter question does not measure the customer experience, customer satisfaction, or loyalty. Instead, it measures likelihood to recommend, which some Net Promoter advocates would claim is a proxy for satisfaction or loyalty. There is little evidence for this claim. In fact, there is extensive proof that NPS is an extremely poor proxy for satisfaction, loyalty, or even detractors.

There are four primary things that drive company growth. One is keeping your current customers, which is often expressed as customer retention and customer loyalty. The second is selling more to your existing customers, also called customer upsell. The third is customer acquisition as a result of marketing initiatives, the ability to attract new prospects through various marketing and advertising efforts and convert them into customers. The fourth is customer acquisition as a result of word of mouth, where your current customers are recommending that others do business with you. One of these is not going to drive or explain all of your revenue growth. It is going to take at least two, if not three, of these to make a business grow. Word of mouth *can sometimes be* correlated with company growth and *can* contribute to future growth but in no way explains the majority of future growth and does not predict future growth. A rising NPS on its own does not cause revenue growth. Revenue growth and a rising NPS can be correlated; on the other hand, rising satisfaction with the customer experience does cause revenue growth. Strong satisfaction with the customer experience *causes* an increase in customer retention, upsell, converting prospects into customers and positive word of mouth. Positive word of mouth will also contribute to future customer acquisition. These positive results from a strong satisfaction with the customer experience will in turn drive revenues. Measure NPS, and you miss the point (see measurement mistake #5 in Appendix B for more discussion on the difference between correlation and causation).

But don't just take my word for it. We asked economists and statisticians at leading national universities to help determine whether a high NPS leads to company growth and whether a low NPS leads to declining revenues. Together, we analyzed NPS over several years to see whether it predicted revenue growth for online retailers.

It did not. Instead, we found that NPS is not a driver of growth, not a measure of or a proxy for customer satisfaction or loyalty, nor does it help businesses decide what steps to take to improve their results.

Insufficient Information

Setting aside the well documented problems with NPS, is it really the one number you need to know? Even if it is a precise and accurate metric, is NPS the one number you would choose?

It is not the one number I would choose. Word of mouth is an outcome of high satisfaction with customer experience, but word of mouth does not explain revenue growth. If I were to pick one number, I would choose revenue—or, better yet, a single number that explains revenue growth and has a direct causal relationship to customer retention, customer upsell, and customer acquisition. That number is the satisfaction with the customer experience.

What can you do with one number? Measurement is critical because we cannot manage what we cannot measure. But where we really need help is in answering three questions:

1. *How am I doing?* What is my performance?
2. *Where should I focus my efforts?* Where will I get the largest return on my investment?
3. *Why should I take action?* Is the payback worth the effort?

One number can help answer the first question, but one number does little to answer the last two questions.

Simple Is Just . . . Simple

I have spent a lot of time on NPS for a reason: It is a prime example of a metric that is simple to use and easy to understand but has no value as a predictive, actionable metric. There will be more and more people like Anna and Alex complaining and more and more CEOs like John becoming disillusioned over time, especially if John is one of the thousands of executives in America whose corporate bonus plan is based in part on NPS. Imagine if *your* corporate bonus were based on a number with a margin of error of $+/-10$ points, among other flaws! I'm glad mine isn't.

My colleagues and I are not the only ones to document the flaws with Net Promoter as part of this research. In a published paper called "A Longitudinal Examination of Net Promoter and Firm Revenue Growth," research by Tim Keiningham, Bruce Cooil, Tor Wallin Andreassen, and Lerzan Aksoy report "our findings indicate that Net Promoter has been vastly oversold to companies worldwide, and demonstrate that claims of the measure's superiority in predicting growth are false." A 2008 article by Bob Hayes in *Quirk's Marketing Research Review* claimed that NPS claims are overstated; that other loyalty questions (such as satisfaction and likelihood to buy again) are just as effective at predicting growth, and that using only NPS can lead to lost revenue. In a January 2007 article in *Marketing Management, D.* Randall Brandt (Ph.D. and Vice President at Maritz Inc.) wrote that NPS "isn't always the best predictor of customer behavior or business results; some measures perform better in particular markets and sectors, or for particular types of customers." In their paper, "The Value of Different Customer Satisfaction and Loyalty Metrics in Predicting Business Performance," published in the *Journal of Marketing Science*, Neil Morgan and Lopo Leotte de Rego found that "metrics based on recommendation intentions (net promoters) and behavior (average number of recommendations) have little or no predictive value." They went on to add, "the number of net promoters is not significantly associated with either firms' sales growth or gross margin performance."

Asking customers about their likelihood to recommend has a definite place in a company's inquiries into their relations with their customers, but it is only one component in a comprehensive, inter-related customer model driven by customer satisfaction.

Predicting the future requires the use of a proven scientific methodology based on reliable metrics and an accurate understanding of the voice of customers; then you can truly manage and grow your business.

Never use metrics based on faulty math, flavors of the month, or measurement by proxy. Faulty metrics are often based on a sloppy approach to data collection, data analysis, and data integrity. Those metrics do more harm than good because they may cause you to make the wrong decisions for what appear to be the right reasons. A proxy measurement is only valuable when it is a very strong proxy that demonstrates great accuracy, precision, and reliability in predicting the elements that it is a proxy for and is easier to collect and measure. I would encourage you to not try to use one measurement as a proxy for another measurement. Customers are the most important asset we have; it is worth the effort to measure the right things to understand our performance and how we can improve the customer relationship. Word of mouth is important enough to measure, but so is the satisfaction with the customer experience and customer loyalty. Don't fall into the trap of giving up accuracy and precision because you are searching for the right proxy.

Also, don't fall into the trap of relying on measurements that may correlate with the success outcomes you are striving for (financial success, loyalty, etc.) but are not causal to those success outcomes. Is there a link between customer recommendations and success outcomes such as revenue growth and customer loyalty? The link is a result of correlation, not causation. You need to find the causal relationships to know where to focus your efforts to improve customer retention, customer upsell, and customer acquisition.

Then, remember that counting is not measuring. It may be natural to look for proxies, because while satisfaction is a concept we all understand, it seems difficult to define and measure because we cannot see it.

Customer satisfaction, measured correctly, is not just a credible, reliable, accurate, and precise measurement of the customer experience, but it is also predictive of future financial results. When you deploy a sound, proven methodology that measures the most important asset you have—your customers—that methodology pays tremendous dividends and helps create truly loyal customers.

But people continue to love Net Promoter, despite its well-documented weaknesses. So we turned ourselves to the task of improving NPS so that companies could use a metric that was still simple, still easy, but more accurate and precise. We also wanted a metric that built upon NPS and was incremental to the measurement of NPS, not a complete replacement for NPS. That is why we have developed WoMI and incorporated it as part of the Customer Experience Measurement Ecosystem. We turn to these concepts in the next chapters as we begin to explore all the dimensions of measuring the customer experience.

Chapter 4

WoMI—The Next Generation of NPS

As I said in Chapter 2, the concept of NPS has done a lot of good for business. However, as customer metrics have evolved over the past decade, NPS has not. While the minimalism of NPS was initially a huge advantage for executives like John who were looking for a simple tool, it has now become apparent that asking one question (or even one question with one or two follow up questions), with what is essentially a three-point scale, is not accurate, precise, or actionable. It is time for the Net Promoter to catch up with the sophistication that companies and managers like Anna and Alex expect from their analytics. It is time for the next generation of NPS. It is time for the Word of Mouth Index, or WoMI.

As you'll read in this chapter, WoMI evolves NPS by measuring both likelihood to recommend and likelihood to detract from a specific brand by adding a second question: "How likely are you to discourage others from doing business with this company?" This additional question helps to deliver on the promise of NPS by creating a more precise, accurate, and actionable measurement that evaluates the customer experience and allows organizations to foster the type of changes that affect the customer experience.

WoMI significantly advances the measurement of the customer experience because its scores offer four primary benefits for businesses operating in today's high-speed, word-of-mouth-driven culture. WoMI provides:

1. A single score—Any measurement with one simple value is easier to communicate and can be used to rally stakeholders (executives, employees, Wall Street, board members, etc.) around the customer experience and across an organization;

2. Valuable insight—Understanding the difference between true detractors and true promoters helps organizations avoid wasting resources trying to convert passives into promoters and eliminates the risk of alienating customers who aren't legitimate detractors; and

3. Proactive data—Adding a second question to understand what drives negative word of mouth as well as positive word of mouth allows companies to take proactive measures to fix issues causing problems for customers by gaining greater insight into what drives sentiment.

4. Improvement to NPS—For the legions of companies already relying on NPS, WoMI services as a simple upgrade that will provide more accuracy, precision, and actionability without needing to remove and replace a system they've relied on for years.

WoMI Distinguishes between Positive Word of Mouth and Negative Word of Mouth

Net Promoter assumes that everyone who is not likely to recommend is an active detractor. WoMI solves that problem by adding a second question, thereby asking customers how likely they are to recommend *and* how likely they are to detract. These are two very different behaviors and you can't measure both using only one question.

In fact, one of the biggest flaws in Net Promoter is its assumption that anyone who rates themselves a 6 or less when asked how likely they are to recommend a company is a detractor. ForeSee research found that Net Promoter overstates detractors by an average of 260 to 270 percent for our clients and by 299 percent on average for the top 100 brands (results vary greatly from company to company, see Appendix A for a list of satisfaction, NPS, and WoMI scores for hundreds of companies, along with the overstatement of detractors for each company.) The overstatement is defined by how many people are mistakenly categorized as detractors by NPS. Net Promoter's overstatement of detractors can be a costly and misleading mistake for companies who are either spending resources pursuing detractors in an attempt to convert them to promoters, as John was doing, or compensating their executives on the basis of what can now be seen as NPS's incomplete measurement.

Our initial research was done using Net Promoter's own definition of *detractor*, people who rate themselves a 6 or lower when asked how likely they are to recommend. However, we also analyzed every combination of answers to the likelihood-to-recommend question and found that by using only the likelihood-to-recommend question, **there is no way to measure detractors as accurately as by asking directly**.

For example, many companies define *super detractors* as people who answer "how likely are you to recommend this company?" with a 2 or less. Surely someone who would rate their recommendation so low would be a detractor, right? Not necessarily. When we asked that same group of people (those who rated their likelihood to recommend very low, 2 or less) how likely they are to discourage others from doing business with the company, fewer than a third say they are highly likely to detract.

Figure 4.1 shows that of people who rate their likelihood to recommend at 1 or 2, only 29 percent fall into what we call the True Detractor category, or people who rate their likelihood to discourage with a 9 or a 10.

We researched every possible combination of detractors (see Appendix B), and there is no way to use likelihood to recommend as an accurate proxy for detraction.

Why does it matter? Why do companies need to add a likely-to-discourage question to get a more accurate measure? Consider Apple as an example.

Apple has stated publicly that it uses NPS surveys to address customer feedback. According to a June 2013 article in the *Business Standard*, negative responses are followed up by store managers.

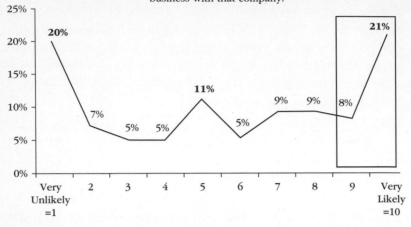

Of people who said they were least likely to recommend (1–2 on NPS scale), only 29% (black box) say they are highly likely to discourage someone from doing business with that company.

Figure 4.1   Likelihood to Discourage

As shown in Appendix A, our research shows that NPS overstates detractors for Apple stores by 57 percent (and by even more in other channels). For Apple stores, this means that instead of contacting the 7 percent of individuals who are likely to discourage others from doing business with Apple, they will be contacting 11 percent of their store customers, 57 percent more than they would have if they were using WoMI. By using an inaccurate metric, Apple is chasing customers who are not true brand detractors that would warrant its attention and thus squandering employee productivity and resources.

In the Apple example, a store manager making $60,000 a year and spending one hour a day following up with so-called detractors (at $29/hour) costs Apple $7,500 annually in wasted time. With more than 400 stores worldwide, this adds up to $3 million in lost productivity—and this is just one initiative based on NPS. Moreover, contacting potentially loyal customers and asking them why they are not satisfied can alienate those customers.

Apple should also be trying to figure out why these customers are detractors: Do they have common attributes, common personas, or are they experiencing similar issues? It is difficult, if not impossible, to determine why these customers are detractors if your identification of those detractors is 57 percent overstated. That kind of margin of error introduces an incredible amount of noise into the analysis and makes coming up with the right answer almost impossible. You can't find out what is broken if your sample of data is 57 percent in error.

Negative Word of Mouth

NPS has a critically flawed assumption: it believes that when a customer is not promoting a company, he or she is engaging in detracting behavior. The NPS scale does not adequately measure the likelihood of a customer saying something negative about a company or its products. Its scale reflects only half of what an ideal word-of-mouth metric should; it measures the concept's midpoint to one extreme (inaction to positive action), rather than from one extreme to an opposite extreme (positive action to negative action). The question used for NPS provides only information about positive word of mouth but does not address negative word of mouth.

Negative word of mouth is an important concept in assessing customer influence in the marketplace. People who truly act as detractors could rate the recommend question the same as someone who is not likely to speak up at all; a customer who is "not at all" likely to recommend is not necessarily likely to discourage others from doing business with a company. In fact, he or she may be a very loyal customer. Moreover, some companies spend substantial sums of money pursuing detractors in an effort to convert them.

WoMI incorporates both positive word of mouth and negative word of mouth by using two survey questions. As with NPS, the likelihood to recommend a company is an important component of the metric. In addition, WoMI includes the likelihood to discourage others from doing business with a company. The WoMI calculation subtracts the percentage of 9 and 10 ratings from the likelihood-to-discourage question ("How likely are you to discourage someone from doing business with this company?") from the percentage of 9 and 10 ratings from the standard likelihood-to-recommend question.

| True Promoters® | True Detractors® | | Promoters | Detractors |

$$\text{WoMI}^{\text{SM}} = \frac{\text{Recommend \%}}{\text{of 9s and 10s}} - \frac{\text{Discourage \%}}{\text{of 9s and 10s}} \qquad \text{NPS} = \frac{\text{Recommend \%}}{\text{of 9s and 10s}} = \frac{\text{Recommend \%}}{\text{of 1s–6s}}$$

Figure 4.2 Promoters and Detractors

Note: NPS traditionally refers to a 0 to 10-point scale; ForeSee has long used a 1 to 10 point scale. Where you see reference to NPS scores that ForeSee has calculated as part of our research, you will see NPS-defined detractors referred to as 1 to 6 rather than 0 to 6.

The WoMI metric is superior to NPS because it incorporates *more* information and it *more* appropriately represents the difference between the proportions of the consumers who report being highly likely to promote or detract via word of mouth.

The WoMI Research Approach and the Validity of the Results

As I said, for almost two years my colleagues and I tested and refined with hundreds of companies and thousands of customers both WoMI questions and how best to calculate the responses we received. On average, NPS overstated detractors by 260 to 270 percent in our tests with clients, though some individual companies saw NPS overstate detractors by more than 1,000 percent. (See Appendix A for a list of publicly-available overstatement scores by company.)

The degree of NPS overstatement of detractors, as well as scores, varied by category and stage of purchase process.

- Product manufacturers have a high average overstatement (425 percent, compared to the overall average of 262 percent).

- Postfulfillment surveys (surveys conducted after a customer has received the product or service they paid for) show the least overstatement (60 percent, on average), but even so, the resulting average WoMI score is nine points higher than the average NPS score for that group.

- Utility companies, especially telecommunications companies, have perhaps the greatest challenges in regard to generating positive word of mouth because they are often monopolies. When is the last time you heard someone recommend his or her power company? I can hear it now: "That is some of the best electricity I have had in years. My lightbulbs have never been brighter. You need to switch to Consolidated Electric." Never going to happen.

While the charts you'll see in Appendix A reflect huge companies (the top brands, retailers, banks, etc.), Figure 4.3 reflects what

Figure 4.3 Benchmarking with NPS and WoMI

	Companies Participating in Testing	Satisfaction	WoMI Score	NPS Score	NPS-Defined Detractors	WoMI-Defined Detractors	Average NPS Overstatement of Detractors*
Overall	70	70	42	22	29%	10%	262%
Fulfillment	7	78	55	46	20%	11%	60%
Retail	23	72	45	26	26%	7%	304%
E-Commerce	26	70	43	22	29%	8%	315%
Product Manufacturers	15	69	43	20	30%	7%	425%
Brick and Martar	10	70	40	19	30%	9%	260%
Content	16	68	39	14	33%	8%	414%
E-Services	14	62	34	9	37%	12%	266%
Utilities	15	56	21	−12	47%	14%	248%
Telecommunication	11	48	12	−27	54%	16%	262%

*Overstatement of detractors is calculated using the following formula: (% of NPS-defined detractors − % of WoMI-defined detractors)/% of WoMI-defined detractors. The average overstatement at the category level is an average of the company-level overstatements of detractors. The overall average overstatement is the average of the overstatements of each underlying category.

WoMI—The Next Generation of NPS

our clients found over 18 months of testing. Our client list includes companies of all sizes and across all industries, from Fortune 100s to midsize companies.

The differences we see in these benchmark categories illustrate that it is important for companies to measure and understand word of mouth among their own customer bases.

Because our intent was to create a metric that would complement NPS and enhance its ability to reflect true detractor behavioral tendencies, we approached our efforts as any scientist would. We created a hypothesis, tested it, evaluated and validated results, retested, engaged in ongoing monitoring, and then conducted a final evaluation. The research involved three phases.

Phase 1: ForeSee Independent Research

Goal: Evaluate options to improve NPS objectively and scientifically.

In conjunction with ForeSee's research on customer satisfaction with the Top 40 online retailers in 2010 and the Top 100 e-retailers in spring 2011, we tested specific questions that would address NPS's missing dimensions: the likelihood to communicate a negative experience, the likelihood to communicate with others about a company at all, the likelihood to make mainly positive or mainly negative comments if the company came up in conversation, and a few others. The question that most optimally allowed us to improve the measurement of detractors was closest to a unidimensional opposite of the NPS question: "How likely are you to discourage others from doing business with this company?"

There are a number of ways that the information from what we call "the discourage question" could be used with NPS to build a single metric—ideally, a full system of metrics that supports good decision making about all of the variation in data collected with scaled questions. This is true of ForeSee's predictive models. However, to maintain Net Promoter's simplicity and meet the needs of executives to track one number, we adjusted NPS by using the data from the new question while keeping the original NPS question intact. Individuals observing and tracking NPS could understand it as a modified score that more accurately reflects the full range of potential word-of-mouth behavior.

Phase 2: Initial Client Testing

Goal: Validate WoMI metric across numerous companies and industries.

The results from the ForeSee large-scale studies led us to believe that the WoMI metric was a notable improvement over NPS, so we moved forward with a client testing phase. The testing opportunity was introduced to ForeSee clients in the fall of 2011 at our user summit (the same one I described in Chapter 1, where I had the great conversations with John, Anna, and Alex, who had such vastly different opinions on NPS). Initially, only attendees to our summit were offered the opportunity to participate, and our first round of client testing involved seven companies. All the remaining clients were invited to participate in November 2011, and the list of companies testing WoMI grew to 55 companies with 78 measures (several companies were measuring more than just one channel). Clients have continued to come on board, and we are currently measuring WoMI for more than 100 customers. During the testing phase, initial results were promising. In October 2011, WoMI seemed to be measuring detractors more accurately than NPS, reducing the overstatement of detractors by 161 percent on average. The initial data also led us to test further refinements of the question and its placement in a survey.

Phase 3: Later Client Testing

Goals: Refine approach and develop best practices.

Certain clients participated in adjustments so that we could test questions to optimize the quality of the resulting metric. Client feedback was also incorporated into the testing process.

Not surprisingly, a portion of respondents answered the recommend and discourage questions in contrary ways: Some people who rated their likelihood to recommend at a high level also rated their likelihood to discourage at a high level. This type of measurement error is commonly found when multiple rating-scale questions are used. After answering a number of questions, some respondents stop reading carefully and assume that the positive and negative ends of the rating questions' scales will not change. This phenomenon is often called "straight lining." Fortunately, the proportion of contrary responses in our research was fairly small. We minimized this source of error by varying the position of the question so as to enhance the chances of respondents reading the question and the anchors more carefully.

In rare cases, we see survey respondents say they are both "very likely to recommend" and "very likely to discourage" not because of "straightlining," but because the respondent is imagining speaking to different audiences.

Imagine taking a survey about Rolex. When asked the two questions, "how likely are you to recommend Rolex?" and "how likely are you to discourage someone from doing business with Rolex?" you think, "For my friends who have a lot of disposable income and appreciate nice watches, I would absolutely recommend Rolex, but I would definitely discourage my son who just graduated from college from buying a Rolex." Another example is a very loyal FoxNews viewer who enthusiastically recommends the channel to conservative friends, but goes out of her way to discourage liberal friends from programming they would probably find irritating. This same equivocation exists across multiple industries and has more to do with to whom the survey respondent is speaking and less to do with the product or service in question.

These instances are rare, but they do happen. When they do, careful investigation of the data and strategic follow up questions can help business leaders uncover the issues at the heart of a seemingly impossible situation—a customer who is likely to recommend *and* likely to discourage someone from doing business with the same company.

Another topic that came up in testing was what to use as the object of the recommend question. Some ForeSee clients measure the likelihood to recommend the channel (such as a website), others measure the likelihood to recommend the company, and still others measure both ways. "Recommend channel" and "recommend company" behaved similarly enough for testing purposes. However, as a best practice, we advocate measuring the same object for both the recommend and discourage questions.

WoMI Testing Results

The Discourage Question

ForeSee's supplemental question measured the likelihood to discourage others from doing business with a company. The average proportion of 9 and 10 ratings within the test group of surveys settled in at 10 percent. However, the level of variation between companies told us that NPS users cannot simply apply an adjustment to their score without actually asking the discourage question. This type of negative word-of-mouth behavior can vary greatly. It needs to be measured separately from the recommend question to be properly understood.

Detractor Overstatement

The NPS overstatement of detractors was determined with the calculation in Figure 4.4.

Here's an example of how the detractor overstatement is derived. If company A has 30 percent detractors as defined by NPS (the percentage of one to six ratings to the recommend question), and it has 10 percent detractors as defined by WoMI (the percentage of

$$\text{NPS Overstatement of Detractors} = \frac{\text{Recommend \% of 1s to 6s} - \text{Discourage \% of 9s and 10s}}{\text{Discourage \% of 9s and 10s}}$$

Figure 4.4 Calculating NPS Overstatement of Detractors

9 or 10 ratings to the discourage question), then that company's NPS score reflects a 200 percent overstatement of detractors: (30 percent – 10 percent)/10 percent = 200 percent). The overstatement percentage varied widely, ranging from 6 to 1,180 percent for individual companies for the entire study period (monthly percentages averaged through August 2012). Detractor overstatement typically fell within a narrower range, however. Most participants' overstatement percentages ranged between 0 and 400 percent. The average overstatement percentage settled in at around 260 to 270 percent for our clients. Companies should measure the discourage question to get a true detractor score and to determine the degree to which detractor overstatement is affecting their NPS scores.

NPS and WoMI Score Differences

If the previous example company has 55 percent promoters (recommend percent of 9s and 10s), then its NPS score is 25 percent (55 percent – 30 percent), and its WoMI score would be 45 percent (55 percent – 10 percent), a 20-point gap. In other words, if we more accurately measure detractors by asking a question that focuses on actual detractor behavior (the likelihood to discourage someone from doing business with a company), as in WoMI, the example company's score is 20 points higher than its NPS score.

Using our August client test data, the average score gap for all 70 participating surveys was similar to this example; the average WoMI score in August was 42 percent, which is 20 points higher than the average NPS score of 22 percent.

Recommend and Discourage Scores

Looking at recommend and discourage scores among the companies who participated in our test, we find a wide range represented. High recommend scores and low discourage scores are most desirable. ForeSee's cause-and-effect models demonstrate the relationship between satisfaction with the customer experience and these potential future behaviors by quantifying them in the form of impacts (further explained in Chapter 5).

Impacts explain the causal relationship between 1) the key drivers of the experience and the satisfaction with the customer experience and 2) the satisfaction with the customer experience and the outcomes of the experience, which we often refer to as the future behaviors of the customer. We use impacts to identify where to focus our improvements to pay the largest dividends in improving the customer experience and the desired future behaviors. The areas with the largest impacts will have the largest return on investment. Another good way to think of impacts is that they identify the slope of the line of the equation that defines the relationship between the drivers of the experience and the satisfaction with the customer experience and the outcomes of the experience. The bigger the impact, the steeper the slope and the bigger the lift in the satisfaction and the future behaviors you should expect to see when you make improvements. So not only do the impacts help you identify the highest priority items to focus your customer experience improvements on but also they help you identify the expected lift in future behaviors you should expect to see with the improvement. The sophisticated calculations to impacts are discussed further in Chapter 5.

Continuing Implementation

We have continued panel research in order to have company-level data we can share publicly (while our clients are enthusiastic participants, testers, and adopters, they don't always want us to share their data!). In Appendix A, you will find WoMI scores (along with satisfaction, NPS scores, and overstatements of detractors) for the 100 biggest brands in the world across all industries, along with lists of scores for online retailers, stores, financial services companies, and mobile experiences in retail, travel, and financial services.

In Virtually Every Industry, We See a Massive Overstatement of Detractors

At this point, we have collected nearly 2 million customer surveys around this concept for nearly 300 companies over two years. In addition, we have collected more than 100 million responses to the Net Promoter question itself over the past 10 years. We have put far more time and research into the development of WoMI than was ever done (or at least disclosed) for Net Promoter, and some may think it's overkill. Maybe it's my Midwestern roots, but I have always tried to balance innovation with thorough testing and tweaking so that I have total confidence in what I'm recommending. And I do. I can say without a shadow of a doubt that WoMI is a better metric, that it accurately measures both positive and negative word of mouth, and that when used as part of a comprehensive customer experience measurement ecosystem, it can be a powerful tool for both CEOs who want one number and analytics superstars who need intelligence to actually move the needle.

> WoMI has been tested with more than 300 companies over two years and represents more than 2 million customer surveys.

Following is a summary of the research from the 100 biggest brands in the world (with additional detail in Appendix A).

As you can see in Figure 4.5, for the top financial services brands on average, NPS would say that 35 percent of their customers are detractors. This 35 percent is based on the percentage of people who, when asked, "How likely are you to recommend this company?" answer with a score of 6 or less. NPS defines those people as detractors. When asked, "How likely are you to discourage people from doing business with this company?" only 8 percent answer that question with a 9 or 10 on a 10-point scale. This is an overstatement of detractors of more than 500 percent for the average financial services company (and you can see how individual companies fare from all these categories in Appendix A).

Figure 4.5 Overstatement of Detractors

Categories	Satisfaction	WOMI Score	NPS Score	NPS-Defined Detractors*	WOMI-Defined Detractors**	NPS Overstatement of Detractors***
Automotive	79	44	38	17%	11%	85%
B2B	79	43	36	17%	11%	96%
Computers/Electronics Manufacturers	78	45	33	18%	6%	264%
Consumer Packaged Goods	78	44	31	19%	5%	399%
Financial Services	70	28	1	35%	8%	527%
Retail	80	47	39	15%	6%	222%
Other	73	33	10	30%	6%	499%

*NPS definition of detractors is anyone who rates their likelihood to recommend a company 6 or lower on a 10-point scale.

**WoMI defines detractors as anyone who rates their likelihood to detract from a company with a 9 or 10 on a 10-point scale. This group is also referred to as "True Detractors."

***Overstatement of detractors is calculated using the following formula: (% of NPS-defined detractors – % of WoMI-defined detractors)/% of WoMI-defined detractors. The average overstatement at the category level is an average of the company-level overstatements of detractors. The overall average overstatement is the average of the overstatements of each underlying category.

WoMI—The Next Generation of NPS

Using WoMI with NPS

If your organization already uses NPS, WoMI builds on what you've already been doing and doesn't require you to stop using NPS. It just requires that you add one additional question and calculation. The following best practices have been developed as a result of this research and will help your company achieve optimal results.

- **Use the recommend question to measure positive word of mouth at the company or brand level.**

    The likelihood-to-recommend question is a very good question to measure and understand positive word of mouth. By keeping this question consistent as you evolve from NPS to WoMI, you will receive the benefit of continuing the trends and leveraging your historical data. Having the question focused on the company or brand level as the source of the recommendation provides the highest level of analysis and the same object as the discourage question.

- **Use the discourage question to measure negative word of mouth at your company or your brand level to reflect the full range of word-of-mouth behavior.**

    By measuring NPS only, you risk excluding an important facet of word-of-mouth behavior. With the discourage question, you are able to identify the potential true detractors to your business.

- **Measure the discourage question toward the end of the survey to minimize the effects of survey straight lining and measurement error.**

- **Use the WoMI score as part of your system of metrics to understand the potential impact of both positive word of mouth and negative word of mouth on your business.** With a measurement of positive word of mouth (true promoters) and negative word of mouth (true detractors), you will have a much deeper understanding of the value of word of mouth.

- **If you are using NPS, you can complement it with the more accurate and precise WoMI.** Since WoMI still involves asking the same recommend question, you can run WoMI and NPS in parallel to better understand the differences.

The benefits of using these best practices are clear. The goal in any measurement system is to get the appropriate level of accuracy and precision so you can make decisions with confidence. You also want to utilize those measurements so you can take action when necessary. An enormous amount of research has been done at ForeSee and by many others to improve the accuracy and precision of measurement.

Let me take a moment to explain the difference between accuracy and precision. Accuracy simply means that your measurement is correct. Think of your wristwatch, the clock on the wall, or the time on your cell phone. Let's say that these show you only the hours, not the minutes. The time is still accurate. When they say it is 10 o'clock, it is. However, accuracy alone doesn't get you to your meetings on time. You need precision to accompany the accuracy. Add minutes to your watch, clock, and cell phone. Now you know when you are precisely on time for a business phone call or a doctor's appointment or when you are late.

Regarding accuracy and precision, one without the other does you very little good. You need to have the accurate time and both hours and minutes on your watch to have the right level of precision to get to your meetings on time. With only hours and minutes on your watch, clock, and cell phone, you won't be late for meetings or appointments, but you would have trouble timing a 100-yard dash. All you could say about Usain Bolt is that he was very fast. You need the right level of precision to make the right business decisions.

As you move from NPS to WoMI, you are increasing your accuracy and precision so you can have better measurement and can take the right actions as a result of your measurement.

NPS is a great example of where a lack of accuracy can lead to wasted effort and missed opportunities. Recently, I was speaking with a financial institution that had been using NPS for a few years. The use of NPS accomplished a few things for this company. The importance of the customer had become its rallying cry, starting with the CEO. NPS was measured across all of their business units and published throughout the organization. It was even a number that was shared with Wall Street analysts and often made its way into their annual report. As a result of NPS, frontline employees became more focused on the importance of customer service than before its introduction.

After a few years, however, a few employees and managers within the company began to question the relationship between NPS and the company's revenue growth. They had assumed that NPS would predict their revenue growth, which is a common mistake. When they modeled the results and compared them to their growth, they did not see the strong relationship that they were expecting. Consultants were brought in to help them figure out what to do, and they had a great idea—reach out to those identified by NPS as detractors and see whether they could be converted into promoters (customers likely to recommend this company to others).

As in any large organization, a great deal of work is needed to roll out a program like this. The company formed a team tasked to convert detractors into promoters. What they found perplexed them at first. Most of the people they contacted who had given a score of less than 6 in response to the likelihood-to-recommend question were good, loyal customers who had no intention of defecting. However, they were also customers who were not likely to recommend this financial institution to others. When the company did what the customers expected, they were satisfied and loyal.

At first, the consultants suspected that a poor measurement device was the culprit. As they dug further, they saw that was not true. They realized that not being likely to recommend the financial institution to others did not mean that the consumers were not loyal or satisfied with the company.

This caused the financial institution to rethink its strategy. It looked for a way to make these data more accurate, precise, and actionable. My discussion with the institution was in the early stages of our testing of WoMI. I shared with the people there the concepts that we were in the process of proving. It opened their eyes to the problems of NPS.

Now does that mean this company should throw out NPS and jump on the WoMI bandwagon? Well, part of the beauty of WoMI is that it enables you to find out who your true detractors are now. You gain better insight to good and bad word of mouth. And you can continue to report your NPS score if you must.

Over time, you will see the difference in clarity, and when you have some history for comparison purposes, then you can make the change. This strategy allows you to gain the benefits of WoMI right away and not lose the value of your history and trends. And that is the strategy that the financial institution decided on: to understand its true detractors and, after gathering some historical data, introduce to Wall Street analysts these more powerful metrics.

As I continued to talk with other companies that were using NPS, I found more and more examples like that of the financial institution. These challenges existed in all industries, from airlines, apparel, and automotive to health care, hospitality, consumer products, retail, telecommunication, and universities. They existed in both business-to-consumer (B2C) and business-to-business (B2B) models.

So is WoMI the new "one number you need to know?" Is it the new ultimate question? No. If you run your business successfully, you need to know more than one number and ask a lot of really important questions. Instead, WoMI is the next generation of NPS that will give you a clear understanding of who the true promoters and true detractors are. Word of mouth is part of the answer to growing your business by bringing in new customers. New customer acquisition is going to be fueled by identifying new prospects by marketing, advertising, and word of mouth. Remember the four drivers of growth: (1) keep your customers, (2) sell more to your existing customers, (3) acquire new customers by utilizing marketing, and (4) acquire new customers as a result of word of mouth. WoMI has an important place in what needs to be your system of metrics used to manage your business and drive growth.

Interview: Jason Faria, ideeli

Ideeli has been using NPS to measure data on all of our call center and post-purchase experiences since August 2010. We decided to utilize NPS based on our executives' use of Net Promoter at previous organizations. And since ideeli was a small startup at the time,

NPS seemed like the easiest and quickest option for an effective in-house approach.

In our call center, we allocated resources to NPS to try and better understand the expectations we were setting for our members, and how to manage those expectations more effectively. We segmented out our top buyers and measured their scores separately: If we saw directional changes, we tried to hypothesize what was driving those directional shifts. But as time passed, we found that we were having to hypothesize more than we should: NPS was too simple and couldn't meet our needs. It only provided two options—to either maintain as-is or to change something, but it never told us what to maintain or what to change. That lack of direction caused us to unnecessarily adjust things that had been performing well.

But since implementing WoMI, we have completely changed how we think about word of mouth and its measurement, because WoMI clearly and accurately defines what action must be taken. WoMI eliminates overstated detractors, and has allowed us to concentrate our efforts on areas where we will get the greatest return.

We plan on using WoMI internally as an educational tool for managers and employees across our business silos. WoMI serves as a strategic starting point for us to finesse how we can best leverage the details of true detractors, while also giving us the ability to benchmark against our competitors and ourselves over time.

The biggest difference between WoMI and NPS: the post-purchase data and the call center data from WoMI is much more clear. WoMI accurately shows us how our brand is holding up, on both web and mobile platforms, in a way NPS didn't.

Jason Faria is director of customer service at ideeli. Ideeli is a flash sale online retailer based in New York City. It acquires excess or sample merchandise and sells it quickly at very steep discounts to their members. Sales typically last less than 48 hours.

Founded in 2006, its $77M in revenue in 2010 led *Inc.* magazine to rank it as the fastest growing company in the United States for 2011. It has raised $70M in venture capital funding.

Chapter 5

The Four Drivers of Business Success

In the previous chapter, we focused on the impact of word of mouth as a driver of your business success and the best way to measure it, WoMI. I briefly mentioned a list of three other major drivers of financial success with customers, making a total list of four:

1. Customer retention, keeping your current customers.

2. Customer upsell, selling more to your existing customers.

3. Marketing-driven customer acquisition, acquiring new customers via various marketing and advertising efforts.

4. Word-of-mouth-driven customer acquisition, acquiring new customers who are brought to your organization by the recommendations of others.

In today's ultracompetitive business environment, what I've called Accelerated Darwinism, only the strong survive, and success and failure can happen at an alarming rate. You need to excel at a *minimum* of one of these drivers to have a chance at survival. If you are great at three or four of these drivers, you have a chance to do great things and be an industry leader. As companies mature, often their strengths shift among these revenue and growth drivers.

Google built its businesses at the beginning by using word of mouth to acquire new customers and did a great job in retaining their current customers (or users). Both of these growth attributes were driven by providing a great customer experience. As its market share growth has slowed, Google is using upsell to continue its growth trajectory. While you could argue that Google doesn't sell anything, so how can it upsell, it is increasing the number of things you do with Google, in essence increasing both the products its customers use and the frequency with which they use the products. Searching for flight information, the weather and sports scores all without leaving Google are a few ways Google is driving upsell, which is getting consumers to use Google for things it didn't before. Consumers are using more of Google's products, for example, Gmail, Google Maps, and, to a lesser extent, Google Plus are newer Google capabilities that existing customers are starting to utilize. And while you may not pay Google in cash to use its products, you are paying it by allowing yourself to be exposed to its advertising which drives revenue for Google.

The growth attributes of McDonald's have evolved over time as well. In the mid-1960s, the food chain grew on the basis of retaining its customers by providing a great customer experience—consistent quality, fast service, and a fun environment. In 1979, McDonald's added the Happy Meal to help keep the customer experience fresh. In those days, word of mouth was also a strong revenue driver. I remember my own first visit to a McDonald's on Telegraph Road in Southfield, Michigan, in the mid-1960s. Back then, it was absolutely a new experience, and people actively recommended McDonald's to others. I was a Big Mac fan back then and will still order one if my wife is not with me! But that was then, and this is now. While I might have raved about a Big Mac as a kid in the 1960s, when is the last time you heard someone recommending McDonald's in the last 20 years? It rarely happens (though the McRib does have its legions of loyal fans, or so I hear!)

While the power of word of mouth is no longer a revenue driver for McDonald's, as it matured and became known to just about everyone, marketing and advertising became far more important than word of mouth to complement its customer retention strategies. In addition, McDonald's has used a strong upsell strategy by expanding its menu choices and offering breakfast, "healthy" menu items, and more types of sandwiches, sides, and desserts. McDonald's is a great example of a company that has evolved its revenue growth attributes over time. Many of those who don't remember the word-of-mouth component that contributed to McDonald's may come to the conclusion that word of mouth doesn't play a role in the fast food industry.

The history of McDonald's shows you that it does—and those were the days that the only way word of mouth happened was when you actually talked with someone. But today, while you may not be recommending that Big Mac to your friends, word of mouth still plays a big role in revenue growth for other fast food chains. Chick-fil-A and In-N-Out Burger are still strong word-of-mouth companies.

Other companies such as Comcast and AT&T work very hard to retain their customers. Competition in their industries is fierce, and reducing customer churn is a key success metric for them. Both companies do a lot of marketing to help them acquire new customers. And they continue to work hard at selling more products to their existing customers. Does the phrase "triple play" ring a bell? It was a campaign by Comcast to upsell their cable TV subscribers to Internet and phone usage.

The strategies any company employs will vary, and to survive over the long run, a company is going to have to evolve its strategy for which of these growth attributes is going to contribute the most to its growth. Going from a good company to a great company and being able to stay there is no easy feat. The key is to continue to evolve. Standing still doesn't work very well in the business world. When you are standing still, you are an easy target for upstart competitors.

What we see way too often are businesses simply living in the moment—resting on their laurels. Company leaders find something (a strategy, sale, measurement, *anything*) that appears to work in this chaotic business world we live in and they stick with it and continue as though all is right in the world.

While I completely understand this, it just doesn't work. Living in the moment sounds great (you're living to the fullest, making the most of a situation). Right? What can be wrong with that? I see a moment as a stagnant interval of time. And standing still (especially in business) can be quite reckless because you are living with little (or no) regard for the future. As business leaders we cannot take our eye off the future. Change is inevitable and constant and moves at a fierce velocity. Conversely, your company should always be moving forward. Therefore, you need to live in the momentum not the moment. Momentum is motion, continuous. Moment is standstill.

Examples of how companies utilize these growth attributes to keep company momentum moving forward in different ways are endless. A good exercise is to look at successful companies and think about which of these growth drivers they used to achieve success and how their strategy has evolved. You can learn a lot from others successes and failures. Ask yourself how Nordstrom, Apple, Starbucks, Facebook, Amazon, and others achieved their growth. Then look at other companies that are struggling or have failed and figure out which attributes they lost and what they could have done to find other growth attributes to replace those lost. Think about companies such as Borders, CompUSA, Blockbuster, and others.

Customer Retention

Keeping your customers is a very important part of revenue growth. It is far easier than replacing them. Many businesses use the words *retention* and *loyalty* interchangeably. In business terms, loyalty is faithfulness or allegiance to a company or brand. In short, when I am loyal to a company, that company is my first choice. According to *Inc.* magazine, acquiring a new customer costs about five to nine times more than it does to sell to an existing one—and, on average, those current customers of yours spend 67 percent more than do new ones.

In broader terms, you should consider five basic forms of customer retention:

1. Purchased Loyalty
2. Convenience Loyalty
3. Restricted Loyalty
4. Competitive Retention
5. True Loyalty

Purchased, convenience, and restricted loyalty are really forms of retention. You can also retain customers by simply winning the competitive battle for the business every time.

Purchased Loyalty

The best example of purchased loyalty is a customer rewards program. Other examples include memberships, coupons, and rebates. Basically, purchased loyalty pays customers to be loyal—and there is nothing wrong with that practice. In many industries and market sectors, the purchased loyalty strategy works well. Best Buy implemented their Rewards Zone a few years ago, and it not only provides them better intelligence about its customers shopping habits but also by giving reward certificates that carry a value when you purchase at Best Buy it incents consumers to come back and buy more from Best Buy than from other electronics retailers. However, the Best Buy rewards program gets some competition from Amazon Prime, the company's membership program that provides free shipping on most products that Amazon carries. This is a good example of an effective attempt at purchasing customer loyalty but also brings to light that others can outbid you for your customers by creating more attractive rewards to the customer.

Grocery stores, drugstores, clothing stores, movie theaters, restaurants, credit card companies, and many others have jumped on the loyalty program bandwagon. Others accomplish similar types of benefits with more of a membership program. Costco is a good example of this. Customers who have paid the yearly dues are more compelled to go to Costco than to a competitor. Amazon is using its Amazon Prime membership to not only provide free shipping but also to supply some free content (books and movies) to its customers as an entry into the very lucrative content business. The most common example of purchased loyalty is the frequent flyer program that virtually every airline has in place. These can be stand-alone programs or tied to credit cards—the more you fly and the more you spend, the more miles you earn.

The main problem with purchased loyalty is that it can be easily stolen. If the only reason a customer is loyal to an airline is the points system of a frequent flyer program, he or she will immediately switch when another airline offers a more advantageous system.

According to Colloquy's Loyalty Census, released last year, the average U.S. household is signed up for 14.1 loyalty programs but participates in only 6.2 of them. Moreover, consumers redeem only an estimated two-thirds of the $48 billion worth of perceived value in reward points and miles distributed annually by American businesses. Companies lose money on time and effort on the remaining third, and customers aren't taking advantage of the value. So while purchased loyalty programs can be part of the mix, you have to make sure they are not the only kind of loyalty your brands engender and are executing well (so that your loyalty program is one of the 6.2 that people use rather than the 7.9 they don't).

Convenience Loyalty

Your corner market, your local dry cleaner, and the coffee shop on your way to work keep customers loyal because of convenience. You may or may not enthusiastically gush about their products or services, you may not even prefer them. But they are convenient enough that you regularly patronize these businesses. Your loyalty may vanish if a competitor becomes equally or even more convenient.

Convenience loyalty can apply to online business as well, although less commonly. If you own the right real estate on a home page or portal (through great placement of Google ad words or if your product is one of the first search results returned on Amazon .com), you may create loyalty through convenience.

Convenience loyalty remains mostly an advantage in the offline world, and even then convenience advantages are generally fleeting. Twenty years ago, if you wanted a television, there may have been one local big-box electronics retailer to visit. Regardless of whether you loved the store's products and services, you probably bought your TV there because it was more convenient.

The Internet has largely eliminated the power of convenience loyalty. Today, even if you have half a dozen stores in your town to buy a TV, you can easily jump online and find the best deal on exactly what you want. And even if you do go to the store to look because it's convenient, you can use your mobile phone in the store (what's known as showrooming) to go online and check out competitors' prices, all while looking at the actual physical television. "Location, location, location" is no longer the most powerful factor in retail success in today's multichannel, Accelerated Darwinism environment.

Restricted Loyalty

Restricted loyalty exists when there is no other game in town. This kind of loyalty is less and less common in the Internet age. Even five years ago, your cable company may have enjoyed restricted loyalty, especially if you lived in a rural setting with no competition. But today you can choose Hulu, Netflix, and network-specific mobile apps (HBO, ABC, Lifetime, etc.) that stream content.

Utilities tend to enjoy restricted loyalty. Most cities do not have multiple electricity providers. Arguably, some Walmart locations enjoy a form of restricted loyalty with a dollop of convenience loyalty mixed in. If Walmart is the only game in your town, naturally you are loyal. We work with a lot of government agencies that we joke have restricted loyalty—after all, no matter how unhappy you are with the IRS, you can't pay your taxes in Canada.

Restricted loyalty is great for a business—if you can get it and maintain it—but it is increasingly a thing of the past. Competition exists in almost every consumer situation, both within an industry or category and in the larger marketplace. Companies compete, especially in down economies, for a larger share of wallets across industries and markets.

Even for companies such as a local electric utility that are providing a service that people truly can't get elsewhere, relying solely on restricted loyalty is a dangerous game. You never know when a competitor will enter the marketplace. It can also be extremely expensive to manage customers who are using you only because they feel they have no other choice. When a customer actively chooses your company, rather than being stuck with it due to a lack of alternatives, complaints go down, call volumes go down, and costs also go down.

Remember that purchased, convenience, and restricted loyalty are not bad and in fact in most cases are good for your business. They have always been hard to sustain. Just ask someone who worked for Ma Bell after its breakup back in the 1980s. In today's world, it is harder than ever to hold onto loyalty. In reality, purchased loyalty, convenience loyalty, and restricted loyalty are really examples of customer retention, not customer loyalty.

Competitive Retention

In addition to purchased, convenience, and restricted loyalty, there are other methods of retaining customers. If you can stay within the considered set of alternatives for your customers, you have a chance to get them to return. It might not be exclusively, but you can still keep them as customers. You can retain customers by winning the competition for their attention and business. When I am looking to buy electronics, I don't have a preferred retailer. I look around and may purchase from one of many retailers. Each one that I return to is an example of customer retention. They may win on product selection, product availability, or price, but each time they are going to have to compete.

True Loyalty

True loyalty is earned loyalty. True loyalty is undying allegiance to a brand or product based on an incredible level of satisfaction. Customer satisfaction breeds true loyalty. When you are highly satisfied, when your needs are completely met, and your expectations are consistently met and even exceeded, you simply cannot imagine using another product or service. True loyalty is the holy grail of the customer experience and what every business should aspire to create.

Examples abound. Whenever Apple introduces a new product, the lines around its stores stretch for blocks. This was true even during the height of the Great Recession. Starbucks customers remain loyal although the coffee at Dunkin' Donuts and even McDonald's has been rated highly and is not as expensive. Google maintains its edge on Bing and the former search champ Yahoo! And Amazon through Amazon Prime streams video perks as a way of maintaining its already intense loyalty from its customers.

The ultimate goal for almost every business is to create and foster true loyalty. When you measure the right things, listen to the voice of the customer, and make changes and improvements that increase customer satisfaction, you can create truly loyal customers.

Loyal customers come back. You do not have to win them or pay to acquire and keep them. They are more profitable as well, since new customers are much more expensive to acquire.

In other words, loyalty is an outcome of satisfaction with the customer experience. To increase loyalty, you need to increase satisfaction. All forms of customer retention and customer loyalty are driven by having a satisfying customer experience. If you have a horrible experience, your likelihood of returning to that company is low. Even if you fall into the convenience loyalty, or purchased loyalty groups, a bad customer experience will drive your desire to go where you are getting a better experience. And if you're in the restricted loyalty group, a bad customer experience will force you jump to another alternative as soon as you have an alternative available to you. Retention programs often put defection obstacles in front of you, but often they are not insurmountable and long lasting. The satisfaction bar for true loyalty is a lot higher to obtain and to hold on to! Achieving and maintaining true loyalty will have a very positive impact on your financial success.

But to increase satisfaction with the customer experience and therefore achieve true loyalty, you must first measure the customer experience, both satisfaction and loyalty. A potential behavior such as likelihood to recommend does not measure loyalty; it measures positive word of mouth.

We recently worked with a fantasy sports provider. Fantasy sports is any sports competition with imaginary teams that the participants own, manage, and coach. Games are based on strategies generated by actual players or teams of a professional sport, such as the Rotisserie League among baseball fans. We found that 27 percent of its users said they would not be likely to recommend the provider, but only 3 percent said they were likely to share such feedback with others. This demonstrated that people not likely to recommend a service would not automatically *volunteer* that information to someone else.

To maintain customer loyalty, always understand customer needs and expectations, continuously measure the customer experience, and then make changes that positively impact the customer experience.

Don't be lazy. Matching a competitor's loyalty program is certainly easier than creating satisfied customers while practicing fiscal responsibility. (After all, satisfying your customers is easy if you don't have to be fiscally responsible. Simply spend what you want!)

Convenience loyalty is wonderful, especially if you work hard to choose the right locations or modes of delivery. Purchased loyalty has its place. Restricted loyalty is great if you can get it. But those forms of loyalty are difficult to obtain and tend to yield fleeting advantages. True loyalty based on customer satisfaction is the ultimate goal of any business and the only long-term competitive advantage.

Upsell

Selling more to your existing customers is always a good strategy for engendering loyalty when done correctly. It can be in a B2B environment where a software company sells multiple products to their clients. It can be a shoe store that sells socks. It can be Apple, who has many of us convinced that we need the newest iPhone every time a new version is released. Now, it is simple to understand that I cannot sell more to my existing customers if they aren't loyal. So customer loyalty is a requirement if I want to upsell to my current customers. Upsell can be a great growth driver and often is a lot easier to execute than bringing in new customers. To sell more to your customers, you are going to have to be delivering a pretty good experience along the way and have satisfied customers.

Marketing-Driven Customer Acquisition

Acquiring new customers is another important revenue driver. There are two primary ways you can acquire new customers. The first is driven by marketing efforts. This could be advertising on television, product placement in movies, billboards, e-mail marketing, search engine marketing, Facebook marketing, and so on. You will find many different methods and many experts, each with their own opinions on the best ways. I leave that discussion and debate to others.

However, I would like you to keep in mind a few points about acquisition. Despite all the innovation in the area of media, from iPhones to the Internet, from digital to mobile, traditional sites and methods of reaching the public continue to exist. We still have stores, billboards, radios, and newspapers. The idea is to use the correct analytics to discover which of this greatly expanded palette of channels is working best and how to achieve customer satisfaction for which group so you can make the right offer at the right time in the right place.

My second point is to think carefully about how much money, resources, and time you should devote to marketing and advertising. It worked wonders for AT&T, IBM, Samsung, Axe, and McDonald's, but be warned: don't become another Pets.com. As you may remember, it was a dot-com enterprise that sold pet supplies to retail customers. It began operations in August 1998 and closed in November 2000.

The company rolled out a regional advertising campaign using a variety of media (TV, print, radio, and eventually a Pets.com magazine). It started with a 5-city advertising campaign rollout and then expanded the campaign to 10 cities by Christmas 1999. The company succeeded wildly in making its mascot, the Pets.com sock puppet, well known. With button eyes, flailing arms, and a stick microphone emblazoned with pets.com, it was a memorable mascot. In January 2000, the company aired its first national commercial as a Super Bowl ad, which cost the company $1.2 million and introduced the country to the answer as to why customers should shop at an online pet store: "Because Pets Can't Drive!" That ad was ranked number one by *USA Today*'s Ad Meter and had the highest recall of any ad that ran during the Super Bowl. The sock puppet mascot was so popular that it was interviewed by *People* magazine and appeared on *Good Morning America*.

The company went public in February 2000; the Nasdaq stock symbol was IPET. Although sales rose dramatically as a result of all this attention, the company was weak on fundamentals. Pets.com lacked a workable business plan and lost money on nearly every sale because, even before the cost of advertising, it was selling merchandise for approximately one-third the price it paid to obtain the products. More than $300 million of investment capital vanished with the company's failure.

So as Sergeant Esterhaus used to say at the beginning of every episode of *Hill Street Blues* when he dispatched the police, "Let's be careful out there."

The important point is that a company is going to use many methods to bring potential customers to the door (and the door here is not necessarily a literal door anymore). Once they are engaged, you need to convert them to actual customers. How do you do that? By providing a great customer experience. That is the key driver to conversion, and it includes all aspects of the experience. So, if the experience meets customers' needs and exceeds their expectations or, in other words, is a satisfying experience, you are going to be able to convert those prospects into customers.

Word-of-Mouth-Driven Customer Acquisition

Another way to acquire new customers is through word of mouth. The process of converting someone from a prospect to a customer is the same as that of the marketing-driven approach. The difference is in what motivated the person to engage with you and potentially become a customer. Here it is word of mouth. It can be social word of mouth via Facebook, Twitter, or LinkedIn, or it might be good old-fashioned word of mouth, where someone talked to someone else and recommended your business. Here the satisfaction of the experience does double duty. A satisfied customer is more likely to recommend your business to others. And once you are engaged with those prospects, if the customer experience is satisfying to them, their prospects of becoming customers increase dramatically.

Customer Intent and True Conversion Rate

Another driver of success is the rate by which a business converts the customers it attracts through marketing and advertising. Conversion rate is one of the most commonly misused behavioral metrics. Conversion rate measures the number of visitors to a particular store, website, or sales call center within a specific period, divided into the number of people who take the desired action (make a purchase, register for a free trial, or any other intended actions). Many businesses feel that conversion rate is one of the most important metrics because they believe it can spell the difference between business success and failure.

What constitutes a good conversion rate depends on the industry and the nature of the action desired. According to Forrester Research, the average conversion rate for a typical e-commerce site is approximately 3.5 percent, which in and of itself is a misleading benchmark to apply.

For example, if your industry conversion rates typically fall between 3 and 5 percent, a 2 percent conversion rate is poor, and a 10 percent conversion rate is outstanding. Figure 5.1 illustrates the relationship between different conversion rates and the revenue they generate.

As conversion rates go up, revenues rise while marketing costs (as a percentage of total sales) fall. That is why these rates matter so much and why they are a basic key performance indicator (KPI): they directly impact revenue and the cost of customer acquisition.

At the same time, focusing solely on an aggregate conversion rate can be misleading. For example, a national jewelry company recently implemented a marketing campaign that flooded TV and print with ads spotlighting a specific product line for Valentine's Day. More

Figure 5.1   Conversion Rate

If Your Conversion Rate Is	You Acquired	At an Acquisition Cost/Customer of	Generating Revenue of
2%	200 customers	$100	$40,000
3%	300 customers	$66.67	$60,000
5%	500 customers	$40	$100,000
10%	1,000 customers	$20	$200,000

people were coming into the company's stores and onto its website, and overall sales went up as a result, but the conversion rate went down. The web analysts were watching conversion rate fall every week, half point by half point. It appeared that the marketing campaign caused the lower rate—but maybe not.

The company needed to look at the goal of its campaign. Was it to attract to its site a new audience segment largely unfamiliar with its brand? If the conversion rate before the campaign was 4 percent and the visitors who arrived because of the campaign converted at a 2 percent rate, the result was that new visitors converted at a lower rate, bringing the aggregate down, even though a greater number of total visitors converted.

This result is not necessarily bad or even surprising. New visitors, especially those unfamiliar with a brand, often convert at a lower rate than existing customers. The net business impact is positive—more people buy products—but using a conversion rate generates misleading information.

Why people visited a store or website is another critical piece of information often missing when businesspeople look at a conversion rate. Take the example of a company that manufactures and sells exterior doors. It added comprehensive service and repair information to its website. Now visitors could quickly find information to make basic home repairs to its products. Over time, more and more visitors sought that information, and the total number of site visitors increased. But the total number of conversions remained flat, and thus the company's conversion rate decreased. Some executives at the company assumed that the website changes were a mistake. They were wrong.

Although the conversion rate of total site visitors declined, the decline was the result of the *additional* visitors who came for information. The company was providing a better experience for those customers seeking support, thus increasing their customer satisfaction and their likelihood to buy more in the future and recommend the company to others. Not only that but also their positive experience lowered support costs elsewhere (fewer request in the company's call centers, for example).

Now a final example. An online electronics retailer that had never sold cell phones added them to its stores. To drive traffic, the retailer advertised heavily. Potential new customers who arrived as a result of advertising did not convert at as high a rate as normal site visitors; normal visitors tend to be repeat customers already familiar with the retailer's products and services. As a result, the aggregate conversion rate naturally decreased. Does a decreased aggregate conversion rate indicate that the decision to expand into the cell phone market was poor? No. It simply means that those sales occurred at a lower rate of conversion.

True Conversion Rate

The metric you should care about is your true conversion rate, which is the number of visitors who came to your site intending to make a purchase *who did in fact make that purchase*. The same is true with the visitors who came to your site seeking support information. You want to know whether they were able to find the information they sought.

True conversion starts with determining your business's specific goals and only then moves to measuring the customer's intent. What do you most want visitors to do in your store or on your site? If you do not define your goals, you cannot measure success or failure. For instance, in most cases your goal is for visitors to perform a specific action. If you are a retailer, your goal is for visitors to buy a product. If you focus on lead generation, your goal is for visitors to become leads. If you run a bank, your goal may be for visitors to open a new account, sign up for online banking, or pay a bill online.

For instance, a multichannel retailer has a website designed to provide two basic services: sell products and provide customer support. But visitors come to this site for different reasons. Some come to purchase a product, some arrive to do research for a potential future purchase, and some look for support. Visitors in the support category want to obtain instructions or maintenance information on purchased products, to check on the status of an order, or to search for a store location.

In fact, when ForeSee evaluated the 40 largest online retailers during the 2012 holiday season, we found the same three segments: 43 percent of visitors came to those sites with the intent of researching, 39 percent came with the intent to purchase, and 18 percent came with other intentions, such as product support or order status checks.

What is an acceptable conversion rate for these three segments? For the first segment, visitors who intend to make a purchase, we have seen true conversion rates as high as 40 percent, depending on the company and the industry. The second segment, visitors researching a product for a potential later purchase, is not easy to convert. They never planned to purchase in the first place; either they are still researching, or they have a plan to buy the item at another place or another time. Low single-digit, near-zero conversion rates for this group are the norm. Your objective then is to meet customer needs and exceed customer expectations—to satisfy the customer. The consumer determines success; you do not. The key is whether visitors found the information they wanted to find. A satisfying experience could potentially lead to an immediate purchase, but a future purchase is more likely, whether from a website or a retail store. Success for this segment cannot be measured by purchase alone at the time of the experience or by other behavioral measurements.

The third segment, the visitors who arrive for support, has no intention of making a purchase. Any conversion from this group is a bonus. Your goal is to satisfy these visitors by increasing their likelihood of becoming loyal customers and making a purchase in the future. You hope these visitors will also recommend you to others. Plus, they could possibly decrease our overall support costs, since the support they receive is online instead of through more costly channels such as a call center.

Let's take a look at some numbers. If 1,000 people visit your bank and 42 open an account, your aggregate conversion rate is 4.2 percent. Now drill down into segments. What is your true conversion rate? If 300 of your visitors arrived with the intent to open an account and you converted 36 of those visitors, your true conversion rate is 12 percent. If 400 arrived to do research and you converted 6 of those visitors, your conversion rate is 1.5 percent for this segment. If none of the 300 that came for support converted, your conversion rate is 0 percent.

Figure 5.2 shows the results.

Your true conversion rate was 12 percent. True conversion is a far more useful metric than an aggregate conversion, which was 4.2 percent.

What did you learn? First, conversion rate alone is not a measure of success. Is a 1.5 percent conversion rate a good or bad result for your researching segment? There is no way to tell by evaluating conversion rate alone. What you must know is whether visitors were satisfied and whether they are likely to purchase from you in the future, either online or off-line. The long-term value created from positive consumer experiences can be far more important to your business than the short-term value.

Success in your support segment cannot be measured by visitor behavior or conversion. Success should be measured by the customer experience satisfaction level of those visitors and by their future likely behaviors, such as whether they will recommend you to others, continue to use the online channel for support, or purchase more from you in the future. In other words, you must use different success metrics than conversion rate to evaluate visitors who arrived with no intent of making a purchase.

The true conversion metric provides a better and more accurate measurement of success. Use voice-of-customer research to find out why customers came in the first place and whether they were satisfied; combine this information with behavioral data to find out whether

Figure 5.2   True Conversion Rate

Intent of Visit	Visitors	Conversions	True Conversion Rate
Open New Account	300	36	12%
Research	400	6	1.50%
Support	300	0	0%
Total	1,000	42	4.20%

they made a purchase. Then you can transform conversion rate, a fundamentally misleading measurement, into a meaningful metric.

The Common Thread

To recap, there are four ways to drive growth in your business. They can be simply thought of as:

1. Customer retention, keeping your current customers.

2. Customer upsell, selling more to your existing customers.

3. Marketing-driven customer acquisition, acquiring new customers via various marketing and advertising efforts.

4. Word-of-mouth-driven customer acquisition, acquiring new customers who are brought to your organization by the recommendations of others.

What do all of these have in common? Each and every one of them is a direct result of a great, satisfying customer experience.

- If you satisfy your customers, they are much more likely to continue to be customers and be loyal with a strong allegiance to your brand or products.

- If you satisfy your customers, they are more likely to buy additional products or services from you and more likely to use you in other ways.

- If you satisfy your prospects, you are more likely to convert those who are driven to engage with you by various marketing methods to become customers.

- If you satisfy your customers, they are more likely to recommend you to others. Those who are driven to engage with you as a result of word of mouth are more likely to convert to customers if you satisfy them.

Satisfaction of the customer experience is the driver of all of these growth revenue attributes.

I am familiar with NPS because of my experience with it at my previous employer in the transportation industry. The executive team made the decision to bring NPS to the company and integrate it into every level of the organization. It was a massive movement to keep our customers at the front of each business decision. General Managers at each local market, as well as their staff, were expected to personally reach out to individuals who were identified as detractors. NPS became one of the key metrics we used to evaluate how each market was performing. We also used NPS to compare ourselves against other companies—not necessarily those solely in our industry but companies with significant size and performance over time.

The major benefit of NPS is in its simplicity. NPS was used as an overall indicator of customer satisfaction, but we asked five questions in addition to the NPS question of referral. One of those questions was about vehicle cleanliness. I remember one market in particular had low scores compared to the others, yet everyone was following the same cleaning schedule. What this simple question with NPS showed us was that this market had different needs than the others we served. We immediately saw a big bump in scores and revenue when we made the business decision to increase cleaning frequency in this market.

Despite the clear usefulness to businesses across all industries, NPS is limited because it isn't scientific and the results are not predictive of future success. Yet it also negatively overstates the impact of your Silent Majority (as Larry Freed calls them). When you have an overstated count of detractors, you focus too much business energy on what's going wrong in your business, but if a person scores you a 6, is that really something wrong? I would argue no. The fact is that a neutral score is really just that—a shrug-of-the-shoulders kind of score about a company you don't think about. WoMI allows for customers to be neutral but gives business leaders the insight they need to focus resources on people who are truly detractors. Business leaders know that a campaign to turn a detractor into a promoter is very different than one to turn neutral customers to promoters. WOMI sees this and does not arbitrarily group these two segments together.

WoMI has just been introduced here at Pear Tree Greetings, so we're watching the scores to get a baseline understanding of our performance. In the short term, we identify customers in the true detractor and true promoter categories and reach out to them. The goal is to understand their experience . . . the good, the bad, and the ugly. By measuring these groups quantitatively and understanding them qualitatively, I can guide my customer service representatives to these groups on either side of the spectrum more easily and more accurately which in turn guides better decision-making at all levels.

WoMI can have a significant positive effect on businesses by adding value to the NPS programs companies already have place.

Stephanie Bottner is general manager of Pear Tree Greetings, an award-winning online greeting card company with a unique collection of high-quality personalized photo cards and announcements, invitations, and innovative paper products. Pear Tree Greetings was founded in 2008.

Chapter 6

Why the Customer Experience Matters

In the previous two chapters, I have argued that customers' satisfaction with their experiences drives customer retention, customer upsell, marketing-driven customer acquisition, and word-of-mouth acquisition—all of which drive financial success. As satisfaction increases, sales increase. As satisfaction increases, transactions increase. As satisfaction increases in one channel, it drives sales in other channels. As satisfaction increases in comparison to the competition, the likelihood to purchase increases while the likelihood of purchasing from a competitor dramatically decreases. And as satisfaction increases, positive word-of-mouth True Promoters increase and negative word-of-mouth True Detractors decrease.

Many people use the terms "customer satisfaction" and "customer experience" interchangeably and there are some overlaps between the two concepts. The first important point is to consider a broad definition of "customer" for both definitions. Customer should mean any person or organization that interacts with a company as a customer, prospect, trading partner, or in some other similar capacity. A customer should be not be restricted to mean a person or organization that buys goods or services from a company.

A customer experience is the interaction between a customer (as defined above) and an organization. A customer experience is the sum of the components of the individual experience, and a few examples are elements such as service, quality, value, price,

(Continued)

(Continued)

and product. In some instances the customer experience will be defined to be a collection of experiences an individual or organization has with a company or other organization.

Customer satisfaction uses the broad definition of customer and is the way we measure the customer experience. A simple definition of customer satisfaction is the level that an experience meets your needs relative to your expectations.

Customer experience is what you are measuring and **satisfaction** is the metric we use to do that measurement. When you are measuring a distance, you can use feet or inches or kilometers or miles. When you are measuring the customer experience, you should use satisfaction because it is the most accurate, precise, credible, predictive, actionable measure of the customer experience.

Customer satisfaction also predicts financial performance. Since 2000, a stock portfolio of companies with strong customer satisfaction has outperformed the S&P 500 every year for 13 years in a row, in both weak and strong economies.

Okay, so we know satisfaction matters. Now, what defines customer satisfaction? Satisfaction is defined as how a customer's experience matches up to their expectation of that experience. Satisfaction is what happens when customers' real needs and expectations are met and potentially exceeded, and satisfaction makes for a good customer experience. It is that simple.

If I go to McDonald's, Burger King, or Wendy's, I don't expect a gourmet meal. I do expect a certain level of quality, fast service, and a relatively low price. Deliver on those expectations, and I am satisfied.

If I go to Fleming's Steakhouse or Wolfgang Puck American Grille, my expectations include great service, delicious food, an amazing atmosphere, and a bill considerably higher than when I glide my car through the takeout window of the Golden Arches.

If I go to Costco, I expect to pay relatively low prices, eat endless free samples (who needs lunch?) and receive the full warehouse experience of buying in bulk and carrying items in boxes instead of bags. At Nordstrom, I expect to pay a premium price and receive no free samples but to get great service, high-end clothing, and a return policy that will never question me.

Deliver on my needs and expectations, no matter how basic or how refined, and I will be satisfied; fail to deliver and I will not—a simple premise but one many businesses often overlook, largely because measuring expectations is difficult unless managers can rely on and trust a rigorous, tested methodology.

However, satisfaction is not binary: a customer is not either dissatisfied or satisfied. Most fall somewhere on a spectrum from very dissatisfied to very satisfied. Companies who say 85 percent of their customers are satisfied are missing the point. Think about an experience you had recently, could you answer a yes/no question on your satisfaction? Probably not. Whether it was the dinner you had at a restaurant, an experience shopping at a store, watching the news on TV or just about any other experience, you likely were somewhere between very dissatisfied and very satisfied. If we say that 85 percent are satisfied, what are we really saying? In most cases, a scale of some sort was used to gather the date, such as 1 = very dissatisfied and 10 = very satisfied. Often a top-box or top-two box-approach is used. The percent of respondents that answered one of the top two choices, for example 9 and 10, we will consider satisfied. The statement 85 percent of customers are satisfied usually will mean that 85 percent of customers are in a top two box of satisfaction. Now, it is sometimes easier to describe satisfaction in percent instead of a mean score, but that view of the data is less precise, less useful, and less actionable. So we may use a top box or top-two box to describe satisfaction to the masses, but we should not ignore the importance of understanding the mean score as well. If I can raise the mean score from a 74 to a 78 that is good for my business even if I don't improve the percentage of respondents that are in a top-two box calculation. Satisfaction is not binary, and using the mean score will give us better insight.

We've talked a lot about the strengths and weaknesses of Net Promoter, and I shared my views on how word-of-mouth marketing is just one of four areas companies need to focus on to achieve success. Why would you manage your business with a KPI such as NPS that measures only one of the four areas?

Most of the measures of success a company uses are actually outcomes of a good customer experience: customer retention, customer upsells, and new customer acquisition (including conversion and true conversion rates), recommendations, word of mouth, customer loyalty, and more. Just about every behavior you want to elicit from your consumers is an outcome of their satisfaction with their experience.

Many companies today (see Chapter 8 for examples) are using comprehensive customer experience analytics to understand, affect, and predict customer behaviors. The subject of this book, WoMI, is one of the critical components of the customer experience ecosystem. But WoMI, like customer retention, loyalty, and upsells, is an *outcome* of satisfaction with the customer experience, not a driver.

So go to the source: measure satisfaction with the customer experience *and* all the possible outcomes of satisfaction, including sales, loyalty, recommendations, and trust. You lose a lot of power when you measure only outcomes without measuring the source that drives all those outcomes. Measure the customer experience, using satisfaction as the metric.

Why Measure Customer Experience?

With the rise of the super consumer, the business landscape has changed, and executives need a tool just as potent as the ones consumers wield (powerful voice, super hearing, unlimited knowledge, and cloning abilities) to level the playing field. They need a precise and reliable technology that not only measures the customer experience but also predicts what impact their satisfaction, or lack thereof, will have on the future success of a company. Companies also need to be aware that consumers are fully immersed in multiple channels, using web, mobile, store locations, contact centers, e-mail, and social media at will, and the experience a customer has in one channel can greatly affect the overall experience with the company as a whole.

Academic research over the past two decades shows that when measured properly, customer satisfaction is a predictor of future success at both macroeconomic and microeconomic levels. At the macroeconomic level, this means that customer satisfaction predicts consumer spending and gross domestic product (GDP). At the company level, this means that satisfaction predicts a company's future financial performance, revenue, and even stock prices. More than 20 years of academic, peer-reviewed research from the University of Michigan and other academic institutions back up this claim (see Appendix D).

Achieving a true customer-centric enterprise requires metrics that track customer behavior in a way that is credible, reliable, accurate, precise, actionable, and predictive. These data also need to be continuously gathered, and organizations need to act on the results. If any of these elements is missing, organizations cannot enact the appropriate customer experience improvements that will positively impact the bottom line.

It has never been easier to collect voice-of-customer data, but the challenge is putting that information into a scientific context that helps companies know how to predict and shape customer behavior in the future. In today's multichannel world, it is also important to understand the customer experience within and across every relevant channel. From customers' perspectives, they see only a single brand, not a channel-specific version of a brand. As a result, every channel must be measured and managed to deliver a customer experience that supports the global objectives of the brand.

When evaluating metrics, it is important to understand that any measure worth tracking should meet all of the following criteria:

- Credible: How widely accepted is the measure? Does it have a good track record of results? Is it based on a scientifically and academically rigorous methodology? Can we trust it to make decisions? Will management trust it?

- Reliable: Is it a consistent standard that can be applied across the customer life cycle and multiple channels? When all factors remain the same, are the results the same with every measurement?

- Precise: Is it specific enough to provide insight? Is it specific enough to allow us to make business decisions based on it? Does it use multiple related questions to deliver greater accuracy and insight? (Remember that a watch without a minute hand may be accurate but it's not precise. Likewise, customer experience data need to be precise to be useful.)

- Accurate: Is the measurement correct? Is it representative of the entire customer base or just an outspoken minority? Do the questions capture self-reported importance, or can they derive importance based on what customers say? (For example, most customers say price is important to them, but in practice price reductions typically do not inspire them to make purchases. Other factors—such as product information—usually have a much greater impact on purchasing behavior.) Does it have an acceptable margin of error and realistic sample sizes?

- Actionable: Does it provide any insight into what can be done to encourage customers to return, buy again, or recommend? Does it prioritize improvements according to the biggest predicted impacts? A score without actionable insights helps keep score but does not help with improvements.

- Predictive: Can it project the future behaviors of customers based on their satisfaction with the experience?

The goal is to focus an organization's efforts on those things that will yield strategic value. The organizations that make the best investments in improvement will be in an advantageous position to win the competitive battles. Without predictive capability, organizations are left to shoot at targets in the dark. They are left to a strategy of trial and error.

Metrics that do not have these qualities will do more harm than good. The only thing worse than having bad data is to have bad data and think that it is good data. Bad data will provide a false sense of security that will lead organizations to make bad decisions.

At the highest level, the customer experience is simply the comparative measure between customer expectations and actual experience: how did what you actually got compare to what you were expecting to get? However, myriad variables go into understanding expectations and experience. Experience with competitors and other organizations, external factors (from the weather to the economy), and customers' intent when they engage the organization all play into their expectations and experience. Because of this, measuring the customer experience can vary with each interaction on the basis of specific customer needs and perceptions at any given time.

Effectively measuring these variables will provide an accurate account of the customer experience. Organizations can understand why customers behave the way they do and also predict how they will behave in the future. They can make business investments based on accurate customer experience analytics that will materially improve the customer experience and, ultimately, the bottom line.

Of course, this begs the question: What is the right set of metrics for measuring the customer experience? And how do we actually do it?

How to Measure the Customer Experience and Answer the Big Three Questions

I've talked a lot about high-level concepts so far, but how do we actually put these concepts into action?

Let's talk about how a comprehensive customer experience measurement can help you answer the three big questions:

1. *How am I doing?* What is my performance?
2. *Where should I focus my efforts?* Where will I get the largest return on my investment?
3. *Why should I take action?* Is the payback worth the effort?

One number can help answer the first question, but one number does little to answer the last two questions.

Let's talk about how a comprehensive measurement system can help you answer all three questions.

How am I doing? *What is my performance?*

This is the first question your analytics should help you answer. In our model, we measure the satisfaction with the experience, the drivers of satisfaction and future behaviors. Customer experience professionals need to know exactly how they are doing in each of these areas. After all, you can't manage what you don't measure!

Simply assessing performance is a start. It allows you to track your progress over time and benchmark against yourself, against competitors, and against best-in-class companies.

The elements of satisfaction and the future behaviors are going to depend somewhat on the channel you're measuring and your industry. You should be able to customize these models to some degree for your own business, adding or subtracting relevant elements or future behaviors as they relate (or don't relate) to your business. But it's useful to use standard questions so you can benchmark against peers and competitors.

Where should I focus my efforts? *Where will I get the largest return on my investment?*

Second, a good methodology will answer the question of where you should focus your efforts. This is where the elements and the prioritization of elements come into play. Customer experience analytics can help a company measure customer perceptions of different elements of the experience, or drivers of satisfaction, in order to prioritize the improvements that will have the greatest return on investment. It's not enough just to know how customers rate various elements of their experience; you need a methodology that goes beyond customers' self-rated importance and assesses which changes will have the greatest impact on behavior and on their likely future behaviors. You can't manage what you don't measure and what you measure will determine what you do.

Why should I take action? *Is the payback worth the effort?*

Third, we want to answer the critical ROI question: Why should I take action? The model we use shows you directly how specific

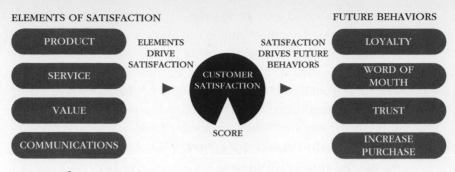

ELEMENTS OF SATISFACTION

FUTURE BEHAVIORS

PRODUCT

ELEMENTS
DRIVE
SATISFACTION

SERVICE

VALUE

COMMUNICATIONS

CUSTOMER
SATISFACTION

SCORE

SATISFACTION
DRIVES FUTURE
BEHAVIORS

LOYALTY

WORD OF
MOUTH

TRUST

INCREASE
PURCHASE

Figure 6.1   Brand-Level Customer Satisfaction Model

improvements to elements lead to improvements to satisfaction and how those improvements to satisfaction increase loyalty, word-of-mouth recommendations, trust, future sales, and more. There are times where the return doesn't justify the investment. It is not a frequent occurrence in the highly competitive environment we operate in, but can still happen. Understanding the payback helps us prioritize our efforts across channels. The companies that make the best investments will yield the greatest results. You can't manage what you don't measure. What you measure will determine what you do. And you can't improve if you don't measure. You may think you can still improve without measurement in place, but how would you know if you improved if you weren't measuring?

Let's look at an example. Figure 6.1 shows a typical model for brand-level or company-level customer experience measurement.

Measuring the Customer Experience at the Brand Level

As they relate to the example of a brand-level customer experience measurement, here is how the three major questions would play out.

1. *How am I doing?*

Let's say the preceding model is used by a fictional national bank called American Bank. American Bank would be answering the "How am I doing?" question by tracking its performance on all of the elements of satisfaction listed here (such as customer perceptions of product, service, value, and company communications). It would also be measuring customer satisfaction. Finally, it would be tracking how likely its customers are to remain loyal, recommend or discourage someone from doing business with the company (WoMI), trust American Bank overall, and increase the number of products or services they buy from American Bank.

2. ***Where should I focus my efforts?*** Where will I get the largest return on my investment?

American Bank can use this model to determine which elements have the greatest impact on improving the satisfaction with the customer experience. In Figure 6.2, we see that product is the lowest-scoring element (at 67 on a 100-point scale). If American Bank didn't have access to the impact component of the methodology, it might decide that because product is the lowest-scoring element, it is the element the bank should focus on. American Bank would use the questions that comprise that element score as well as other custom questions to decide how to improve the various types of savings accounts, checking accounts, loans, CDs, and other products it offers.

But when we look at impacts, we see that value (customers' perception of the value provided to them by American

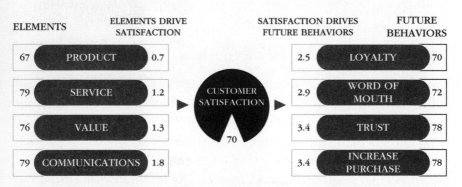

Figure 6.2 American Bank: Prioritizing Elements with the Greatest Impact on Future Behaviors

Bank) actually has a much higher impact than product. Here's how it works: a 5-point increase to product will result in a 0.7-point increase in satisfaction. A 5-point increase to value would result in a 1.3-point increase to satisfaction. (A 5-point scale is used to keep the math straightforward. If you increase the value by four points, you will see 80 percent of the impact, or in the example of the value element, a four point increase in value would result in a 1.04 increase to satisfaction). Therefore, even though customers are relatively happy with American Bank's value, improving value is still the area that will have the greatest impact on improving their satisfaction with the customer experience—nearly twice that of improving the product. An investment in improving the value that customers see in American Bank will provide the greatest ROI.

3. ***Why should I take action?*** Is the payback worth the effort?

For question 3, look to the future behavior side of the model. Every increase to satisfaction will drive increased loyalty, trust, and more purchases of American Bank's products and services. It will also increase positive word-of-mouth recommendations while reducing negative word of mouth.

For every 5-point increase in satisfaction, customers' likelihood to be loyal to American Bank will go up 2.5 points, their likelihood to recommend will go up 2.9 points, their likelihood to trust American Bank will go up 3.4 points, and their likelihood to spend more in the future will go up 3.4 points.

The companies that choose to tie these customer experience analytics to financial metrics are able to quantify ROI. For example, American Bank decides that it will work on increasing perceived value, since that is the highest-priority element, by changing its communications about value. It will spend $2 million on revamping web copy and changing the language on various printed materials handed out at the bank. That improvement to perceived value increases satisfaction by two points, which in turn increases customers' likelihood to purchase additional services. American Bank can quantify additional sales made and make a direct link to ROI. If it sells an additional $10 million in products and services, it knows the $2 million it spent on increasing perceived value was money well spent.

This type of modeling is tremendously useful in understanding where to make improvements and *why* they should be made.

Moreover, it's worth pointing out (again) that WoMI and NPS are both outcomes of satisfaction. If a company were measuring only NPS (or even if it is just measuring WoMI), it would have no idea where to focus efforts or how changes to the customer experience drive word-of-mouth recommendations and detractions.

Let's look at another example.

Measuring the Customer Experience in Contact Centers

Figure 6.3 is a model for a contact center that supports an electronics manufacturer. Let's call the company iMicro.

iMicro sells products on its own website (and on other websites such as Amazon and Target), and it also provides service, support, and sales via call centers, live chat, and e-mail.

1. *How is iMicro doing?*

Not bad. A score of 73 is pretty good for a contact center, actually. This is where benchmarking comes in. A score of 73 is decent for a call center but fairly poor for a retailer. You

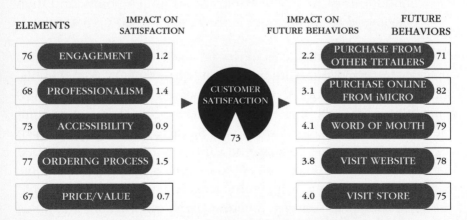

Figure 6.3   Contact Center Customer Satisfaction Model

have to know what to compare yourself to. iMicro's scores for the various elements of satisfaction and for future behaviors are also in line with industry benchmarks.

2. *Where should iMicro focus its efforts?*

We see from the model that price/value is the lowest-scoring element. When iMicro looks at open-ended e-mails and complaints, the thing that customers complain about the most is price. Executives are worried, and there have been closed-door meetings about adjusting prices to be more competitive, but they can't really afford to take the hit on profit margin.

Then, they take a look at their customer experience analytics, which show them that price is actually the lowest-scoring element but also the lowest-impact element. Improvements to price (or improvements to perceptions of price) will have a lower ROI than improvements to the ordering process (the highest-scoring element) and professionalism (a fairly low-scoring element).

Now they know that they should focus on the ordering process (more specifically, they know from additional analysis that they should focus on closing the sale with an e-mail confirming the order that is delivered while the customer is on the phone) and professionalism (customers don't like being cut off to be placed on hold).

Executives are nervous about "ignoring" the complaints about price, but they aren't ignoring them, they're focusing their effort on the areas that will actually satisfy their customers most in the long run: ordering process and professionalism.

3. *Why should iMicro take action and make these changes?*

iMicro can see from its future behaviors that improving the ordering process and the associates' professionalism will have a greater return on investment when it comes to driving sales through iMicro's website and its retailers, along with positive word of mouth. A 5-point increase in satisfaction will increase customers' likelihood to purchase at an iMicro retail partner by 2.2 points, their likelihood to purchase from iMicro's website by 3.1 points, their likelihood to recommend the company by

4.1 points, their likelihood to visit the website (which is a lot cheaper for iMicro than when they come to the contact center) by 3.8 points, and their likelihood to visit a store by 4.0 points.

Measuring the Customer Experience in Stores

Let's look next at the customer experience at Daisy Chain, a large, national, multichannel apparel and accessories store with an online presence (see Figure 6.4).

1. *How is Daisy Chain doing?*

   It is doing very well in customer satisfaction, with a score of 84. We generally say that 80 is the threshold for excellence, so 84 is good, especially since we know that other apparel and accessories retailers average 81.

2. *Where should Daisy Chain focus its efforts?*

   Well, the first response would seem to be price, which had the lowest rating at 62. But it is often true that price is the lowest-scoring element and rarely the highest-impact element.

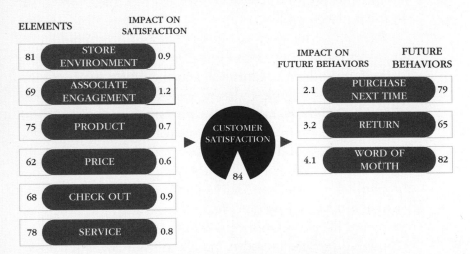

Figure 6.4   Store Customer Satisfaction Model

Customers are always looking for the lowest price possible, but dropping prices will have little impact on customer satisfaction—only 0.6 points. Rather, Daisy Chain should focus its efforts on improving associate engagement, which scored only 69 but will improve customer satisfaction more (a 1.2-point increase to overall customer satisfaction if Daisy Chain can improve associate engagement by 5 points). This would mean making sure that employees introduce themselves, wear nametags, assist customers in the fitting room, and suggest additional merchandise. These changes will have the highest impact on satisfaction.

3. **Why should Daisy Chain take action and make these changes?**

It is clear from a ForeSee analysis that each of these actions will substantially improve Daisy Chain's bottom line. We can see from the model that improved associate engagement will lead to improved satisfaction and that improved satisfaction will lead to increased sales. But Daisy Chain can track these through external data sources as well. For instance, the value of greeting a customer improves each customer's spending by $0.70, wearing a name tag jumps spending another $0.50, assisting customers in the fitting room adds $1.27, and suggesting additional merchandise increases spending a whopping $5.00. The total for each customer is thus an additional $7.47 per customer by doing just these four relatively easy things. We know that customers' average order size is currently $35. If staff members simply do a better job of greeting their customers and wearing name tags, average order size will increase by $1.20, or 3.4 percent. If they are able to make improvements and realize the full $7.47, they will see a 21 percent improvement in sales.

Measuring the Customer Experience on Websites

Let's look at an example of customer satisfaction from the point of view of a website (see Figure 6.5). The *Daily Reporter* is a large

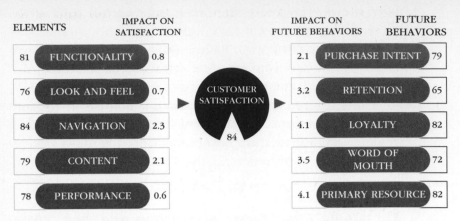

Figure 6.5 Website Customer Satisfaction Model

metropolitan newspaper that, in reaction to declining circulation for its print version, has spent a lot of money in the past few years building up the functionality of its website, with the possibility that over time it might end the print edition. But despite the outflow of money, the *Daily Reporter* hasn't seen its functionality or satisfaction scores change significantly.

1. ***How is the* Daily Reporter *doing?***
   Like Daisy Chain, for the *Daily Reporter*, overall customer satisfaction is 84, which is very good.
2. ***Where should the* Daily Reporter *focus its efforts?***
   At first glance, based solely on scores, it should try to improve the look and feel of the website, but doing so will have only a 0.7-point impact on satisfaction. Rather, the *Daily Reporter* should focus its efforts on navigation, which can have an impact on satisfaction far above any of the other areas. The *Daily Reporter* can look at the model and then dig deeper into customer questions and even have a usability audit review to identify exactly which changes should be made to navigation.

3. *Why should the* Daily Reporter *take action and make these changes?*

By making changes in navigation, the *Daily Reporter* will see an increase in satisfaction, which will lead to an increase in subscriptions and renewals, an increase in customer loyalty, an increase in word of mouth, and an increase in referred links on social networks and in the use of the website as a primary resource for information.

Measuring the Customer Experience with Mobile Experiences

Last, let's take a look at customer satisfaction with mobile experiences (see Figure 6.6). Here we are dealing with the Rest Well international budget hotel chain, which allows customers to research rates and book rooms via a call center, website, or mobile site and app. The app allows visitors to determine the availability of hotel rooms and the rate for each one.

1. *How is Rest Well doing?*

Not so well. Its customer satisfaction score is only 70, which is not good at all, especially compared to the average satisfaction for a hotel travel app or mobile site, which is 78.

2. *Where should Rest Well focus its efforts?*

While content is the lowest-scoring element, improving the look and feel of its app will provide the biggest boost to Rest Well's poor satisfaction score. It needs to improve the

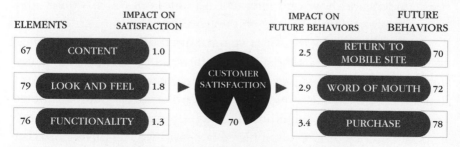

Figure 6.6 Mobile Customer Satisfaction Model

app's buttons in terms of readability and make them larger so items are easier to tap and swipe.

3. *Why should Rest Well take action and make changes?*

By improving the look and feel of the app, Rest Well will increase customer satisfaction, which will drive more people to make reservations and recommend the hotel.

How to Measure the Multichannel Consumer

Today's consumers are multichannel; some business leaders prefer the term *omnichannel*. No matter what word you use, the reality is that consumers are going to interface with companies across multiple channels. To further complicate measuring the customer experience, within a digital channel, consumers often use multiple devices. They may start on a computer at work, continue on a home computer, and then move to a tablet or phone. And in most cases they are not logging into each site so from the company's perspective they are unique experience, not experiences by the same consumer as they move through the customer experience spanning multiple channels and multiple devices. Companies have been thinking about the customer experience within a single channel. Consumers think about the customer experience with the brand.

To measure the customer experience of the multichannel, multidevice consumer, you must measure all consumer touch points and fully understand the relationship between those touch points. You must understand the intent and purpose of each interaction. You must understand how one interaction influences the customer and the next interaction he or she will engage in.

At ForeSee, one of the ways we measure the customer experience of the multichannel, multidevice consumer is by gauging customer intent through initial surveys, followed up with subsequent surveys that comprehensively evaluate the overall process and customer experience, including a methodology to determine which actions the respondent took as a result of his or her visit. We call this a post-visit measurement.

The process of determining customer satisfaction starts with intentions and ends with outcomes. Our goal is to understand intentions and expectations, whether and to what extent those intentions and expectations were met, and what the customer actually did as a result of his or her visit or experience.

There are five possible outcomes of an interaction with a potential customer for a multichannel retailer:

1. The customer made no purchase.
2. The customer made the purchase from the retailer online.
3. The customer made the purchase from the retailer off-line.
4. The customer made the purchase from a competitor online.
5. The customer made the purchase from a competitor off-line.

This approach applies to a broader range of behaviors and outcomes than within retail activity alone. *Purchase* can take on different meanings. For instance, if your goal is to sign up new members, that action can be considered a purchase, even if no money changes hands. If you run a government agency and your goal is for citizens to fill out Social Security benefit applications online as opposed to in person at a local office, then a successfully completed application can be considered a purchase.

Potential outcomes can vary, but those different outcomes are easy to define on the basis of your particular business model.

A manufacturer with an online channel and no direct brick and mortar channel that also sells to retailers for online and off-line distribution has six potential outcomes:

1. The customer made no purchase.
2. The customer made the purchase from the manufacturer online.
3. The customer purchased the manufacturer's product from a retailer online.
4. The customer purchased the manufacturer's product from a retailer off-line.
5. The customer purchased a competitor's product online.
6. The customer purchased a competitor's product off-line.

By asking what actually occurred after and as a result of a visit (no purchase, purchased online, purchased from a competitor, etc.), we can determine what happened and how satisfied customers were with their experience.

Traditional metrics are flawed because they take into account only behaviors. Behavioral metrics struggle to provide insight into the multichannel and multiservice consumer. Voice of Customer measurement overcomes the behavioral metrics limitations by understanding the customer's intent, prior experiences (channels and devices) and what they are likely to do next. The only way to truly understand customer satisfaction is to employ a methodology that captures the voice of the customer. Listening to customers helps identify intent and as a result is a key component used to evaluate whether you satisfy your customers, whether your customers will be loyal, whether your customers will recommend you to others, and whether your customers will return. We never *infer* satisfaction, loyalty, or intentions from correlated data; we go to the source and ask. Understanding intent and outcomes by using a scientific methodology allows us to determine causal factors that predict the future instead of relying on correlations that may not predict anything.

Let's look at conversion rates again, only in a different way. Say overall conversion rates at your company have remained static for years. Relatively flat results make sense if for no other reason than the weight of statistical data; when you look at results in aggregate, the needle is incredibly hard to move.

So what can you do? Instead of trying to move the aggregate, segment your audience and your customers, as we did in the earlier example. Determine which people come to your store or site to make a purchase. Then make sure you do the right things to enable them to make that purchase. Determine which people look for product or service information, and do the right things to provide that information quickly and conveniently.

The goal is for the audience that can be converted based on intent. Make changes and evaluate the success of those changes. Then take the process a step further. Consider segmenting intent by the source of acquisition. Was the visit due to awareness of your brand, a recommendation from a friend, or off-line or digital advertising or search? Understanding how you attracted a visitor to your site or how you acquired that visitor can be an illuminating segmentation to layer onto your initial analysis.

With the right information, you can turn data into intelligence and determine that while your overall conversion rate may have decreased, your true conversion rate actually increased.

Traditional metrics and traditional measurements are useful and important but often leave out a key indicator of overall performance. My guess is that you use a number of traditional metrics. And you should. But it is time to look to the next generation of customer experience analytics and complement the traditional metrics with more actionable and insightful metrics.

Interview: Josh Chapman, Cars.com

In a previous organization, I was brought in to build a customer experience program from scratch. We used NPS at the direction of our executive management team; they were adamant that we have a single metric to evaluate customer loyalty. Unfortunately, using NPS did not allow us to shape our business strategy as much as it was used for benchmark purposes and to punish or reward leaders of the respective business units.

In this organization, our response to NPS-defined detractors was to build a system that required the local manager to contact each customer labeled a detractor. Our hope was that the manager could resolve any issues customers had and convert them into promoters. This was a huge missed opportunity. Our more detailed analysis identified key customer pain points that should have been addressed at a global level before diving into the local issues.

With my prior company, our executive management team attempted to benchmark against other businesses using NPS.

Within our own organization, we found four different permutations of how departments were measuring NPS—a real limitation to the credibility of any benchmarks. How could we know if the other organizations we benchmarked were measuring NPS using the same methodology? Also, the sources being used for benchmarking were third parties and not the firm actually measuring NPS. By the time I left that company, many within management were satisfied by a belief that our NPS put us in the top 10 percent of like companies. They filed for bankruptcy seven months later and were completely out of business within one year of my leaving. Many factors contributed to this company's failure, but it is hard to believe that if we were truly in the top 10 percent of like companies, in terms of brand loyalty, that the business would have collapsed so quickly.

At Cars.com we have been using WoMI, and it has finally proven something I have believed throughout my career—NPS is not the paramount metric for measuring customer loyalty. The challenge has always been finding an alternative method and obtaining enough data to prove this theory. Since we began utilizing WoMI, the data has proven, beyond a shadow of a doubt, that NPS was overstating our detractors.

We began using WoMI internally about a year ago when measuring our dealer satisfaction. For the first year, we reported WoMI alongside NPS to illustrate the difference in the two measures. After two quarters, we solely discussed WoMI when reporting out to our executive team, leaving NPS in as a data point to reinforce the increased accuracy provided by WoMI. Customer experience is a key objective in our balanced scorecard that is reviewed at a more detailed level quarterly. As we move forward, WoMI will be the metric used to illustrate promoters and detractors, ultimately driving key strategic decisions such as the allocation of resources or increased investment.

For Cars.com, the fact that WoMI is a more accurate measure of detractors than NPS is highly relevant, especially when it comes to our dealers. These are B2B relationships where our dealers are thinking about whether they would recommend us to someone else. Their first thought often centered on whether they would recommend us to their competitors. As a result, we often had dealers with mixed feelings about whether they would recommend us, but not because they were true detractors to our brand. With WoMI, we were able to see that NPS overstated our detractors by more than 120 percent.

Josh Chapman is vice president of operations for Cars.com, which was recently named the Best Overall Customer Experience by Keynote Systems, the world's leading Internet usage research company. Cars.com is an online destination for car shoppers that offers information from consumers and experts to help buyers formulate opinions on what to buy, where to buy, and how much to pay for a car. With price listings, side-by-side comparison tools, photo galleries, videos, unbiased editorial content, and a large selection of new- and used-car inventory, Cars.com puts millions of car buyers in control of their shopping process with the information they need to make buying decisions.

Chapter 7

The Customer Experience Measurement Ecosystem

The key to understanding your customers is to comprehensively measure and operate within what ForeSee calls the Customer Experience Measurement Ecosystem, a set of data and analysis that allows you to measure the customer experience and predict the future. Using a measurement ecosystem is based on using different types of metrics, methodologies, and tools to make the whole significantly stronger and more robust than its individual parts.

Using the Customer Experience Measurement Ecosystem helps solve a long-standing problem. Most traditional metrics attempt to determine—or, at best, infer—the success of an experience within a channel such as a website by counting events, including the number of pages viewed, the number of unique customer visits, the number of items sold, the average order size, or the number of subscribers.

But counting is not the same as measuring. Recording, sifting, sorting, or displaying data is not the same as generating usable information. I deeply believe in the value of behavioral data, but these metrics are often not measuring the experience the customer had but rather what the customer did. Understanding behavior is not the same as understanding the experience. And the problem gets compounded as the consumer experience evolves from an experience that resides in one channel via one device to a multichannel, multidevice experience. All too often we see that people find something they can count and they turn it into a KPI. Just because we can count it doesn't make it a KPI.

The key is to use best-in-class metrics, working together, to provide a complete picture of your customers and their experience and

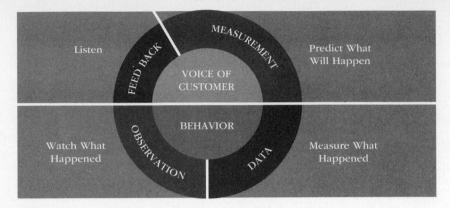

Figure 7.1 The Customer Experience Measurement Ecosystem

their actions, including their needs, expectations, and likely future behaviors. No single tool or measurement can provide all of that information.

Notice that each element of the ecosystem (Figure 7.1) revolves around the customer because the customer is the most important asset of every company.

Let's look at the fundamental elements of the ecosystem: behavioral data, feedback or service data, observation, and the customer experience.

Behavioral Data

When we are dealing with customer metrics, there are many pieces of behavioral data that can be captured. Each one provides some value in the ecosystem. They help us understand what the customer has done and how he or she interacted with your company.

On websites, mobile apps, and mobile sites, you can measure all the transactions that happen and a whole lot more. Compared with other channels, the web and mobile channels can provide you with the richest and broadest record of activity. One of the most important aspects of behavioral data (after financial transactions) is referred to as *clickstream data*, which creates a record of each user's activity on a website and includes traditional measurements such as page views, time on site, shopping cart usage, and transactions completed—in short, the events that occurred while a visitor was on a website, from the instant the visitor arrived until the instant the visitor departed.

When studying customer behavior in stores or other physical locations, companies generally look at the traffic into the location. When transactions or purchases are involved, this also includes items such as the number of transactions, average purchase size, and number of items in the purchase or basket. The more sophisticated metrics involve conversion rates (or percentage of traffic that purchases or transacts). Newer technologies including video tracking and mobile phone tracking can follow the user's pathway through stores or locations and can even create heat maps of customer movement.

When looking at what happens at call centers, companies check agent activity, e-mail exchanges, and live chat. For instance, behavioral metrics view an agent's average hold time, how many calls he or she handles, and first call resolution.

But because such behavioral metrics are backward looking, it is often hard to tell what is going on. ForeSee conducts an analysis that segments calls as up to four minutes, four to six minutes, and six minutes or longer. When we did this for one particular company's call center, we found that its satisfaction score for up to four minutes was in the mid-70s, for four to six minutes it dropped to the low 60s, and for 6 minutes and longer it was in high 70s. The client's assumption that the worst experience would result from the longest call was wrong. Using traditional behavioral metrics, they didn't realize that the agents had to attend to complex issues. Those agents who spent a significant amount of time helping customers were in fact increasing their satisfaction and improving their experience. It turned out that the customers' time and the effort involved by the agents were not directly related to customer satisfaction and future loyalty. When looking at broad aggregated scores, one might think that there is a relationship between effort and satisfaction and loyalty, but this example proves that when one is properly analyzing the data and looking at the right segments, the relationship between effort and satisfaction or loyalty does not consistently exist. Making assumptions without the analysis to prove or disprove those assumptions can get us into trouble.

Behavioral data are a KPI, a set of backward-looking tools that *measure what already happened*. Behavioral data are useful information that every company should track, but they make up only one piece of the puzzle.

Let's look at some of the kinds of behavioral information many companies are still collecting and why they may be an inadequate measure of the true customer experience.

Getting Sticky

In the business world before Accelerated Darwinism and the super consumer, a primary business goal was to find ways to make customers stick to the environment. The typical department store or retail outlet wanted customers in the store as long as possible. The longer they stayed, the greater the likelihood they would make a purchase, whether due to sales pressure or simply because they had already invested a lot of time in the process of shopping at that store. Customers were captive to the store. And the concept of stickiness was applied in other areas. For instance, TV networks wanted to keep viewers glued to that channel for as long as possible so their ratings would be higher. "Must See TV" was coined by NBC in the 1990s to describe the block of comedy shows led by *Friends*, and *Seinfeld* that dominated Thursday nights. From eight o'clock to the late-night news, viewers never touched the remote control so that they could watch the adventures of Sam and Diane, Ross and Rachel, and Jerry, Kramer, George, and Elaine.

Stickiness worked for NBC and many other companies during that era. Due to the cost of switching—even if switching meant only flipping to CBS or ABC or driving to another bank branch or walking across the street to a rival shoe store—business success by creating a sticky environment was extremely high.

Today, sticky has lost its power. Let's look at what happens when a website tries to hold a visitor's attention. At one time, it was thought to be a good idea if users were stuck on a website. This could be done by having the visitor engage in extensive navigation to find desired results or by spreading content or search results across multiple pages. Unfortunately, this concept of stickiness does not apply in today's web world. In fact, it often can drive visitors away from a site. Most people won't waste their time like this anymore. With switching costs low and competition high, they just depart.

Unfortunately, tools designed to measure and evaluate stickiness in pre-super-consumer terms are still commonly referenced and widely used. The main problem is that sticky measurements are strictly behavioral and therefore often misleading.

Take a simple and widely used behavioral web metric many companies use to evaluate the success, failure, and stickiness of a website: page views. Each time a visitor views a page on a website, a page view is generated. Say that three months ago, visitors to a site viewed an average of five pages before exiting. Was that good? Was that bad? In the absence of other data, it is difficult to tell. Faced with such a situation, many CEOs and managers might decide to measure trends over time to gauge site performance, spend thousands of dollars on site modifications, and then evaluate the results of changes made to the site. In some cases, they would find that the page view average had decreased from five pages per visitor to three. What happened? Were they worse off than when they started? It seemed that the site had become less sticky, not more.

Maybe.

It could be that the changes resulted in greater visitor satisfaction and a better customer experience. Stickiness could be irrelevant, depending on the needs and expectations of the visitors. If visitors were more satisfied because they found exactly what they wanted within three page views, the result could be increased loyalty and more recommendations to the site and to the business. Deeper metrics are necessary.

Here's a personal example that illustrates my point. I received my undergraduate degree from the University of Michigan. My family has season tickets to Michigan football games, and I follow Michigan football closely. One Sunday morning, I wanted to check a few stats to settle a friendly wager with one of my sons, Jake. I went to the Michigan football home page, MGoBlue.com, clicked a couple of links, and within seconds found exactly what I wanted to know. I was looking up the name of a running back, Tshimanga Biakabutuka, who was from Zaire by way of Canada and was known as "Touchdown Tim" (which is a lot easier for fans and announcers to pronounce than, well, his real name). He rushed for 313 yards against Ohio State on November 25, 1995, the second-highest number of yards ever gained by a Michigan running back in one game. The Michigan Wolverines won that game 31–23. Those were the days! But Jake was right, because no one knows Michigan football trivia like he does. The single-game record is held by Ron Johnson, with 347 yards in 1967 against Wisconsin.

I got exactly what I wanted from the website, but I viewed only three pages.

Following the stickiness paradigm could lead officials at my university to believe that the Michigan football website does a terrible job of creating a sticky environment. I viewed three pages. I didn't stay. I didn't browse. I didn't consume page after page after page. I was on the website for seconds, not minutes.

But think about what *really* happened. My intent was to find a specific football statistic. I did. I found it quickly and easily, which is what I wanted. I was highly satisfied by my experience.

Measuring my page views, and *only* my page views, in no way indicated my level of satisfaction, my likelihood of returning to the site, the probability of my purchasing a Michigan football jersey—or my likelihood of taking *any* future action. In fact, I was satisfied. I will be loyal. I will be back, and I will recommend the site to others (by the way, you really should check out MGoBlue.com).

My page view statistics indicate only one thing: I viewed three pages. Observation of my actions could not provide insight into my level of satisfaction because observation cannot measure satisfaction.

On the other hand, what if when I went to the site, finding the stats I wanted meant sifting through 15 or 20 pages and spending 5 or 10 frustrating minutes on the site? Measured in a vacuum, without consideration of intent or expectation or future behaviors, that type of visit to the site could easily be considered a success based on the high number of page views and the lengthy amount of time I spent on the site.

Even as a University of Michigan alumnus, I would not be inclined to return if I had such an experience. (Whom am I kidding—with my background, I would be making a phone call to the football department on Monday to file a complaint!) I have too many options at my disposal. Technology allows me to be on multiple sites at the same time, and any number of sports and information websites such as ESPN.com and Wikipedia contain the same basic information and statistics. Plus, my switching costs are nonexistent. Exiting the site, never to return, is for me a zero-cost action.

Another example happened with one of our customers whose business model was 100 percent driven by ad revenue. They had just implemented a major overhaul of their system that was somewhat revolutionary to how other sites were designed. Within a day or two of their launch, their CEO was reviewing the revenue statistics and saw that revenue was dropping. He immediately called the team and said, "The new release is not working, we are losing revenue, let's immediately go back to the older design." Luckily, they were measuring not only the behavioral data but also the customer experience, which showed people were more satisfied with the new experience. As a result, they were significantly more likely to be loyal to this site, for it to be their first choice, when looking for similar information. The new release was more effective, allowing people to find what they were looking for more quickly than before. This resulted in fewer page views per sessions and less revenue. The result of the better experience was higher satisfaction, increased loyalty, and the site becoming the destination choice for many users—a very positive long-term impact on revenue, but in the short term it was negative. The team shared the customer experience data with the CEO, and he agreed with their analysis. The long-term value of increased customer loyalty would pay back dividends far greater than any short-term impact on revenue. They kept the new release, and the long-term results proved it out: higher revenue driven by increased loyalty, which was driven by a better customer experience.

The same holds true for virtually all kinds of websites and businesses. If retail sites follow a stickiness paradigm and use traditional web analytics—such as time on a site and pages viewed—to measure site success, their chances of performing an accurate analysis are hardly better than flipping a coin. The intent of customers is critical and cannot be determined by simply observing where they visited and what they did.

Mobile Complexity

When the Internet started to hit critical mass, with companies having a web presence and users reaching significant size, the web both created a new channel of interaction between customers and businesses and changed how existing channels were being used, thereby greatly complicating the world of customer experience analytics. The Internet dramatically increased our capability to count, observe, and measure. But just because we can count something doesn't make it a good metric.

The web served many purposes as a new channel—a channel of interaction that could stand on its own (Yahoo!, Amazon, Zappos, eBay, etc.) but also a channel that worked in conjunction with existing channels (Target, Home Depot, AT&T, ESPN, etc.) in many different ways. Behavioral metrics thus became more complex and confusing, less valuable, and sometimes downright misleading.

Two relatively recent events have taken such complexity to the next level and then some. The first event is the proliferation of Internet-connected computers in people's lives (I am not yet even talking about mobile). Many people have access to more than one computer on a daily basis. You have your work computer and your home computer. Sometimes you have a shared computer at home. Moving among these devices is difficult for behavioral systems. Most often, businesses won't know that the same users are accessing their sites from multiple computers unless customers are logging into the site from all devices.

The second event, the use of mobile devices, both phones and tablets, has taken the multiple-device situation to even greater complexity. In addition to work and home computers, many of us now have smartphones and tablets armed with apps and Internet access. Soon, wearable computers will be widely available, such as Google glasses and smart watches. Thus, users will have more and more devices with which to interact with a company, thus complicating what a business sees as many discrete, unrelated visits—when, in fact, each is part of the journey as customers interact and engage with a company.

Mobile use also adds complications. It performs most if not all the same functions as traditional laptops and desktops but adds some new twists. Often, mobile is used as a companion channel, for example, while in a store using a smartphone or while in a library or in front of the TV with a tablet. Mobile has changed the customer experience world in many ways. It has raised the competition level and further reduced the switching costs. With tablets on their laps and smartphones in their hands, consumers have even more control and more options.

Let's explore mobile use a little more. I've asked my colleague Eric Feinberg, ForeSee's Senior Director of Mobile, Media, and Entertainment, to expand on mobile usage.

Mobile Context, Location, and Intent

Eric Feinberg

In mobile, content is no longer king (although still important)—context is. It reigns supreme because as mobile and tablet sites and apps are developed, context is hierarchically the top of the design pyramid. Merriam Webster tells us that *context* is "the interrelated conditions in which something exists or occurs." In mobile especially, everything is interrelated. A mobile or tablet site or app cannot exist without the business need it represents and the customer or prospect that actively uses it. There are so many moving pieces—interrelated, moving pieces—that make a mobile experience successful and profitable.

(Continued)

At ForeSee, we think of context as being composed of location and intent:

Location is where a customer is in the world. Not geographical location but contextual location. Sure, you can determine his or her latitude and longitude, but what does 34.063601, 118.359709 mean without having the context, that the location is at home? Our analysis indicated that two-thirds of the audience is using mobile from home, not a harried customer zipping around in his or her car.

Intent involves asking: Why is the customer at the mobile site today—to research, to purchase, to find a local store, to comparison shop, to check inventory, to check a balance, to do something else? Each one of these can and should necessitate a unique user experience. Some of those experiences will be speedy, quick-hit experiences; others will be more immersive and engaging.

All too often businesses are optimizing for a conversion event when, in fact, they should be optimizing for a contribution event.

Together, location and intent provide context—the context that behavioral analytics simply cannot deliver alone. Companies must strive to optimize their contribution rate. To solve for *contribution* (the active, unidirectional word for the term of the moment *attribution*), companies must connect the dots between channels and experiences and predict the impact that a particular experience in one channel has on a conversion event in another channel.

You know that a high-quality mobile experience can influence a store purchase, right? That a web visit influences a call center purchase, right? That a mobile site experience can lead to someone downloading our app, right? Connecting the dots is the tough part.

Companies are often looking at app store ratings as a kind of feedback. Unfortunately, the ForeSee Mobile Satisfaction Index: Financial Services Edition demonstrated some interesting facts about app store ratings and feedback.

So, what do app store star ratings tell you? Not much at all.

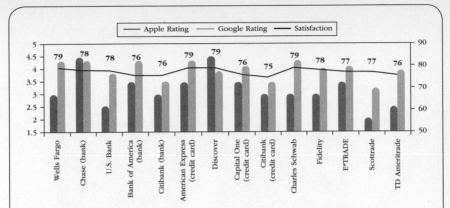

Figure 7.2   Stars and Downloads Can be Misleading

The feedback provided by tracking how many stars an app gets in an app store is questionable at best. Usually only the most satisfied and the least satisfied provide feedback, leaving the silent majority—the segment you want to hear from—unrepresented. That feedback proves to be more useful for customers than it is for companies and provides no direction or insight as to how you might improve the customer experience. Figure 7.2 demonstrates how misleading star ratings can be when it comes to truly understanding the mobile customer experience.

The Art and Science of Measuring the Customer Experience

Tablets are moving toward the forefront of mobile-first thinking. These devices are playing an increasing role in your customers' experience, and critical patterns are starting to emerge. More and more companies are considering developing their digital user experiences for the tablet first and then scaling up for the big browser and down for the mobile handset browser. So, what are we seeing?

ForeSee has a front-row seat to the massive impact mobile is having on digital strategy. With more than 100 measures of

(Continued)

The Customer Experience Measurement Ecosystem

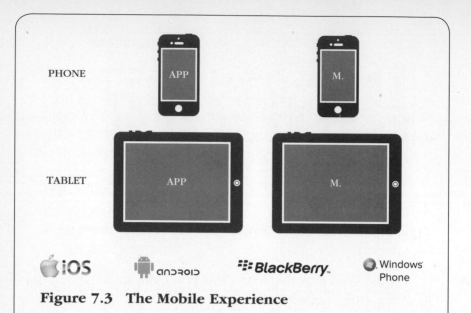

PHONE

TABLET

Figure 7.3 The Mobile Experience

mobile experience spanning tablets, apps, and m-dot sites, we have unique and intimate knowledge on critical trends of why, where, and how customers use mobile devices. For the record, we define *mobile* inclusively: handset and tablet experiences across web and apps (see Figure 7.3). To us, it doesn't matter whether it is optimized. The reality is that while many are optimizing their handset experiences, a good amount are still hybrid experiences (some parts mobile optimized, some not), and well over 90 percent of our 600 clients are serving their traditional website to the tablet audience.

Most notable is the increasing impact of the tablet experience. More and more of our clients say they are starting to see higher conversion rates of tablet visitors over desktop users, as well as spikes in evening traffic when the majority of site visitors are coming from tablet devices. These trends are easily spotted with basic web analytics (behavioral data). However, the real insight comes from measuring what you cannot see; it comes from understanding customers and their wants, needs, and (most important) expectations. This cannot be done by using feedback.

The mind-set of the customer visiting your tablet site is decidedly different from a web visitor or a mobile phone visitor. Customer expectations of how a site works in tablet form are increasingly diverging from the expectations of the web. The form factor of tablets is closely aligned functionally with that of the mobile phone world (touchscreen, portable), but the customer expectations are rooted in the full-featured experience from the web. Sure, it is the same content, but it is a different experience. Same content, different experience. Will this change over time? Maybe. But it is this way now and for the foreseeable future.

We see a lot of companies pushing their desktop website experience to tablet visitors because it offers them presence at virtually no cost. Thus, why optimize the web experience for tablet when it works already? Further, many of our clients are seeing tablet conversion rates higher than those of desktop, with traffic growing amazingly. This beguiles us into thinking that a winning strategy is afoot. It might work for a little while, but just because traffic numbers are high doesn't necessarily mean it is the best long-term strategy. It could just mean that more people are using mobile as a preferred tool of engagement. That is part of the problem with behavioral data: you miss a big chunk of the full picture. And what we see from our front-row seat is mobile being used not only because it is the best available screen but also because customers expect that it will be closer to their ideal experience.

What we do not see in traditional analytics is who your audience is, where they are engaging via mobile (on their couch, in a store, at a competitor's store, at home, on a train, on a plane), and why. This intelligence begins to paint a different picture and is essential in leading your mobile strategy forward.

In our experience, tablet audiences skew higher on affluence and education and are more tech savvy than a desktop audience.

(Continued)

So shouldn't we expect higher conversion from an audience with more disposable income? How much higher should *t-conversion* (tablet conversion) be? Also, tablets are increasingly becoming the preferred point of Internet access within the home and at night. So we're seeing customers bring a different engagement persona when coming from a tablet experience. Their mind-set is different. They are often more relaxed, sometimes referred to as in lean-back mode, that is, leaning back on their couch while using their tablet. In retail, we refer to this as couch commerce. Tablet engagement is not often characterized by the microtasking persona that is typical of handheld mobile. Customers desire a more engaging experience on tablets, and tablet strategy is lagging behind on capitalizing within this medium.

Desktop web usability breaks down when customers are *trowsing* (tablet browsing). Orientation preferences have tremendous impact on the tapability of top navigation, and content above the fold changes for tablet screen size, greatly impacting customer engagement. Cascading navigation has been the preferred navigational scheme on the web for some time, but even though it works in tablets, it is by no means optimal. Most times, you need to tap thrice to get to the next page (tap to engage the menu, tap to open the submenu, and, finally, tap to get to your page). In fact, 70 percent of the 20 retailers measured in both web and mobile in the ForeSee Mobile Satisfaction Index: Retail Experience recorded lower customer satisfaction scores in their mobile experience than in their web experience. When we compare tablet against handheld mobile experience, we see a similar trend: tablet experiences score lower than handheld site experiences, according to the ForeSee Mobile Benchmark analysis (see Figure 7.4).

Simply stated, companies are failing to recognize that tablets are a different experience that provides a unique medium to engage with customers. Service and feedback measures that were useful in the past now must be viewed in a much larger context.

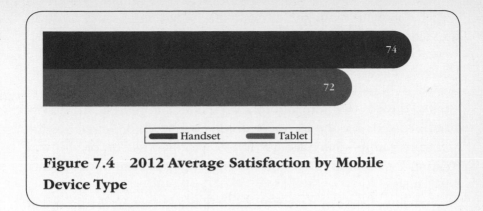

Figure 7.4   2012 Average Satisfaction by Mobile Device Type

Challenging Behavioral Metrics

Bounce rates and shopping cart abandonments are among the more challenging behavioral metrics.

Bounce Rate

Bounce rate is a useful but generally misapplied behavioral metric. It calculates the percentage of visitors who view one page and then bounce off that page to a different site instead of viewing additional pages on the original site. Exit rate, sometimes called page exit ratio, is a similar metric that measures the percentage of visitors who leave a site from individual pages. (By definition, all visitors eventually exit, but not all visitors bounce.)

Bounce rate is calculated by dividing the total number of visits by the total number of visitors who view one page. If 1,000 people visit and 200 leave after viewing one page, the bounce rate is 20 percent.

Exit rate is calculated by dividing the total number of visitors to a page by the total number of visitors who exit the site after viewing that page. If 1,000 people view a page and 400 leave after viewing that page, the exit rate for that specific page is 40 percent.

The traditional use of these two metrics assumes the lower the bounce rate and exit rate, the better. Why? The basic assumption is that unsatisfied visitors bounce or exit.

That assumption is not always correct because it does not take into account the impact of visitor intent, especially in a multichannel world. Many companies assume that the pages on their sites with the highest exit rates need to be fixed. But if a customer visits a product page, finds the information wanted (say, a product price), and exits to drive to the store and pick up the item in person, should the page be fixed? Was the customer dissatisfied by his or her visit to the website? Hardly—the customer found exactly what he or she was looking for and left after viewing one page *because* the customer was satisfied.

In many cases, the page with the highest exit rate is the page that best meets the visitor's needs and expectations. To truly understand behavioral metrics such as bounce rate or exit rate, other factors, such as initial intent and subsequent actions, must be taken into account. Otherwise, CEOs and managers may fix what is not broken and ignore what may be, in fact, a real problem and a real opportunity for improvement.

Data do not equal actionable intelligence, especially when you jump to conclusions or simply follow conventional wisdom based on those data—no matter how accurate the metric itself may be.

Shopping Cart Abandonment

Shopping cart abandonment is another classic example of a frequently misused metric.

The shopping cart abandonment rate is calculated by dividing the number of visitors who start but then abandon a shopping cart (in other words, they do not complete the transaction) by the total number of visitors who initially create a shopping cart.

Abandoned shopping carts are the bane of an e-commerce site's existence. (Picture business owners with their heads in hands crying, "They were this close . . . and then they left!")

A business that knows a consumer abandoned the shopping cart can certainly infer that the customer was not satisfied with some portion of the shopping or checkout process. Maybe the customer could not easily delete an item no longer wanted. Maybe the customer could not determine the shipping cost for the order. Maybe the customer felt that there were too many steps in the process and got frustrated.

Or maybe the customer never intended to buy at all and was only doing a little virtual window-shopping.

Instead of attempting to *infer* what happened and why, the business should instead *ask* the customer about the experience. A business that knows why a customer abandoned the shopping cart and what he or she planned to do as a result can then start to understand the customer's needs and expectations. A business that knows the causal factors behind a customer's actions can determine what to do and can predict the results of changes to better satisfy the customer.

That is why behavioral data can be misleading, especially in extreme circumstances.

Beware of False Positives and False Negatives

All data needs to be analyzed within the context of the bigger picture. You don't want to fall in the trap of being nearsighted, where the only thing that appears to be clear to you is the number in front of you. You need to understand the environment and how it may require you to look at the analysis in different ways. For example, many times when companies are struggling or even near bankruptcy, their customer satisfaction rates actually go up instead of down. Why? Because often the only customers left are loyal customers who remain satisfied with the company, for whatever reason. I call this the *mother's love syndrome:* No matter what other people think, your mother still loves you. Kmart, for instance, entered bankruptcy in 2002 after a period of rising customer satisfaction, and AOL also showed the same pattern: customer satisfaction increased in 2005 and 2006 while customers left in droves to take advantage of free services; the company's for-pay model was no longer relevant to any but the most die-hard AOL users. Looking at satisfaction outside the context of the struggling economics of the business and the declining customer base could have driven you to the wrong assumption.

No data can exist entirely on its own. The combination of data can be very powerful, provide you the insights you need, and lead you to a competitive advantage driven by analytics.

Voice of Customer Feedback Metrics

Besides behavioral metrics, companies use feedback metrics to evaluate how they are satisfying customers. Feedback has always existed, but technology has opened newer and easier feedback mechanisms, resulting in more feedback being given by consumers and received by companies. It can be as simple as a letter, phone call, or e-mail to a CEO; an old-school suggestion box or an online version of one; or a tweet, Facebook post, or blog in the social networks. In-store service metrics involve receiving feedback from customers and how quickly managers are able to resolve problems presented by customers within a 24-hour period. Call centers may provide simple surveys to ask how they did.

Providing a mechanism for your consumers to give feedback is a great way to hear their voices. But you need to be cautious in how you use the information they provide. The difference between feedback and customer experience analytics is that feedback is opt in (people come to you to tell you what they think), while good customer experience analytics randomly intercepts users to create a representative sample of your entire customer base. Feedback is typically nonrepresentative. Some customers seek out such mechanisms and provide feedback, and others do not. When the feedback is direct to the company, we typically see a very high percentage of feedback that is extremely negative, a much smaller percentage that is extremely positive—and almost no feedback that represents the majority of a company's customer base, the middle ground. When the feedback comes via social networks such as Facebook and Twitter, we typically see a high percentage of feedback that is extremely positive, a smaller percentage that is extremely negative, and almost no feedback that is in the middle, representing the majority of a company's customer base. I cannot recall seeing a tweet like "I had a decent dinner last night, might go back there" or "not bad looking clothes at the store today." If you listen to only feedback, you could completely ignore the silent majority.

Listen to feedback, but do not overreact to only the squeakiest wheels on the far ends of your customer spectrum. Decide where to allocate resources by determining which improvements will make the biggest impact on your business—which does not always mean fixing what the most people complain about the loudest.

Another problem with feedback is that it leads to reaction. It is easier to react to complaints than it is to proactively identify and measure potential problems. If you wait for feedback to determine where to focus your resources, how many potential customers will be lost because their needs were not met—and who never provided feedback you could have acted on?

Remember that feedback is not inherently bad—it's just reactive. Feedback shows what already happened. To succeed, you must be proactive and future directed.

Observation and Usability

Observation tools are also behavioral in nature but are based on direct and, at times, real-time studies; some take place in a consumer's natural environment, while others are simulated studies that take place in a lab environment. Some of the most popular and valuable kinds of observational tools are those in the usability field. Usability is the study of the ease with which people are able to use a particular tool, product, or software, and the field of usability has exploded along with the Internet explosion.

There are a few kinds of usability testing that are most commonly used for websites:

- **Usability in the Lab.** Users are asked to interact with a website while their actions and sometimes even their eye movements are tracked. This type of testing can provide very specific results for how a single user (or a small group of users) interacted with a website. Usability experts can see where the user struggled, where the user lingered, what he or she could not find, and what caught his or her attention and then use those results to suggest improvements for a website that will improve usability and, in theory, improve the overall customer experience.

The results of a usability lab test are beneficial, but remember that usability labs evaluate a few users in a controlled environment performing tasks they were asked to perform instead of operating in their own environment and doing what they want to do.

- **Online Usability Tests or Remote Usability Tests.** Technology is deployed to capture or record a user's web session, allowing analysts to view what, in effect, is a replay or movie of visitor behavior as it occurred. Typically, these tests do not observe real users in a real environment who are unaware they are being observed but instead observe recruited users (or people expected to be similar to users) who were asked to participate in the test. The tests allow analysts to view a user's mouse movements, mouse clicks, and other site interactions in a way that points out the strengths and weaknesses of the site.

- **Session Replays.** This type of observation allows for the most natural environment possible: a user environment where visitors pursue their own objectives, not the objectives of the testers, and can do so in their natural environment. The replays allow analysts to view a user's mouse movements, mouse clicks, and other site interactions as the user goes about his or her business unaware of observation.

- **Usability Audits or Heuristic Reviews.** These reviews are performed by skilled web navigation specialists who evaluate a website using a range of criteria including site architecture and navigation, user friendliness, page design and layout, functionality, and shopping cart and checkout design. These reviews can be costly when applied to an entire site, but when we choose to focus on specific problem areas, a usability audit on the customer experience of just one element of a site can be performed.

- **Focus Groups and Listening Sessions.** Bringing users together to share ideas and give feedback can be very helpful. Although users are not in their natural environment, you have the ability to interact with them and probe deeper into key issues. There are online versions as well that take the form of online discussion groups and online communities.

Call center recordings are another form of observation. Being able to listen to the conversation can be an effective tool. However, be aware that while you are listening to the exact conversation, knowing how the consumer felt about the conversation and its resolution is a very important aspect that you can't ascertain simply from the conversation.

In-store observation has traditionally involved operational issues. One of the most frequently used methods is the mystery shopper. The shopper observes whether salespeople greet customers, have their name tags displayed, provide assistance with the items customers are interested in, and give other information that is necessary to make a purchase. Although this provides information, it is backward looking and episodic, and the checklist that the mystery shopper uses is generated from the company's viewpoint. In-store video tracking has become another tool in the retailer's arsenal. Counting the user traffic, tracking their movements around the store, and in some cases even trying to identify some basic demographical information based on leading-edge video technology are now all possible ways to monitor and observe your customers. The newest method is using consumers' mobile phones to track their movement within a location. While there are some concerns that these methods might infringe on consumers' privacy, it is a technology that adds to your observation capabilities.

Far more effective is the kind of customer experience analytics survey that ForeSee conducts that enables managers to act in a proactive manner. Designed to obtain customers' opinions through a randomized survey, questions are located at the bottom of the receipt and then are analyzed. This information can even be used by the mystery shopper when making his or her assessments, which will be based on the customer's viewpoint and not just the company's concerns.

Voice of Customer Measurement

The key *performance* indicators that we have been discussing are based on past results, provide valuable information, and definitely should not be ignored. Key *success* indicators measure success rather than just performance.

Some metrics fit into both categories, and some clearly do not. Does a fast-loading page indicate success? What about the number of unique visitors? How about a short duration of a call into the call center or a long visit in a store? While these are important metrics, an increase or decrease in results does not indicate success or failure. Reducing page load times from an average of 1.2 seconds to 1 second is definitely a positive change, but that change alone will not cause a site visitor to consider his or her experience a success. On the other hand, if your page load times increase from 1.2 seconds to 8 seconds, your visitor may definitely consider his or her experience a failure—and so will you.

If you are concerned with future success, track success indicators in addition to performance indicators. Our goal is to truly understand the totality of the customer experience. That is why all elements of the Ecosystem Model provide value and help businesses manage forward. In every customer experience, success is defined from your customers' perspective. Did you meet their needs and exceed their expectations? In short, were your customers satisfied?

Let's take a hypothetical example. Say you run a huge national insurance company called the National. Two critical customer behaviors contribute to bottom-line success for your company, above all others:

1. The customers' likelihood to use the website, mobile, and call centers as the primary channels to receive insurance quotes and service their accounts.

2. The customers' likelihood to purchase a policy on your website or through an agent.

You implement a customer satisfaction model based on the Customer Experience Analytics Ecosystem. The model will show which element will have the greatest impact on satisfaction. That element may not be the lowest-scoring element. Say it is the price of an insurance policy. Customers always complain about prices, and many of our clients find that price is their lowest-scoring element. Even so—and this is very often the case—other elements such as site navigation, ease of downloading your app, or a call center agent's friendly manner may be higher priorities than the price of a policy.

So what do you need to do? Put your resources behind those drivers of satisfaction. Improve your site navigation capacity, make downloading your app easier, and ensure that your call center agents reply to questions about coverage in a friendly manner. If you do, the customer experience improves, satisfaction increases, and so should the number of policies purchased.

Here's another example. You are the head of marketing for Ford. You decide to run a television commercial. You think it is powerful. Your goal is obviously to sell more cars, but your more immediate goal is to drive visits to dealerships, your website, and your app.

How will you know whether your television commercial drives more traffic to the Ford website, to downloading the Ford app, or to visiting a dealership showroom? The problem in answering that question lies in the data available.

Some potential customers arrive at Ford by typing the URL www.ford.com. Others search Google for a term such as "Ford" and click on a link in the natural search results. More visitors arrive via banner ads you place on a variety of sites. Still others arrive by watching your commercial during a sports event or a situation comedy. Others read a favorable review in *Motor Trend* magazine—or was it a photo they saw of a celebrity driving a Ford?

Gauging the impact of a single influencing item in an environment where multiple channels exist is difficult. Unfortunately, we do not live in a lab environment where we can evaluate one new potential influencer at a time.

Using a customer experience measurement ecosystem, you can use your attitudinal tools (such as customer satisfaction and voice-of-customer measurement) to know what influenced visitors, to know whether their expectations were met on the basis of expectations set by the ad, to know whether they were satisfied with their experience, and to know whether they are likely to visit a dealership or to consider buying a Ford as a result of their experience.

Using the customer experience measurement ecosystem allows you to gain intelligence previously unavailable and make decisions that allow you to manage your business forward. That is why behavioral analytics, deployed on their own, can be misleading. Although you are certainly able to count, you are unable to turn data into intelligence, and the ability to measure success is lost.

Measuring the customer experience is based on understanding and measuring attitudes, perceptions, expectations, and intentions. We know, not only intuitively but also from empirical research, that satisfied customers become loyal, long-term customers more likely to make recommendations. Dissatisfied customers go elsewhere when they have the opportunity and may provide negative word of mouth by sharing their poor experiences with others. Customer satisfaction not only helps us measure success today but also provides a leading indicator of what users and customers will do in the future.

Satisfaction with the customer experience, when measured correctly, is a key success indicator rather than a key performance indicator because it measures success today and predicts what will happen in the future. A satisfied customer today is much more likely to be a customer in the future and recommend you to others. What we did last time is not predictive of the future, but whether we were satisfied with the experience is predictive of the future. Satisfaction is proactive and predictive rather than reactive and backward looking.

At the same time, if you only measured the satisfaction with the customer experience without a proper integration with the rest of the ecosystem, you miss data that help develop a forward-looking action plan.

While the ecosystem is by its nature input and output driven, the process does not stop when customer satisfaction is measured. The Customer Experience Measurement ecosystem, like any other ecosystem, continually evolves and constantly renews. Changes in each area can affect results in other areas. Correct those problems, and satisfaction will increase—and so will financial performance.

Interview: Mario Castano, Nikon, Inc.

I had used NPS before I came to Nikon as a gauge of customer satisfaction. At Nikon, NPS allowed us a way to assess how our brand awareness was penetrating our customers. It allowed us to put together strategies to work with our customers. In addition, it permitted us a quick way from an industry perspective to see how we ranked with customers. NPS did help us understand our customers' point of view and provided us with a way to improve our website.

But on the other hand, NPS doesn't provide a lot of details and help in deciding what I should focus on in regards to the customer experience. Particularly in an e-commerce environment, NPS doesn't distinguish between a very active member and a passive customer.

WoMI supplies us with information that is much more actionable, which makes it easier for us to understand what our customers are saying and the specific improvements that they want us to make. This helps us prioritize our resources and determine what moves the needle the most for our customers. WoMI helps us have aha! moments. We can sit down with our groups and plan projects and allocate budgets so we can achieve our objectives. WoMI is much more surgically precise in the information it gives us. Unlike NPS, WoMI enables us to clearly understand our ROI.

Furthermore, WoMI helps our developers understand how well some of our innovations are working. Customer concerns that would have been overlooked by NPS are captured by WoMI. Our developers can observe a common theme by customers, which they will investigate and then take a proactive approach to resolving the issue. WoMI allows us to see both positive and negative comments, which NPS doesn't do.

Mario Castano is Internet and eCommerce Technology manager at Nikon, Inc., which is involved in a broad spectrum of businesses centered around specializations in imaging products, precision equipment, and instruments. Nikon products and technologies play a significant role in defining the digital imaging industry.

Chapter 8

Best Customer Experience Practices

As WoMI becomes a widespread tool and the Customer Experience Measurement Ecosystem achieves greater acceptance, more and more companies will have the ability to provide a great customer experience. But even now some companies and organizations already are creating a superior customer experience, a number of which use ForeSee analytics. Let's examine first the efforts and history of three companies and a government agency, all of which exemplify superior customer experience, and then of several companies ForeSee has recently worked with to improve the customer experience through the measurement and improvement of satisfaction. And finally, we'll see how some companies are using WoMI to improve on Net Promoter.

Amazon

Amazon.com was founded by Jeff Bezos in 1994 in his garage in Bellevue, Washington, and went online in 1995. Since that time, Amazon, now headquartered in Seattle, Washington, has become the world's largest online retailer. It started as an online bookstore but soon diversified to sell DVDs, CDs, MP3 downloads, software, video games, electronics, apparel, furniture, food, toys, and jewelry. The company also produces consumer electronics, including the Amazon Kindle e-book reader and the Kindle Fire tablet computer and is a major provider of cloud computing services.

Bezos wanted a name for his company that began with *A* so that it would appear early in alphabetic order. He looked through the dictionary and settled on *Amazon* because it was a place that was "exotic and different" and it was one of the biggest rivers in the world.

Bezos's business plan was unusual; he did not expect to make a profit for four to five years (he wrote the plan during a cross-country trip to Seattle). Amazon survived the dot-com bubble around 2000 and finally started turning its first profit in the fourth quarter of 2001: $5 million, on revenues of more than $1 billion. This profit margin, though extremely modest, proved to skeptics that Bezos's unconventional business model could succeed.

The confidence Jeff Bezos displayed to burst through traditional ways of thinking showed up early in his life—as a toddler, he tried dismantling his crib. He went on to be his high school's valedictorian and then attended Princeton University, graduating *summa cum laude* with a bachelor of science in electrical engineering and computer science in 1986. He worked on Wall Street at Bankers Trust and D. E. Shaw & Co. but left New York City to start Amazon when he learned about the rapid growth in Internet use and when the U.S. Supreme Court ruled that online retailers didn't have to collect sales taxes in states where they had no physical presence. Bezos's concern for his customers began with his initial decisions at Amazon: He had headed to Washington because its relatively small population meant fewer of his future customers would have to pay sales tax.

The impact Bezos is having in transforming shopping and enhancing the customer experience has drawn continued praise. In 1999, *Time* magazine named Bezos its Person of the Year, recognizing the company's success in popularizing online shopping. In 2008, *U.S. News & World Report* selected him as one of America's best leaders. In 2011, the *Economist* presented him and Gregg Zehr, president of Lab 126, an Amazon subsidiary, with an Innovation Award for the Kindle. The next year, *Fortune* named him Businessperson of the Year. The *Harvard Business Review* recently ranked him as the second-best CEO after the late Steve Jobs of Apple, making him the best living CEO.

ForeSee Analysis of Amazon

All these press accolades of Bezos's leadership were confirmed by our own analysis.

During a recent holiday season, ForeSee Online Retail Satisfaction Index found that overall retail satisfaction scores were up compared to the previous year and that top e-retailers in particular did very well. The study also showed many increases in satisfaction on a year-to-year basis.

Who was the big winner? It came as no surprise. The gold standard of online customer satisfaction is Amazon.com. Not only did Amazon achieve the highest score any company had ever received on our holiday index but also its financials backed up that result. Amazon grew revenues at a higher rate than several of the next retailers combined. Since Amazon sells almost everything, almost every online shopper has been to the site. Even if your company does not directly compete with Amazon, your customers may expect your website to provide as satisfying an experience.

Amazon's commitment to the customer experience began in its formative years, when Bezos decided not to use call centers but to instead provide incredible service via e-mail. Amazon took returns with no questions asked. It worked hard to overstock inventory for peak holiday periods. Those service strategies helped the company grow market share, loyalty, and trust.

The commitment to a great customer experience required a significant financial commitment, but Amazon stayed the course and had the internal fortitude and (possibly more important) the capital to stick to the overall plan of *first* becoming great and *then* figuring out the economics.

Along the way there were definite missteps. A widespread customer relationship issue occurred when Amazon transitioned to selling products for other retailers. The transition was not apparent to customers. Most did not realize they no longer bought directly from Amazon. Customers placed the order with and paid Amazon, but another retailer delivered the product. The system worked fine until people had problems or concerns. When customers needed help from a customer service representative, Amazon forwarded them to the retailer's customer service department.

Customers had developed the expectation of receiving Amazon-level customer service, and suddenly those expectations were not met. Customer satisfaction levels dropped. Amazon worked hard to change expectations and better support its associated retailers and their mutual customers. For example, Lisa Dias was looking for books that could help her start a home business. She found a used workbook for entrepreneurs that was described as "like new." The seller wasn't Amazon itself but one of the merchants that marketed through its website. Still, Dias ordered the $24.95 paperback.

When the book arrived, its worksheets were already filled in. Upset, Dias first tried the merchant and didn't get any response. Then she called Amazon. The company immediately gave her a refund, without her having to return the book. She was impressed: "I felt like they stood up for me."

For the most part, Amazon has earned a reputation for strong service by letting customers get what they want without ever talking to an employee. Orders ship with a few mouse clicks. Packages arrive rapidly. But when things go wrong at Amazon—and they occasionally do—the company's employees get involved.

Jeff Bezos has talked about the distinctions Amazon makes between customer experience and customer service. The latter is only when customers deal with Amazon employees—and Bezos wants that to be the exception rather than the rule. "Internally, customer service is a component of customer experience," he says. "Customer experience includes having the lowest price, having the fastest delivery, having it reliable enough so that you don't need to contact [anyone]. Then you save customer service for those truly unusual situations. You know, I got my book and its missing pages 47 through 58."

Fixing customers' problems builds loyalty with people like Dias, says Bezos. But it's also a good way to spot recurring issues that need to be addressed more systematically. Outside merchants, like the one Dias dealt with, are a prime example.

So Bezos is trying to bring the quality of service from Amazon's outside merchants up to the same level as its own. The company has long let customers rate their experience with merchants and has instituted many internal safeguards to track the behavior of merchants. For instance, retailers have to use an e-mail service on the Amazon site to communicate with customers so Amazon can monitor conversations.

The company also uses metrics such as how frequently customers complain about a merchant and how often a merchant cancels an order because the product isn't in stock. Partners who have problems with more than 1 percent of their orders can get booted off the site.

To refine the experience with outside merchants, Amazon launched an initiative called Fulfillment by Amazon. Merchants simply send boxes of their products to Amazon's warehouses, and Amazon does the rest. It takes the orders online, packs the box, answers questions, and processes returns.

Though Amazon charges the merchants, Bezos says that's not why it launched the service. "It's important because it improves the consumer experience so much. It doesn't make us more money; it's heavy lifting. If you think long term, I think it's very important for us." The ultimate goal is to gain more control over the shopping experience, making it more consistent and reliable. The idea is that more people will use the online retailer and spend more.

Customer Complaints

Amazon has gotten many ideas from trying to address customer complaints. One gripe from years past was that popular items were at times out of stock. The last thing Amazon wants is for a frustrated shopper to head to another site or the mall.

Amazon has developed programs to keep hot items in stock and ready for quick delivery. One initiative is something Amazon calls the Milk Run. Instead of waiting for suppliers to deliver to Amazon's warehouses, Amazon picks up top-selling goods, reducing the number of late or incomplete orders the company receives.

One of the drawbacks to shopping online, of course, is that people don't feel the instant gratification of getting their purchases right when they buy them. That's one reason Bezos expanded Amazon Prime, the program for which customers pay $79 a year to get free two-day shipping on many in-stock products. Bezos has taken it international and increased the number of products that qualify for Prime. "Our vision is to have every item made anywhere in the world in stock and available for free two-day delivery," he says.

Still, things go wrong. Lindsey Smolan splurged on an iPod and a pink case from Amazon. The iPod arrived, but the case didn't. Two weeks later, Smolan e-mailed Amazon and asked for a refund. After a little thought, she e-mailed again, asking for a free cover. "I didn't use my iPod because I was waiting for my case, and I'm a valuable customer," she says. Amazon agreed. She got the iPod case free.

Zappos

Zappos was started by Nick Swinmurn, who grew up in the California Bay Area and graduated from the University of California, Santa Barbara, with a degree in film studies. After college, Swinmurn worked for the San Diego Padres and then Autoweb.com. His inspiration for Zappos came when he couldn't find a pair of brown Airwalks at his local mall. Swinmurn then became a contractor for Silicon Graphics to raise funds for an online shoe store he initially called Shoesite.com. (Swinmurn left Zappos in 2006. With his brother Dan, he started the Dethrone clothing line, which caters to fans of Ultimate Fighting Championship.)

In 1999, Swinmurn approached Tony Hsieh and Alfred Lin with his idea of selling shoes online. Hsieh is an American Internet entrepreneur and venture capitalist, a graduate of Harvard University with a degree in computer science. While at Harvard, he managed the Quincy House Grille, selling pizza. His best customer was Alfred Lin, who would become his business partner. Lin graduated from Harvard with a BA in applied mathematics and then got an MS in statistics from Stanford.

After college, Hsieh founded LinkExchange in 1996, and Lin became VP of finance and administration. At LinkExchange, members were allowed to advertise their site over LinkExchange's network through display banner ads. Within 90 days of launch, LinkExchange had more than 20,000 participating web pages and had its banner ads displayed more than 10 million times. By 1998, the site had more than 400,000 members, and 5 million ads rotated daily. In 1999, LinkExchange was sold to Microsoft for $265 million.

After LinkExchange, Hsieh and Lin cofounded Venture Frogs, an incubator and investment firm that invested in companies such as Ask Jeeves, Open Table, and MongoMusic.

Hsieh was initially skeptical about Swinmurn's idea about a new way to sell shoes but became interested when he realized footwear in the United States was a $40 billion market, and 5 percent of that was already being sold by mail-order catalogs. Hsieh and Lin decided to invest $2 million through Venture Frogs.

A few months following its launch, the company's name was changed from ShoeSite to Zappos (a variation of *zapatos*, the Spanish word for "shoes") so as not to limit itself to selling only footwear. In January 2000, Venture Frogs supplied additional capital and allowed Zappos to move into its office space. During this time, Hsieh became co-CEO with Nick Swinmurn and Lin became the chairman, COO, and CFO.

Advertising costs were minimal at the beginning, and the company grew mostly by word of mouth. It was around this time that Hsieh and Zappos executives set long-term goals for 2010: achieve $1 billion in sales and receive inclusion on *Fortune*'s list of the Best Companies to Work For.

In 2003, Zappos reached $70 million in gross sales and abandoned drop shipping, which accounted for 25 percent of their revenue base. The decision was based on supplying superior customer service. As Hsieh says, "I wanted us to have a whole company built around [customer service], and we couldn't control the customer experience when a quarter of the inventory was out of our control." In 2004, Zappos did $184 million in gross sales and received its first round of venture capital, a $35 million investment from Sequoia Capital. That same year, Zappos moved its headquarters from San Francisco to Henderson, Nevada (it is now in Las Vegas).

Over the next three years, Zappos doubled its annual revenues, hitting $840 million in gross sales by 2007. Zappos expanded its inventory to include handbags, eyewear, clothing, watches, and kids' merchandise. Hsieh summarized this transition, saying, "Back in 2003, we thought of ourselves as a shoe company that offered great service. Today, we really think of the Zappos brand as about great service, and we just happen to sell shoes."

In 2008, Zappos hit $1 billion in annual sales, two years earlier than expected. One year later, it fulfilled its other long-term goal, debuting at number 23 on *Fortune*'s Top 100 Companies to Work For.

Zappos's primary selling base is shoes, which accounts for about 80 percent of its business. There are currently about 50,000 varieties of shoes sold in the Zappos store, from brands such as Nike, Uggs, and Steve Madden. It also serves the niche shoe markets, including narrow and wide widths, hard-to-find sizes, American-made shoes, and vegan shoes. In 2004, it launched a line of high-end shoes called Zappos Couture.

In 2007, Zappos expanded its inventory to include clothing (including petite, big and tall, and plus sizes), handbags, eyewear, watches, and kids' merchandise, which currently account for 20 percent of annual revenues. Zappos expects that clothing and apparel will bring in $1 billion worth of revenue by 2015, as the apparel market is four times the size of the footwear market. Hsieh states that "our whole goal is we want to build the best brand of customer service. Hopefully, 10 years from now, people won't even realize that we started selling shoes."

Hsieh received the Ernst & Young Entrepreneur of the Year Award in 2007. In 2009, Amazon.com announced the acquisition of Zappos .com in a deal valued at approximately $1.2 billion.

Delivering Happiness

In June 2010, Hsieh authored *Delivering Happiness: A Path to Profits, Passion, and Purpose*. In it, he lays out the customer-driven philosophy that underlies the success of Zappos. He details 10 core values of the company, two of which are "Deliver WOW through Service" and "Build Open and Honest Relationships with Communication."

For Hsieh, it's all about the customer. *Delivering Happiness* states that Zappos is willing to make short-term sacrifices such as lost revenue or profits if it will result in long-term benefits. Hsieh believes in the loyalty business model and relationship marketing. The primary sources of the company's rapid growth have been repeat customers and numerous word-of-mouth recommendations. Of its customers, 75 percent are repeat buyers.

Company Culture and Core Values

Zappos places great emphasis on company culture and core values. Hsieh's belief is that "if we get the culture right, then everything else, including the customer service, will fall into place." The company publishes an annual 480-page *Culture Book*, which is composed of two- to three-paragraph entries from employees describing Zappos's company culture. The entries are unedited, and a copy of the *Culture Book* is given to all employees (although anyone can receive a copy of the book upon request).

Zappos applicants must go through two interviews: one for their professional aptitude and one for their personality, both equally important. In the personality interview, they are asked questions to see whether they would fit in with Zappos culturally, such as "How weird are you on a scale from 1 to 10?" and "What is your theme song?" All newly hired employees, even executives, are required to undergo a four-week customer loyalty training course, which includes at least two weeks of talking on the phone with customers in the call center. After training, the new employees are offered $2,000 to quit, which weeds out people who would jump ship anyway and allows those who remain to make a public statement of commitment to their new employer. More than 97 percent turn down the offer.

The Zappos website states that "we've been asked by a lot of people how we've grown so quickly, and the answer is actually really simple. . . . We've aligned the entire organization around one mission: to provide the best customer service possible." On average, Zappos employees answer 5,000 calls a day and 1,200 e-mails a week (except in the holiday season, when call frequency increases significantly). Call center employees don't have scripts, and there are no limits on call times.

Zappos employees are encouraged to go above and beyond traditional customer service. In particular, after a late night of barhopping and closed-room service, Hsieh bet a Skecher rep that if he called the Zappos hotline, the employee would be able to locate the nearest late-night pizza delivery. The call center employee, although initially confused, returned two minutes later with a list of the five closest late-night pizza restaurants. *Inc.* magazine notes another example: A woman called Zappos to return a pair of boots for her husband because he died in a car accident. The next day, she received a flower delivery, which the call center rep had billed to the company without checking with her supervisor.

Social Media

Hsieh encourages his employees to use social media networks to put a human face on the company and engage with customers, following their core value number 6: "Build Open and Honest Relationships with Communication." Zappos employees maintain an active presence on:

- **Twitter:** Zappos run its own Twitter microsite for its 500 employees registered on Twitter. Among them, Tony Hsieh is one of the most followed persons on Twitter, with 1.85 million followers. Employees are encouraged to use their Twitter accounts for casual communication rather than promotions or marketing pitches. He also encourages customers to use Twitter to give positive as well as negative feedback.

- **YouTube:** Zappos's content on YouTube supplements its other networks, hosting videos that primarily highlight the work culture at Zappos headquarters, including behind-the-scenes clips, humorous sketches by employees, and contests for customers.

- **Facebook:** Its Facebook page provides an effective route for feedback and discussion with customers.

- **Corporate blogs:** Zappos runs several blogs covering many topics related to its business: CEO blog, COO blog, Couture blog, Fashion Culture.

Panera Bread

I love eating at Panera Bread. Walk into any one with its open spaces, red and yellow walls, wooden chairs, and usually a gas fireplace, and they give you great sandwiches made with artisan bread on real dishware at $7 a pop, as well as soups, salads, and baked goods.

Panera is one of the fastest-growing chains in the United States, with 1,652 stores and a roughly $4.7 billion market capitalization. During the depths of the Great Recession, when most companies contracted, Panera's management invested in its product line and increased the number of stores. The strategy worked: In 2012, the company posted revenues of $4.78 billion, up from $640 million in 2005.

The reason for Panera's success is twofold. The chain has pursued a niche strategy, differentiating itself as a fast-food restaurant that serves healthy, tasty, affordable food. Panera offers a wholesome alternative to purveyors of fatty burgers and burritos. Equally important, it provides an appealing customer experience.

As Wharton Business School professor Lawrence G. Hrebiniak has said, "Panera is a symbol of warmth. In advertisements, they position themselves as a warm, welcoming place. They want you to bring your friends and family. They want you to come to Panera to have lunch with a good old friend. . . . When times are tough, people go back to the basics. You can't go out to dinner and drop $250, but you can go to Panera with a friend and have a tasty bowl of soup and smell the bread baking."

Panera started out as the St. Louis Bread Co., a modest chain that ran 19 bakery-cafes in urban Missouri. In 1993, Ron Shaich, a graduate of Clark University and the Harvard Business School who, at the time, was head of the similarly minded chain Au Bon Pain, bought the company for $23 million and renamed it Panera, Latin for "time of bread." By 1999, Shaich had sold off Au Bon Pain to concentrate on Panera. "At the highest level—and I've been doing this for 30 years—what I am trying to do is bring real food to people in environments that engage them," says Shaich.

According to Shaich, Panera's growth is due to a larger trend driven by American consumers' rejection of commodities: "My vision for how Panera would compete was rooted in specialty artisan bread, made with no chemicals and no preservatives."

And grow it has. By the beginning of the financial downturn, Panera was one of the best-performing restaurant stocks. Between 2007 and 2009, its earnings per share grew by more than 50 percent. Panera, which appears in the Quick-Serve and Quick-Casual market grouping, consistently ranks third in financial performance, trailing only McDonald's and Chipotle.

"As we began the recession, we made a decision to increase our investment," says Shaich. "At a time when almost every other restaurant was driven to cost cutting, and pulling back, we invested in the quality of the product, in growth, and in marketing."

During the recession, Panera introduced a range of low-fat fruit smoothies and brought out new dishware for its dine-in customers. It retooled its salad line, introducing new dressings, and developed new signature dishes. The company also started growing its own lettuce. "These details actually matter," Shaich states. "In the middle of a recession, our salad business was up 30 percent."

The company increased its labor force, paid bonuses, and gave raises. It made significant investments in the quality of its stores and built new ones, taking advantage of the fact that construction costs were down 20 percent.

The Customer Experience

Besides having good, healthy food at a reasonable price, Panera focuses on the customer experience. Panera rolled out a loyalty program during the recession, giving its most devoted customers opportunities to earn free pastries and coffees and offering invitations to cooking demonstrations.

Panera also recognizes that its customers want to sit, drink coffee, talk, read, and use their computers and tablets. In many cities and towns, Panera has become a de facto community center. "We're seeing the evolution of the common space and the community space, and Panera is a part of that," says John Ballantine, a senior lecturer who specializes in strategic management at Brandeis University International Business School. "It's become a place where people gather. There is ample room, plenty of comfortable chairs. You often see the elderly gathered there for clubs, as well as young people and students hanging out, and others with their laptops using it as their virtual office. It's welcoming, and it's comfortable. It's almost an extension of the café world of Europe."

Government Agencies

In the past few years, the federal government has been attempting to overcome its image of bureaucratic indifference to the needs of American citizens. It has placed a particular emphasis on developing websites that allow citizens access to their government. In 2013, ForeSee, in partnership with the American Customer Satisfaction E-Government Index, shows government maintaining high satisfaction scores, even outpacing satisfaction averages for private-sector news and information sites, portals, and search engines.

What were the underlying factors for improvement over the past decade? Let's start with a little background.

First, analysis showed that the longer a federal website had measured satisfaction, the greater the level of improvement was, both short- and long-term. (Once again, you cannot manage—much less improve—what you do not measure.) So while the Obama administration does deserve at least some of the credit for improvements in satisfaction, the fact remains that sites enjoying the largest increases have measured the customer experience and evaluated customer satisfaction—and acted on those findings—for years.

Clearly, federal web managers are committed to listening to the voice of the citizen. The people in charge of e-government worked hard to understand what we want, need, and expect online.

The Social Security Administration website is just one example. In 2010, the Internet Social Security Benefits Application site, where citizens can apply for benefits online instead of in person at a local office, scored an 87 in customer satisfaction. (An ACSI score of 80 or higher is considered to be excellent.)

They have maintained their excellence and even improved on it; in early 2013, their score was as high as 92.

Those are outstanding results and just one of the ways we have determined that citizens are more satisfied with e-government services than with traditional off-line services.

The old joke "If you don't like the government, it's not like you can start paying taxes to Canada" contains a kernel of truth. Dissatisfied citizens have few options because, where public services are concerned, the government is the purest example of restricted loyalty. Even so, the government officials we work with display a sincere and dedicated focus on improving the experience of the people they serve.

Other gains from increased satisfaction are easier to quantify. Processing benefit applications online is significantly less expensive than processing applications at a local office. Budget cuts and shrinking tax revenues, combined with a growing population that puts ever-increasing pressure on government agencies, make cutting costs while improving the customer experience a win-win for both officials and citizens.

More and more of us prefer to handle certain transactions online. The easier those transactions are and the more often our expectations for those transactions are met, the more satisfied we become—and, in most cases, the less expensive we become to serve.

Eddie Bauer

The Eddie Bauer clothing store chain is headquartered in Bellevue, Washington. It has grown into a major high-quality merchandiser, with retail stores, which sell premium Eddie Bauer merchandise; outlet stores, which offer Eddie Bauer merchandise and inventory overstocks at lower prices than the retail stores; and its direct-orders center, which provides Eddie Bauer merchandise through call centers and its website. The company also selectively licenses the Eddie Bauer brand name and logo for various products sold through other companies, including eyewear, furniture, and bicycles.

In 1920, Eddie Bauer, at the age of 21, established his first store in downtown Seattle. He opened Eddie Bauer's Tennis Shop in the back of a local hunting and fishing store and specialized in building and repairing tennis rackets. Over time, he expanded his line of merchandise to include his own handmade golf clubs and fishing tackle. He designed a standardized shuttlecock that helped popularize badminton in America. While operating this first store, Bauer developed his creed—"To give you such outstanding quality, value, service, and guarantee that we may be worthy of your high esteem"—still used by the company.

While on a winter fishing trip, Eddie contracted hypothermia, which led him to create a goose down–insulated jacket, which he called the Skyliner. In 1942, the U.S. Army Air Corps commissioned Bauer to develop the B-9 Flight Parka to keep pilots warm at high altitudes. More than 50,000 parkas were manufactured for World War II airmen. Of all government suppliers, Eddie Bauer alone was granted permission to affix his company logo to his products used by the army. In addition to the parkas, Bauer supplied the army with backpacks, pants, and sleeping bags, which became standard issue for American troops in the war.

In 1945, soon after he began selling women's clothing as well as men's, Eddie Bauer issued his first mail-order catalog. The original mailing list included the names of 14,000 soldiers who had worn Eddie Bauer clothing provided by the army during their service. He eventually closed his downtown store and left retailing, except for showroom sales at his Seattle factory, to focus on the company's mail-order catalog.

Throughout the 1950s and 1960s, Eddie Bauer outfitted various scientific and exploratory expeditions. Eddie Bauer went on to supply his equipment for the American K2 Himalayan Expedition. In 1963, James W. Whittaker, wearing Eddie Bauer clothing, became the first American to climb Mount Everest.

In 1968, Eddie Bauer retired, and he and his son sold their half of the business to William Niemi (Bauer's business and hunting partner) and his son for $1.5 million. That same year, the first store outside Seattle opened in San Francisco. To appeal to a broader range of consumers, Niemi shifted the company's focus to feature casual lifestyle apparel. The emphasis on women's apparel and accessories was greatly expanded in all stores.

In 1971, Niemi sold the company to General Mills. After the sale, the company focused on casual clothing and expanded to 61 stores. Spiegel purchased Eddie Bauer from General Mills in 1988. Aggressive expansion continued, and within the first year, the company had expanded to 99 stores. By 1996, an additional 300 stores had been opened. Eddie Bauer continued to expand in North America and internationally.

Touch Points

Eddie Bauer partnered with ForeSee recently to provide consistent insights into its customer experience at all touch points. Our analytics were used to quantify the impact of increasing customer satisfaction on future customer behavior. Using this work, the company established corporate-wide initiatives to improve end-to-end customer experience, to better manage the store operations, and to gain specific customer feedback at the store level.

Store improvement became based on customers' perspective. Bauer customer suggestions included improving product and pricing, creating a positive fitting room experience, and suggesting how employees could provide better service. For example, Eddie Bauer identified several ways to improve the fitting room experience: personalizing service, arranging different items of clothing in a way that makes it clear how they are worn together, and adding coordinating pieces and accessories. The company also encouraged associates to recommend merchandise to complete an outfit or to help customers try something additional, which increased their upsell business.

While retailers often see a decrease in satisfaction during the holiday season because of increased traffic and a shift in the customer mix, Eddie Bauer was not willing to accept the status quo. By continuously measuring the customer experience, Eddie Bauer was able to identify and gain insight into seasonal trends. Heading into the 2011 holiday season, the company decided to take a proactive approach by starting holiday preparations earlier in the season. The company held meetings to help associates prepare to take on the challenges of the season and deliver a high level of customer service, despite a number of unpredictable variables. The company redefined job descriptions and established specific roles during the holiday season for employees, including designated greeters, cashiers, fitting room associates, and stock room associates, to adequately address customers' needs. Employees now are more conscious of taking on these specific roles during their shifts.

As a result, customer satisfaction during the 2011 holiday season was better than the previous year, validating the decision to begin preparations earlier in the year. Beyond the holiday season, Eddie Bauer keeps customer satisfaction front of mind. Its store managers monitor progress on an ongoing basis and share insights with their teams during weekly meetings. ForeSee provides a store-level scorecard for Eddie Bauer that is customized to include key metrics such as making customers aware of the company's creed and guarantee, processing returns in a satisfying manner, and ensuring that customers leave with the item they came to purchase. Reports are posted for associates to review their achievements and recognize areas for improvement. Linking actual comments from customers and customer experience analytics provides a reliable performance metric to identify actions that will have the greatest impact on satisfaction and purchases.

Nutrisystem

Nutrisystem, headquartered in Fort Washington, Pennsylvania, is a commercial provider of weight loss products and services. Initially, the company offered weight loss counseling and products in brick-and-mortar centers. In 1999, the company moved to a direct-to-consumer business model, selling its products and programs on the Internet and through a call center. Nutrisystem's programs have been sold on the QVC television home shopping network since 2001 and in Costco stores since 2009. The company entered the retail arena in 2012 with the launch of its Everyday line of breakfast and snack items in Kroger grocery stores. It has enjoyed brand awareness through its commercials featuring singer Marie Osmond, television host Jillian Reynolds, and ex-quarterback greats Terry Bradshaw and Dan Marino.

The company's mission is to provide a weight loss program based on quality foods and a nutritionally balanced meal plan. The foundation of all Nutrisystem programs is the home delivery of portion-controlled entrees and snacks. Separate plans are offered for women and men at calorie levels that support a weight loss of one to two pounds per week (approximately 1,200 calories per day for women and 1,500 per day for men). The Nutrisystem products provide approximately 60 percent of daily calorie needs. The remaining 40 percent of daily calorie intake comes from grocery foods, which the customer purchases separately. These grocery food additions include fresh fruits and vegetables and low-fat dairy and protein sources. The program supplies specific guidance on how to choose and when to use these grocery additions. When followed, the diet is low in the glycemic index and provides nutrition consistent with the Dietary Guidelines for Americans.

The Nutrisystem program offers more than 150 menu choices in four categories: breakfast, lunch, dinner, and snacks and desserts. Most options are shelf-stable products, including bars, muffins, pretzel snacks, and pancake mix, as well as microwavable soups and dinner entrees. Nutrisystem also has a line of frozen food choices available, called Nutrisystem Select.

The program, however, includes several resources intended to promote motivation, behavior change, and success. Customers have free access to trained counselors via telephone, online chat, and e-mail. Nutrisystem provides paper, online, and mobile device applications to encourage customers to record their food intake and physical activity. Customers can also keep track of their progress (weight loss and changes in measurements) on the company's website. The Nutrisystem website supports an online community, which allows members to participate in discussion boards and chats with their peers or to keep a blog if they wish to do so. Participation in the online community is not a required aspect of the program.

Customer Analytics

Nutrisystem has a sophisticated e-commerce team that ForeSee has armed with a variety of metrics to ensure that Nutrisystem is providing the best customer experience. Using ForeSee analytics, the team has identified the top priorities for improving customer experience. For instance, the team discovered that a number of site visitors were having difficulty finding key information needed to complete transactions. The web analytics team knew the information was on the website, so why couldn't people find it? By watching session replays, including the scrolling, mouse clicks, and mouse movements of customers who said they had trouble finding what they were searching for, the team could finally see where frustrated customers were looking and, more important, where they weren't looking. This type of insight about what visitors experience at a site is critical to delivering a high-quality customer experience.

The team made website improvements that made information more accessible to visitors. Finding key information went from the number one issue to number six on the list of issues. The ForeSee analytics ensured that Nutrisystem focused on fixing the concerns that will have the greatest impact on the customer experience and the bottom line.

House of Fraser

House of Fraser is a British premium department store group with more than 60 stores across the United Kingdom and Ireland. It was acquired by Icelandic investor the Bauger Group in 2006.

The company's acquisitions have included numerous household names in England, some of which are no longer used as part of the company's long-term strategy of rebranding its stores under the House of Fraser name. Over the years, House of Fraser purchased a number of such famous stores, including Army & Navy, Dickins & Jones, Jenners, Howells, Kendals, Rackhams, Binns, and Harrods of Knightsbride (which is now owned privately). D. H. Evans's Oxford Street store in London was rebranded as House of Fraser in 2001 and became the chain's flagship store.

The Early Years

The company was founded by Hugh Fraser and James Arthur in 1849 as a small drapery shop on the corner of Argyle Street and Buchanan Street in Glasgow, Scotland, trading as Arthur and Fraser. Hugh Fraser had been apprenticed to Stewart & McDonald Ltd, a Glasgow drapery warehouse, where he rose to the position of warehouse manager and from which he brought many of the initial customers. James Arthur also owned a retail drapery business in Paisley, near Glasgow.

The company established a wholesale trade in adjoining premises in Argyle Street. In 1856, the wholesale business moved to a larger site in Miller Street, Glasgow, and started to trade under the name Arthur & Co. The retail side of the business expanded into the vacant buildings left by the wholesale site. In 1865, the partnership was dissolved, and Fraser assumed control of the retail business, leaving Arthur with the wholesale business. Also in 1865, Alexander McLaren joined the retail business, and the name was changed to Fraser & McLaren.

When the first Hugh Fraser died in 1873, his three eldest sons, James, John, and Hugh, acquired stakes in the business. James and John Fraser were initially directors in the business. In 1891, Hugh also joined the partnership, which by then was called Fraser & Sons. By 1900, Hugh Fraser II was in charge: he incorporated the business as Fraser & Sons Ltd. in 1909 and introduced the famous stag's head logo.

After Hugh Fraser II died in 1927, his son Hugh Fraser III, an accountant, became chairman. He opened new departments, enlarged the tearoom, opened a restaurant, and also began to look at possible acquisitions. In 1948, the company, now named House of Fraser, was first listed on the London Stock Exchange. Throughout the 1950s, House of Fraser expanded. Sir Hugh Fraser succeeded his father as chairman in 1966. Sir Hugh resumed the expansion of the company in 1969, and more than 50 stores were acquired in the 1970s.

In 1981, Professor Roland Smith succeeded Sir Hugh Fraser as chairman. The company diversified into sporting goods under the name Astral Sports and Leisure and into funerals with Wylie & Lochhead. It also launched the YOU range of cosmetics and jewelry shops and in 1985 acquired Turnbull & Asser shirtmakers of London and Kurt Geiger Holdings Ltd., shoe retailers.

In 1985, the Al Fayed family bought the business for £615 million. The Al Fayeds supported the continuing expansion of the company and replaced the stag's head logo with a stag leaping from a green triangle. In 1988, a five-year strategic business plan was announced that saw a rationalization of stores. Small branches were to be relinquished and replaced with larger units.

In the mid-1990s, there were many store closures. In the early 2000s, there was a large reduction in the number of House of Fraser stores in Scotland.

In May 2006, House of Fraser was taken over by the Icelandic Baugur Group. As part of the takeover, all brand names for their stores were replaced with the House of Fraser name, with the exception of Jenners, and the stag logo was axed. In September 2007, House of Fraser launched its online store.

The company had three major openings in 2008, including its first store in Northern Ireland. House of Fraser launched its HouseofFraser .co.uk Buy and Collect concept shop in October 2011 with its first location in Aberdeen. These much smaller shop units have PC terminals allowing customers to order from their website using their Buy and Collect service.

Consistent Customer Experience

Until working with ForeSee, the company didn't have consistent customer experience metrics that would enable it to see the interconnected relationships between its contact center experience and its other channels so it could identify root causes of service issues and improve operations. The House of Fraser's call center management team had used a variety of behavioral metrics to manage, motivate, and train contact center agents.

Our customer experience analytics allowed them to connect the dots between customer-specific issues, the stores, and the online site. The ability to compare the contact center's score to the scores from the website and store locations provided managers with a greater context and better understanding of the contact center's role within the organization.

House of Fraser launched a new delivery service that posed challenges with customer-facing tracking. Through continuous measurement, the company recognized a simultaneous increase in customer calls and a decline in satisfaction scores related to the knowledge possessed by agents. Using our data, they discovered that many customers who called were frustrated with the visibility of the delivery status of their purchase on the website. They rated their overall experience poorly, regardless of their experience with a contact center agent. Agents faced similar challenges when trying to assist customers, which reflected poorly on agent knowledge. The contact center management now could identify the root cause of dissatisfaction and focus resources on solving it.

ForeSee customer experience analytics provided agent-specific verbatim feedback to recognize outstanding performance in the contact center team, which is an essential tool for motivating agents to deliver on an exceptional House of Fraser experience. At the same time, by identifying underperforming individuals based on specific feedback, contact center management customized development plans to coach its staff to achieve their best performance and reinforced the brand's commitment to service.

ABC

The American Broadcasting Company (ABC) is one of the major commercial broadcasting television networks. Headquartered in New York, ABC was created in 1943 from the former NBC Blue radio network and is owned by the Walt Disney Company as of 1996.

For many years, it lacked the resources and programs to compete with NBC and CBS. However, under the leadership of Leonard Goldenson, in the mid-1950s it launched its first major hit, *Disneyland*, hosted by Walt Disney himself, and a slew of Warner Brothers programs followed, including *Maverick, Cheyenne, 77 Sunset Strip*, and *Hawaiian Eye*. Other classic shows of that period were *The Lone Ranger, The Adventures of Ozzie and Harriet, The Lawrence Welk Show*, and, of course, *Leave It to Beaver*.

In the 1960s, ABC brought cartoons to prime time with *The Flintstones* and *The Jetsons* and pioneered with the *Wide World of Sports* headed by Roone Arledge, who then created *Monday Night Football* a few years later. In the middle of the decade, ABC launched what became a cultural phenomenon with the introduction of *Batman*, starring Adam West as the caped crusader.

The 1970s saw *Happy Days, Three's Company, Taxi, Laverne & Shirley, Charlie's Angels, Love Boat*, and *Dynasty*. Perhaps the network's greatest accomplishment was its production of *Roots*, which galvanized the nation with Alex Haley's epic tale of slavery and survival. Combined with ratings for ABC's regular weekly series, *Roots* propelled ABC to a first-place finish in the national Nielsen ratings for the 1976–1977 season—a first in the then 30-year history of the network.

The 1980s brought such major hits as *Moonlighting, MacGyver, Who's the Boss?, The Wonder Years, Thirtysomething*, and *Roseanne*. In 1984, ABC acquired majority control of 24-hour cable sports channel ESPN.

A decline in top shows then ushered in the Walt Disney Company as the network's new owner. Despite intense efforts by the Disney management, ABC was slow to turn around. In 1999, the network had a big hit game show in *Who Wants to Be a Millionaire?* and dramas such as *The Practice* (which gave birth to a successful spin-off, *Boston Legal*, in 2004) and *Alias*.

ABC was able to find success in ratings beginning in 2004. Under new entertainment president Stephen McPherson, in the fall of that year ABC premiered *Desperate Housewives* and *Lost*. Immediately, the network's ratings skyrocketed to unprecedented levels, thanks, in part, to the shows' critical praise, high publicity, and heavy marketing over the summer. It followed up its prosperity with the premieres of *Grey's Anatomy* and *Dancing with the Stars* in 2005.

Through the early 2000s, the ABC Sports division and ESPN merged operations. ESPN, which had been broadcasting its own popular package of Sunday night games since 1987, took over the *Monday Night Football* franchise in 2006. Beginning that fall, all sports broadcasts on ABC were produced and presented on the ABC network with ESPN graphics and announcers.

At present, ABC operates a schedule of 86 weekly regular hours of network programming. It provides 22 hours of prime-time programming to affiliated stations: 8 to 11 p.m. Monday to Saturday (all times ET/PT) and 7 to 11 p.m. on Sundays. Daytime programming is also provided 11 a.m. to 3 p.m. weekdays (with an hour break at noon for local stations to air news or other programming), featuring the talk-lifestyle shows *The View* and *The Chew* and the soap opera *General Hospital*. ABC News programming includes *Good Morning America* from 7 to 9 a.m. weekdays (along with one-hour weekend editions), nightly editions of *ABC World News*, the Sunday political talk show *This Week*, and the late-night newsmagazine *Nightline*. Late nights also feature the talk show *Jimmy Kimmel Live!*

ABC.com was the first network website to offer full-length episodes online from May to June 2006. Beginning with the 2006–2007 television season, ABC.com has regularly been airing full-length episodes of most of its popular and new shows on its website the day after they aired on ABC, with some advertisements. It also has episode player applications for multiple platforms. On November 20, 2006, ABC and Comcast reached a landmark deal to offer hit shows through video on demand.

iPad App

ABC was the first network to provide viewers the opportunity to watch their favorite series on a mobile device through the ABC iPad app. With the rapid expansion of their viewership, ABC needed to know who was watching programming via the app and how they could leverage this touch point to increase consumer reach and engagement. Although ABC could track downloads and the millions of video streams viewed, it needed better insight into these viewers' demographics and experience.

As one of the few firms to offer in-app mobile satisfaction measurement, ForeSee provided ABC with a comprehensive solution that collects feedback from users during their experience, without viewers leaving the ABC app to go to a website. The survey's intuitive touch, swipe, and tap functionality aligns with the experience itself, allowing ABC to achieve a response rate much greater than traditional web surveys.

ABC knew its mobile audience would vary from its television viewers and web viewers, but it wanted to establish parameters around the various groups that interacted with its app to inform advertisers and guide future improvements.

ForeSee analytics provided demographic and satisfaction data in both aggregates, by demographic group, device, and programming segment. This information supplied the research team with strong, customer-based feedback that could be used to identify app improvements and to share ForeSee analytics and insights throughout the organization. The predictive nature of the analytics allowed ABC to see how small updates could have a large impact on users' likelihood to continue using the app, recommend, or view ABC programming through another channel, such as a television broadcast. The analytics also supported both the sales team in its efforts to promote advertising across platforms and management that was seeking reliable demographic information.

ForeSee customer experience analytics revealed that a large segment of users were using the app to view a television series for the first time. ABC had anticipated a higher level of engagement. It expected most viewers to use the app to catch up on episodes of their favorite series or to watch their usual programming at a more convenient time. Further analysis revealed that this important viewer segment had needs and levels of satisfaction different from those of more frequent users. First-time viewers were less aware of some ABC programs, thus identifying the need for content updates, such as series overviews and episode description information. This insight allowed ABC to discuss improvements that would encourage viewers to return to view more programming and, in turn, support the advertising value of the app.

We also conducted a usability audit review to assess the mobile app and provide recommendations for improvement on the basis of mobile's best practices. While the overall user experience was quite strong, enhancements could be made to help ABC stay ahead of the curve and make the experience easier and more enjoyable for viewers. The usability team provided actionable insights aimed to help ABC increase its reach by encouraging the discovery of new programming for both new and existing users.

Understanding the mobile viewer helps advertiser clients and the current viewing experience to guide future improvements to the mobile app. ForeSee Satisfaction Analytics for Mobile allowed ABC to gain valuable feedback by collecting data from viewers during their mobile app experience.

Testing New Store Programs Impact on the Customer Experience

Here is a final example of improving the customer experience. A major women's apparel retailer planned to implement custom fitting programs in its stores. The program was rolled out to a test group of stores across the country. By segmenting and comparing stores in the test pilot program to other stores in the chain, the retailer was able to measure the execution of the rollout and the impact it would make on customer satisfaction, purchase intent, and loyalty.

Consumers who made purchases were asked whether they had been offered a custom fitting and, if so, were asked a series of additional questions about the specifics of that fitting. The retailer used the ongoing customer experience measurement program to test compliance with the new program in pilot stores. It thus created a more cost-effective and accurate way to test for compliance than by implementing a mystery-shopping program.

The success of the program was analyzed by comparing customer satisfaction, future purchase intent, and loyalty across various segments of customers:

- Customers in stores that were not participating in the pilot.
- Customers in stores participating in the pilot who were not offered the custom fitting.
- Customers in stores participating in the pilot who were offered the custom fitting but declined.
- Customers in stores participating in the pilot who were offered the custom fitting and accepted.

The results of the analysis showed that the program was a major success, increasing customer satisfaction and customer loyalty. The program was then rolled out across all stores, and the ongoing measurement was used to monitor compliance and evaluate the impact of the program. The results were improved near-term financial success and improved customer loyalty.

Word-of-Mouth Index (WoMI)

A number of companies today have been using Net Promoter Score (NPS) in various ways within their organizations. Let's discuss a few cases of how they have used them and what WoMI will provide them above and beyond NPS.

A Multichannel Retailer

A multichannel retailer has been using NPS as a metric it shares with its board of directors and with Wall Street. It has discussed NPS on analysts' calls and reported it in the annual report. It introduced NPS to the organization four years ago. The executives felt that it really helped the organization have a common rallying cry around the importance of the customer. The retailer started by introducing it as a corporate initiative. For the first two years, it shared NPS every month with the entire company via its intranet. It was a topic of executive management and regional meetings. The company was focused on making the customer a more important part of the internal dialogue—a very noble effort.

As the company moved into the third and fourth years of the program, it decided to up the stakes by having store managers contact every customer who was labeled a detractor by NPS standards. The program faced some challenges. Store managers were spending time every day calling their customers who had scored them poorly. Soon, the managers' conversations turned beyond the original goal. The managers began to ask their customers for higher ratings the next time. The managers shared with their customers the importance of the NPS metric because, as they talked with them, they found out that they were not detractors but loyal customers who were planning to buy more items from the store. In addition to these issues, customer follow-up was time consuming for the store managers.

The four years of the NPS programs provided some interesting results. Year 1 saw a 15 percent rise in the NPS score. Year 2 saw it jump around a lot, sometimes increasing by 10 percent and sometimes decreasing by 10 percent. At the end of year 2, it was flat compared to the prior year. Year 3 saw NPS drop by 5 percent while still showing signs of jumping up and down throughout the year. And in year 4, NPS improved by about 5 percent. Over the four-year period it jumped by about 15 percent. The problem the retailer had was in its attempt to model the change in NPS to the change in revenue: It could not identify a strong and consistent relationship. Sometimes it thought it was on the right track, but that hope would fade as it continued the NPS modeling.

I was not surprised when I heard this story from the retailer's customer insights team. We discussed in detail the strengths of NPS (bringing focus to the importance of customers). We also discussed the challenges (they couldn't find the causal relationship between NPS and financial results because there isn't one). We spent a lot of time talking about the key drivers for revenue growth for a retailer: keeping your existing customers, selling more to those customers, and attracting new customers. The lightbulb went off for the customer insights team. They were trying to model the relationship with only one of the potential revenue growth drivers (attracting new customers via word of mouth), and during those four years, many other corporate initiatives focused on some of the other drivers.

I thought I had made progress until Jessica, the manager of the team, told me that she would not be able to convince the store's CEO that NPS wasn't working because it was his initiative. I understood her dilemma and offered her another option. We had just begun testing WoMI. I encouraged her to add the additional question and to gather data for a while before we approached the CEO. I told Jessica that if we had the data and the test was well thought out, he would want to hear the result. I also suggested that the model we tested would allow us to measure not only positive and negative word of mouth but also the other drivers of revenue growth, such as customer retention, customer upsell, and new customer acquisition via marketing efforts. She agreed to my strategy, and work got under way.

After six months, Jessica, the team, and I met again to look at all the data. She had decided to focus the team's efforts on the web channel first, and, if the results were positive, she would roll it out to stores as well. As we started the meeting, Jessica was all smiles. She said, "We're beginning to see the relationships between our metrics and our financial results." About 60 percent of its revenue growth was coming from existing customers buying more frequently. A number of initiatives both in the loyalty program and in the marketing program explained the increase in frequency. The remainder of the growth was attributed to new customer acquisition. About three-fourths of it was the result of marketing-driven customer acquisition, and one-fourth was a result of word-of-mouth acquisition. In addition, Jessica and her team saw that as a result of the "discourage" question, they were overstating detractors by about 210 percent.

Armed with these data and results, Jessica was confident that it was time to go to the CEO and other senior executives. We discussed the best strategy of how to present this information. We decided that

Jessica would recommend that the retailer add the discourage question across its channels and use the True Detractors (those very likely to discourage others from doing business with the retailer) as the target for store managers when they conducted outreach to their customers. This would be an easy thing for the CEO and other senior executives to embrace since it would make the store managers more efficient in their jobs. As part of her second recommendation, Jessica would share the modeling that was done to explain the revenue growth. She would then propose that ForeSee continue to track revenue growth for the next six months, now utilizing both web and store data, and report back results to the executives.

Jessica carried the day, and the CEO and the senior team backed her recommendations. Making the store managers more efficient will prove to be a big win for the retailer. Being able to run WoMI and NPS for the next six months will allow us to better understand the true drivers of revenue growth in their business. I am eager to see how this plays out and to share the results with Jessica, the store executives, and the readers of our next book!

Consumer Products Company

Not long ago, I received a call from a long-time customer named Juan who had taken a new job about seven months ago at a consumer products company. When he arrived, Juan found that the company was using NPS as part of its variable compensation program. Juan had heard me speak about the topic of compensation, and now that it was going to impact his bonus check, he wanted to know more.

As we chatted, he shared the details of the company's current program. It was a typical NPS program: run surveys on both web visitors and those who registered products. It was a simple two-question survey, with one being the "How likely are you to recommend?" question and the other question asking those who gave a score of six or less to describe why they wouldn't recommend the company. Lots of data were collected, and the NPS scores were gathered and used in determining year-end bonuses.

Not only did Juan's bonus rely on NPS but also one of his responsibilities was to improve the customer experience with the website, and his manager wanted the NPS score to go higher. Unfortunately, the data being generated weren't giving him any clear direction. Juan was a fan of ForeSee from his prior job but was given strict instructions from his new manager that the NPS survey needed to stay in place. I agreed to meet with Juan to discuss the situation.

A few days later, we sat down and went over the data Juan was receiving from the NPS system and what data he was missing. He told me frankly that he couldn't decipher what was driving NPS from the open-ended comments that were coming in as part of the second question in the survey. We talked about the importance of a causal model, and I reminded Juan that positive word of mouth is an outcome of the customer experience with satisfaction. If you improve the consumer's satisfaction with the experience, it will have a positive impact not only on positive word of mouth but also on retention, loyalty, and frequency of purchases. We put together a plan to implement the ForeSee model on his site and to continue to use the recommend question used in NPS. I also shared with him the discourage question and how WoMI would be an added benefit to the new system of metrics we were going to implement.

Juan is a smart guy and had no problem embracing the importance of multiple metrics such as KPIs for the business. The company's NPS score had not moved much over the past few years, and that was the main reason Juan was hired (and his predecessor fired). Juan moved quickly to implement the ForeSee Customer Experience measurement model, along with SessionReplay.

Within weeks, he was able to identify opportunities to improve the customer experience that would have a positive impact on improving the likelihood to recommend and, as a result, NPS. Juan became a hero because he was able to drive NPS up, and his division was rewarded with big bonus checks. After about nine months of continuous improvement to the site, he was called into a meeting with the CEO, who asked, "What was the strategy you used for driving up NPS?" Juan proceeded to explain to him that while word of mouth is an important metric, it is an outcome of the customer experience. He shared with him the data that supported his position. Juan explained that he was able to focus on improving the customer experience and it resulted in higher satisfaction, stronger word of mouth, and higher customer loyalty. But, he added, focusing only on word of mouth won't get any company very far; you need to focus on what drives word of mouth: simple in concept yet powerful in action. By the time Juan got back to his desk, he had received a personal e-mail from the CEO thanking him for his insight.

Insurance Company

A couple of months ago, I was at a conference and met an executive named Lois, who was from an insurance company. I had just finished giving a keynote presentation about the importance of measuring the customer experience and how excelling at customer experience analytics could give you a competitive advantage. Lois came up to me after the presentation and said that she was a big NPS fan. I asked why. Her answer was a good one, just like John told me at our annual user summit: she told me that NPS gave the company focus on the customer. She went on to say that the insurance company's challenge was improving NPS. I explained that the challenge with NPS is assuming that those who don't recommend are detractors, when many are in fact very loyal, good customers. I said, "You may be improving loyalty and customer acquisition but not having much impact on NPS." I could see her mental wheels turning. Lois replied, "We are growing market share, but our NPS number is not improving." We set up a meeting to discuss this challenge in more detail.

A few weeks later, as Lois and I sat down, I drew for her a diagram showing the drivers of revenue growth that included customer retention, customer upsell, and new customer acquisition.

She agreed that the diagram described her business. I then added to the diagram by showing customer acquisition split into two groups: those driven by marketing and those driven by word of mouth. I said to Lois, "Last time we spoke, you mentioned how customer acquisition was so important to the growth of your business and your company, which is known for its aggressive marketing programs, right?" She shook her head yes. I asked Lois what the NPS score was across the customer base, and she replied that it ranged between 25 and 30. I then inquired whether she could segment this NPS by looking at new customers compared to existing customers. Lois flipped open her laptop, spent a couple of minutes banging on the keyboard, and replied, "They are the same." The next question was how many new customers came as a result of word of mouth. Again a few minutes of banging on the keyboard and Lois had the answer. Only a small percentage of their new customers indicated they were influenced by word of mouth. The answer was an easy one—growth was being driven by marketing efforts that resulted in new customer acquisition, which was very good for business. However, new customers were just as likely to recommend the company as were existing customers. Growth was not explained by NPS but rather by marketing-driven customer acquisition. Lois had her answer and asked what good was NPS for them. I responded by saying, "Focusing a company on the customer is never bad, and NPS can do that. However, as a metric by itself, it isn't going to be very insightful to your business. You need a system of metrics to better understand your business and be able to focus on how to continue to accelerate growth." Lois now understood the importance of a system of metrics, not just having one number to rely on.

Best Practices

When you think about best practices and how you implement them within your organization, you need to make sure they fit your business, strategy, and culture. In customer experience analytics, there is not a one-size-fits-all approach available. I have yet to see where you can boil things down to one number that you need to know. Your customers are complex and getting more complex. No one number that I have seen is going to help you understand the relationship you have with your customers.

Yet there are some threads that run through most, if not all, of the successful approaches. Remember that you cannot manage what you do not measure, and what you measure will determine what you do.

- Focus on a set of metrics that map to the revenue drivers of your business. Even if word of mouth is not a driver today, don't ignore it as part of these metrics. You need a metric for each of the drivers of revenue growth: customer retention, upsell to existing customers, and customer acquisition. But don't stop there.

- Take those metrics and model them with your financial results. When you get the models right, the relationships will be clear.

- Make sure you are measuring what drives those outcomes. It starts with the satisfaction with the customer experience.

- It continues with the drivers of satisfaction. Satisfaction and its outcomes will be pretty consistent throughout your business. The drivers will be different, based on the channel and the stage of the customer life cycle you are measuring.

- Any measurement system is only as good as its accuracy, precision, and reliability. Develop a measurement system that can continually have the level of accuracy, precision, and reliability you need to make the decisions for your business.

Chapter 9

Big Data and the Future of Analytics

When you truly measure the satisfaction with the customer experience and turn the resulting data into intelligence you can use, you make the right decisions that lead to success—for you, for your customers, for everyone. That seems as worthy a goal as any I have known, and it is what makes every day for me and my colleagues so challenging and fulfilling.

To compete and win in today's ultracompetitive environment, where consumers are in control and switching costs are very low, the customer experience is more important than it has ever been. Businesses cannot stand still in the field of customer experience analytics; they must continue to push the envelope and evolve—not only products, services, and marketing but also analytics. If businesses don't evolve, they will be overrun by competitors and will cease to exist. There are a lot of examples to look at. Of the 1955 Fortune 500 companies, 87 percent are no longer in the Fortune 500. Some of the companies have fallen out of the 500 but still exist, and others no longer exist, including Studebaker, Bethlehem Steel, Bendix, Sperry, Fruehauf, and Pullman.

Businesses can gain a competitive advantage by having the most accurate, precise, reliable, insightful, and actionable customer experience analytics. Such analytics give companies the ability to make good decisions, decisions that most often will lead to success. The companies that make the best use of their investment—that is, get the biggest return on their investment—will win the competitive game. Companies with insightful and actionable analytics can respond to the market and their customers quicker than their competitors. Success and failure of companies can often be traced back to their good decisions and their bad decisions. With the right analytics, the probability of making good decisions is greatly increased. Superior customer experience analytics can become a company's competitive advantage.

Companies cannot stand still with their analytics. You need to continue to evolve them to meet the evolving consumer and the evolving market and to stay ahead of the evolving competition. Billy Beane, general manager of the Oakland As, takes this approach to continue to outperform his peers and do it with a significantly smaller investment. His approach was chronicled by the book *Moneyball* by Michael Lewis, who has almost turned the word *moneyball* into a verb to describe the evolving analytics approach. Tomorrow's winners will be defined by the innovative strength of the customer experience analytics they use and implement. That is what will allow companies that have gone from good to great to remain on top.

And the key to measuring this new world of customer experience analytics is to understand the rise of big data, which is a very new phenomenon. In 2000, only one-quarter of all the stored information in the world was digital; paper, film, and other analog media ruled. Remember microfiche? Remember stacks of old, yellowing newspapers and magazines in libraries? No more. I bet my sons have never even used microfiche. With the amount of digital data doubling every three years, as of 2013 less than 2 percent of all stored information is nondigital. An extraordinary change.

So what is a workable definition of *big data?* For me, it is the explosion of structured and unstructured data about people caused by the digitization and networking of everything: computers, smartphones, GPS devices, embedded microprocessors, and sensors, all connected by the mobile Internet that is generating data about people at an exponential rate. Big data is driven by the three Vs: an increasing Volume of data with a wide range of Variety and gathered and processed at a higher Velocity.

Big Data Volume

The increase in volume provides us a bigger set of data to manipulate. This provides higher accuracy, a lower margin of error, and the ability to analyze the data into many more discrete segments. As entrepreneur and former director of the MIT Media Lab Frank Moss explains in an interview on MSN[1]:

Every time we perform a search, tweet, send an e-mail, post a blog, comment on one, use a cell phone, shop online, update our profile on a social networking site, use a credit card, or even go to the gym, we leave behind a mountain of data, a digital footprint, that provides a treasure trove of information about our lifestyles, financial activities, health habits, social interactions, and much more.

He adds that this trend has been "accelerated by the spectacular success of social networks like Facebook, Twitter, Foursquare, and LinkedIn and video- or picture-sharing services like YouTube and Flickr. When acting together, these services generate exponential rates of growth of data about people in astonishingly short periods of time."

More statistics show the scope of big data. In 2010, over 4 billion people, or 60 percent of the world's population, were using mobile phones, and about 12 percent of those people had smartphones, whose penetration is growing at more than 20 percent a year. More than 30 million networked sensor nodes are now present in the transportation, automotive, industrial, utilities, and retail sectors. The number of these sensors is increasing at a rate of more than 30 percent a year. The new data stored by enterprises exceeded seven exabytes of data globally in 2010, and new data stored by consumers around the world that year was an additional six exabytes. To put these very large numbers in context, the data that companies and individuals are producing and storing is equivalent to filling more than 60,000 U.S. Libraries of Congress.

Big Data Variety

The wider variety will unlock data relationships we haven't been able to see before. There are endless examples. The digital environment

---

[1] http://businessonmain.msn.com/browseresources/articles/inventingandnewideas.aspx?cp-documentid=30009963#fbid=UJRE-ODLUd9

Big Data and the Future of Analytics

has allowed us to gather more data about more interactions than ever before. Let's think about the experience you have reading a newspaper compared to visiting the newspaper's website. I am a faithful *Wall Street Journal* reader. I have a subscription that gets delivered to my home. I also read it on the website, my iPad, or iPhone from time to time. So what does the *Wall Street Journal* know about my experiences with the paper version? They know I am a subscriber and for how long. They know when I stop delivery. They know what credit card I use to pay for the subscription. They know where I live. They don't know much else. They don't know how many days I read the paper. They don't know what sections and articles I read. They don't know which ads I have seen. They don't know how long I spend reading it or how many different times I may pick up and read that day's paper. They don't know that I start by scanning the What's New column and never miss the Marketplace and Opinion sections. They can have focus groups, do surveys, and get some samples of how people interact with the paper, but those methods are costly and time consuming and are not often done on a continuous basis.

Now let's switch to the digital world. They know how many times I visit the website, iPad app, and iPhone app. They know what articles I see, what ads I see, how many articles I see per day, how long my average session is, and how many times I go back to the site or app to read the same issue. If they are measuring the customer experience and voice of the customer, they will know if I am satisfied with the content, navigation, functionality, and performance of the site. If they are using the ForeSee SessionReplay product, they will know how I scroll, how active I am with the page, how I navigate between articles, and how I search for information, where I got stuck, what I could and couldn't find, and they will be able to see exactly what I saw and replay the session I had with the WSJ.com site. And if they are measuring the customer experience across all channels, they can understand the omnichannel experience as I move between channels and devices. The variety of data about interaction with the *Wall Street Journal* that you can learn from the digital versions is far-reaching and ever increasing in usage and value.

Let's look at a retail example. Here the technology has not only increased the variety of the data available in the digital world but also increased the variety of data in the physical world. There is technology that will allow me to track people as they walk through the store, where they spend their time, which aisles they go down, which sections of the store they ignore. They will know if usage patterns of the store vary by time of day, day of the week, or season.

In a contact center bringing together the consumer's satisfaction with the agent, the length of time of the call, the prior purchase history of the consumer, the seniority and training of the agent, and the demographics of the customer can enable analysis that will lead to better and quicker improvements to the consumer experience. These data integrations that expand the variety of data can be game changers.

Big Data Velocity

The increased velocity in gathering and, more important, processing the data can turn what used to be a once-a-year project into an everyday analysis. Increasing the velocity of analysis is critical to keep up with ever-faster evolving consumers, markets, and competitors. In yesterday's analytics environment, we would be left to deal with the sources of data independently. With today's multichannel, multidevice consumers, we would be missing the omnichannel experience. Being able to gather data quickly and process data quickly is a game changer. It allows us to analyze faster, make decisions faster, and get returns faster. Today's consumers have many choices, and we cannot afford to miss meeting their expectations for long before they go elsewhere. The increased velocity in today's big data environment gives us the ability to move faster and keep up with the dynamic nature of the consumer experience.

But for me, big data involves more than just the dramatic increase in volume, velocity, and variety; it also implies the ability to render into data many aspects of the world and business that have never been quantified before. The authors Kenneth Cukier and Viktor Mayer-Schoenberger call this *datafication*. For example, Google treats words as data as it digitizes millions of public domain books from the libraries of our greatest universities, creating new value.

The World of Big Data

Since the beginning of time, researchers have had to work with relatively small amounts of data because the methods of collecting, organizing, storing, and analyzing information were very limited. Researchers reduced the information they studied to the minimum so they could examine it more closely and with some degree of ease. This is how statistics has worked until very recently. Sampling was the key in this world. It is founded on the idea that within a certain margin of error—you hear those words with every exit poll conducted in every political campaign—a well-trained analyst could infer something about a total population from a small subset, as long as the sample is chosen at random. This is highly useful when you are looking for gross impressions. But good luck making predictions when you want to know how left-handed, Hispanic men over 40 who have a postgraduate degree in the sciences will vote. Or what televisions, cars, or smartphones they want. When pollsters collect all the data, however, insights appear. Big data is, as Cukier and Mayer-Schoenberger argue, not just about creating somewhat larger samples but about harnessing as much of the existing data as possible about what is being studied.

As a major McKinsey study indicated, the use of big data is becoming a key way for leading companies to outperform their peers. However to outperform their peers, companies need more than big data, they need great analytics. One retailer that embraced big data had the potential to increase its operating margin by more than 60 percent, while other retailers used it to capture significant market share from its competitors. The study proclaims that across all business sectors a significant competitive advantage will be gained by leading users of big data at the expense of those companies that are slow off the mark or never quite grasp the importance of the trend. Ultimately, they will be left behind.

The study shows that big data will also help to create new growth opportunities and entirely new categories of companies. Opportunities will exist for companies that sit in the middle of large information flows where data about products and services, buyers and suppliers, and consumer preferences and intent can be captured and analyzed. Such companies include those that interface with large numbers of consumers buying a wide range of products and services, companies that enable global supply chains, companies that process millions of transactions, and companies that provide platforms for consumer digital experiences. They will be the big-data-advantaged businesses. Other businesses will flourish when they realize they have access to valuable pools of data generated by their products and services.

Early movers that secure access to the data necessary to create value are likely to reap the most benefit. From the standpoint of competitiveness and the potential capture of value, all companies need to take big data seriously. In most industries, established competitors and new entrants alike will leverage data-driven strategies to innovate, compete, and capture value.

Big data will also play an important part in small business. Several forces are democratizing big data, including affordable cloud computing storage, open-source software for processing large volumes of data, and big data sets being made available in the public domain.

The stage is now set for entrepreneurs and small-business owners to reap tremendous rewards from big data by creating new businesses or finding ways to accelerate the growth of existing ones. There are an almost unlimited number of such opportunities, but here are just a few:

- Mobile phones and wireless sensors can now collect huge volumes of data about people's behavior where they live, work, and play. These data sets reveal important patterns that can revolutionize how consumer products are conceived, designed, and marketed. For example, Affeciva Inc. is marketing an innovative system, based on years of research in affective computing by Rosalind Picard of MIT's Media Lab, using webcams to read people's emotional states and levels of attention from their facial expressions. It gives marketers faster, more accurate insight into consumer response to their products and services.

- Today, many people watch TV and use social media to simultaneously comment about the programs and advertisements they're viewing. It would provide a huge insight to businesses and advertising agencies if they measure this big data in real time to get up-to-the-minute insights into audience sentiment about programming and products. Bluefin Labs Inc. is creating a big data set called TV Genome, which is a real-time mapping of vast amounts of social media commentary traceable back to its stimulus on TV. Every month, Bluefin fingerprints and analyzes all domestic U.S. TV broadcasts—more than 2 million minutes!

- In the decade ahead, consumer-centric health will radically transform health care, moving it out of hospitals and doctors' offices and into our everyday lives. This will be made possible by the exploding volume of big data about our lives and our bodies, enabling ordinary people to take control of their health and wellness. An early mover in this market is Ginger.io Inc., which uses cell phones to collect data about people's daily behavior and then visualizes it to reveal important health patterns, like the early signs of illness. For example, when people are getting sick, they often sleep more, use their phones less, and change eating habits. By analyzing such data, doctors could prevent illness.

Besides these examples, there are many ways that big data can be used to create value across all sectors of the global economy. I firmly believe that American businesses are on the cusp of a tremendous wave of innovation, productivity, and growth, as well as new modes of competition and value capture—all driven by big data as consumers and companies exploit its potential.

Big Data Creates Value

Companies can use big data and more sophisticated analytics to create value in a number of other ways that will improve the customer experience.

For example, big data allows businesses to create highly specific segmentations and to tailor products and services precisely to meet those needs. Even consumer goods and service companies that have used segmentation for many years are beginning to deploy ever more sophisticated big data techniques, such as the real-time microsegmentation of customers to target promotions and advertising.

Also, sophisticated analytics can substantially improve decision making, minimize risks, and unearth valuable insights that would otherwise remain hidden. Retailers can use algorithms to optimize decision processes such as the automatic fine-tuning of inventories and pricing in response to real-time in-store and online sales. In some cases, decisions will not necessarily be automated but augmented by analyzing huge, entire data sets using big data techniques and technologies rather than smaller samples.

In addition, big data will become a key basis of competition and growth for firms. These opportunities involve improving efficiency and effectiveness, enabling organizations both to do more with less and to produce higher-quality outputs, that is, increase the value-added content of products and services. For example, companies can leverage data to design products that better match customer needs. Data can even be leveraged to improve products as they are used. An example is a mobile phone that has learned its owner's habits and preferences, that holds applications and data tailored to that particular user's needs, and that will therefore be more valuable than a new device that is not customized to a user's needs.

Big Data and Retail

Let's take a look at how big data will impact one area of the economy—retail. In the past, the use of information technology and digital data has helped boost the profitability of individual companies and the productivity of an entire sector. In the coming years, big data could significantly increase operating margins and play an increasing role as consumers search, research, compare, buy, and obtain support online and as the products sold by retailers increasingly generate their own digital data. Of course, the value that retailers and their customers capture will depend on how retailers overcome barriers related to technology, talent, and organizational culture.

Retailers will be able to not only record every customer transaction and operation but also keep track of emerging data sources such as radio-frequency identification (RFID) chips that track the location of products.

In fact, U.S. retail has been leveraging information technology for decades. Point-of-sale transactional data, primarily obtained from the use of bar codes, first appeared in the 1970s. Since the 1990s, many leading retailers have been using store-level and supply chain data to optimize distribution and logistics, sharpen merchandise planning and management, and upgrade store operations. Walmart pioneered the expansion of an electronic data interchange system to connect its supply chain electronically. Walmart also developed Retail Link, a tool that gives its suppliers a view of demand in its stores so that they know when stores should be restocked, rather than waiting for an order from Walmart.

Today, leading companies mine customer data to inform decisions they make about managing their supply chain, merchandising, and pricing. Retailers are also increasingly sophisticated in using the big data they collect from multiple sales channels, catalogs, stores, and online interactions. Granular customer data can enable retailers to improve the effectiveness of their marketing and merchandising.

Big data can also be used in marketing products and services in these ways:

- **Cross-selling.** State-of-the-art cross-selling uses all data known about a customer, including the customer's demographics, purchase history, preferences, and real-time location, to increase the average purchase size. For example, Amazon.com employs collaborative filtering to generate "you might also want" prompts for each product bought or visited. At one point, Amazon reported that 30 percent of sales were due to its recommendation engine. Another example of this lever is using big data analyses to optimize in-store promotions that link complementary items and bundled products.

- **Location-based marketing.** Location-based marketing utilizes smartphones and other personal location data-enabled mobile devices to target consumers close to stores or already in them. For instance, as a consumer approaches an apparel store, that store sends a special offer on a sweater to the customer's smartphone. The start-up PlaceCast claims that more than 50 percent of its users have made a purchase as a result of such location-based ads.

- **In-store behavior analysis.** Such analysis can improve store layout, product mix, and shelf positioning. Retailers can now track customers' shopping patterns (e.g., footpath and time spent in different parts of a store), drawing real-time location data from smartphone applications, shopping cart transponders, or passively monitoring the location of mobile phones within a retail environment.

- **Customer microsegmentation.** The amount of data available for segmentation has exploded, and new analytical tools can provide ever more granular microsegments. Retailers can now track and leverage data on the behavior of individual customers—including click stream data from the web—and update the data in near real time. Neiman Marcus has developed both behavioral segmentation and a multitier membership reward program, and this combination has led to substantially more purchases of higher-margin products from its most affluent, high-margin customers.

- **Sentiment analysis.** This methodology leverages consumer data in the various forms of social media to help inform a variety of business decisions. For example, retailers can use sentiment analysis to gauge the real-time response to marketing campaigns and adjust course accordingly.

- **Analyzing the multichannel consumer experience**. Enhancing the multichannel experience for consumers can be a powerful driver of sales, customer satisfaction, and loyalty. Retailers can use big data to integrate promotions and pricing for shoppers seamlessly, whether those consumers are online, in-store, or perusing a catalog. Williams-Sonoma, for example, has integrated customer databases with information on some 60 million households, tracking such things as their income, housing values, and number of children. Targeted e-mails based on this information obtain 10 to 18 times the response rate of e-mails that are not targeted. The company created multiple versions of its catalogs attuned to the behavior and preferences of different groups of customers.

The Trap of Big Data

One of my favorite sayings these days is that big data without great analytics is a waste of time. The trap of big data is that we can get a false sense of confidence. Bad data will still lead to bad decisions, regardless of the volume, variety, and velocity of that data. All of the measurement mistakes I discuss in Appendix C are relevant to Big Data. Gathering more data doesn't eliminate the need for accuracy, precision, and reliability. We can take a poorly defined set of data that has measurement error and, by increasing the volume, eventually lower the margin of error to an acceptable level. While low margins of error are generally good, if we are not measuring the right things or if we have sample bias or measurement bias, a low margin of error will not lead us to an analysis that provides value.

The accuracy and precision level needs to fit the business decision we are making. As a society, we have very low tolerance for a measurement error when it comes to drug trials that can have life-threatening side effects. We have a low tolerance for an error when it comes to our bank's processing of our transactions. We have a higher tolerance when weathermen predict next week's weather.

We also don't want to fall into the trap of correlation over causation, just because we have a lot of data. A lot of data will create more correlated relationships, but that doesn't mean a causal relationship can be determined.

The right kind of data is even more important than the volume of data. All too often the big data advocates gather more and more of the same data. We need to compliment the behavioral data with the attitudinal, or voice of customer, data. Bigger data that is only behavioral in nature will not give us the customer's perspective and with today's multi-channel, multi-device consumer, that can be disastrous mistake.

The final trap to avoid is the bad metric trap. A designed limited metric like NPS that has not evolved over time will not give us the insights and actionability we need to be successful. We need to apply the right analytics and the right metrics to make Big Data valuable.

Big data *and* great analytics will give you the opportunity to gain the competitive advantage that all companies are seeking.

Innovation

The classic definition of *innovation* is introducing something new. From a practical business perspective, the word *innovation* has come to mean something more than that. Innovation is about change that is significant and positive, creating a new dimension of performance. Innovation can create a competitive advantage and set the target for others to aim at. Most of us, when thinking about innovation, recall innovative products and companies like Apple, Amazon, and 3M. Much like the innovation that has led to great success for Apple, Amazon, and 3M, companies that innovate in customer experience analytics can also gain a competitive advantage.

When I think about innovation, these are some of the guiding principles I follow:

- Don't accept the status quo; question it.
- Challenge the assumptions.

- Reward ideas, good or bad.
- Try it and test it . . . and test it . . . and test it some more.
- "If you always do what you always did, you will always get what you always got" (Albert Einstein).
- "You miss 100 percent of the shots you never take" (Wayne Gretzky).

I had the opportunity to host Billy Beane at an event recently. In discussing *Moneyball* and the concepts he used to create a competitive advantage in baseball, it was clear that he had to continue to innovate or his ideas would, to borrow a pop music term while mixing metaphors, make him a one-hit wonder. Other baseball clubs would catch up to what the Oakland As were doing. To stay ahead, Billy had to keep innovating analytics to maintain that advantage. He is using new metrics, in new ways, to enable him to make better player personnel decisions than his competitors. Billy's story continues to be a great example of using analytics to get a competitive advantage and innovating with analytics to keep that competitive advantage.

Customer Experience Analytics is the new competitive battleground where companies will fight for the loyalty of the consumer. Striving to continue to innovate your analytics is what will allow you to gain and keep that competitive advantage. We use at ForeSee to sustain our competitive advantage and to enable our customers to gain a competitive advantage and keep it.

Measuring Customer Experience—A Broader Impact and the Start of a Journey

When Peter Drucker died in 2005, he was widely regarded as one of the most profound thinkers about business and one of the creators of management as a formal discipline. Having witnessed almost a century of turmoil and change, from the rise of Hitler in his native Austria, to the ascendance of the corporation, to the prominence of the Internet, Drucker could assess the complex realities of his time and still find the simple truths that underlie our institutions. He once said, "The single most important thing to remember about any enterprise is that there are no results inside its four walls. The result of a business is a satisfied customer." He added, with equal insight, "The quality of a service or product is not what you put into it. It is what the customer gets out of it."

Drucker knew that customer satisfaction is the key to success for a company. His was knowledge gleaned from decades of observations of businesses and conversations with their leaders. Our assertions about customer satisfaction and the customer experience are based on the new science of analytics, of which WoMI and the Measurement Ecosystem are two recent examples. As the interactions between customers and businesses grow more complex and intricate, this new science will continue to evolve, producing better and more accurate ways to describe these situations and providing companies with the tools to better serve their customers.

Like Drucker, we believe that business's purpose is to create a customer. Good companies become great companies when they satisfy the customers they create and are rewarded for their efforts. Companies that fail to satisfy their customers over time will be punished, both by deserting customers and by the capital markets.

When you truly measure the satisfaction of the customer experience and turn data into intelligence, you make the right decisions that lead to success—for you, for your customers, for everyone. That seems as worthy a goal as any I have known, and it is what makes every day for me and my colleagues so challenging and fulfilling.

To compete and win in today's ultracompetitive environment, where consumers are in control and switching costs are very low, the customer experience is more important than it has ever been. Businesses cannot stand still in the field of customer experience analytics; they must continue to push the envelope and evolve—not only products, services, and marketing, but also analytics. Businesses can gain a competitive advantage by having the most accurate, precise, reliable, insightful, and actionable customer experience analytics. Tomorrow's winners will be defined by the innovative strength of customer experience analytics. That is what will allow companies that have gone from good to great to remain on top.

Satisfaction, WoMI, Net Promoter, and Overstatement of Detractors for Top Companies

In addition to testing and perfecting WoMI with clients, ForeSee also conducted extensive research from 2011 to 2013 to collect satisfaction, WoMI, and Net Promoter Score for hundreds of private companies across industries. Collecting NPS and WoMI scores allowed us to calculate how much Net Promoter overstates detractors.

According to Net Promoter, anyone who answers 6 or lower when asked "how likely are you to recommend this company?" is a detractor. According to WoMI, anyone who answers a 9 or 10 when asked "how likely are you to discourage people from doing business with this company?" is a True Detractor. By subtracting WoMI detractors (or True Detractors) from NPS detractors and dividing by WoMi detractors, we can find out how much Net Promoter is overstating detractors for each of these companies. (See Figure A.1.)

This appendix contains tables with satisfaction, WoMI, NPS, and overstatement of detractors for the following categories:

- 100 U.S. brands
- 100 online U.S. retailers
- 40 online U.K. retailers
- 7 largest U.S. banks
- 29 American retail stores
- 25 mobile retail sites and apps

$$\text{NPS Overstatement of Detractors} = \frac{\text{Recommend \% of 1s to 6s} - \text{Discourage \% of 9s and 10s}}{\text{Discourage \% of 9s and 10s}}$$

Figure A.1   Calculation of Overstatement of Detractors

- 17 mobile financial services sites and apps
- 25 mobile travel sites and apps

Figure A.2 shows an overview of the research we conducted in various industries and various channels.

Note that in the following charts satisfaction is always measured at a channel level, while WoMI and NPS are always measured at a brand level. For example, we have conducted various surveys of Apple's customers. We have surveyed Apple's customers about their brand-level satisfaction with Apple, their satisfaction with Apple stores, their satisfaction with Apple's website, and their satisfaction with Apple's mobile site and app. Each satisfaction score reflects satisfaction with the specified channel. However, WoMI and NPS are always referring to the company overall. In Figure A.3, you will see that Apple has different satisfaction scores for various experiences (brand-level, store, web, and mobile). But since WoMI and NPS are always asked about the brand level, shouldn't all the WoMI and NPS scores be the same?

Not necessarily. A mobile user might have a different overall likelihood to promote or detract than a store visitor.

So which one is Apple's true satisfaction, WoMI or NPS score? Arguably, the brand-level scores are the highest level and would be the most appropriate for someone looking for a company-wide tracking metric. With today's consumers being multi-channel, the individual channel scores are very important and play an important role in the success of Apple. Most Apple consumers are going to interact with Apple in more than one channel. Channel managers will find the differences useful and instructive, especially when viewed within a comprehensive system of metrics that makes these numbers actionable.

Figure A.2   Satisfaction, NPS, WoMI, and Average Overstatement of Detractors by Category

Industry	Channel	Satisfaction (on a 100-point scale)	WoMI Score	NPS Score	NPS-Defined Detractors*	WoMI-Defined Detractors**	Average Overstatement of Detractors***
Automotive	Brand-level	79	44	38	17%	11%	85%
Business-to-Business	Brand-level	79	43	36	17%	11%	96%
Computers/ Electronics Manufacturers	Brand-level	78	45	33	18%	6%	264%
Consumer Packaged Goods	Brand-level	78	44	31	19%	5%	399%
Financial Services	Brand-level	70	28	1	35%	8%	527%
Retail: Brand Level	Brand-level	80	47	39	15%	6%	222%
Top 100 Retailers	Web	78	41	29	20%	7%	271%
Top 25 Retailers	Mobile	78	44	35	17%	8%	130%
Top 40 U.K. Retailers	Web	74	33	12	25%	5%	516%
Top 29 Retailers	Stores	78	48	33	18%	4%	450%

(Continued)

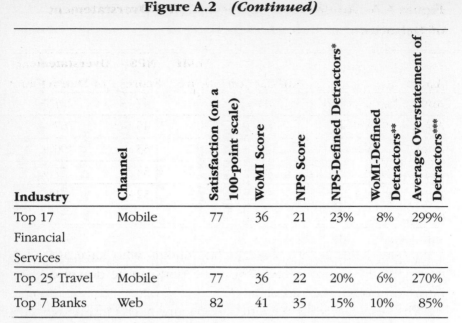

Industry	Channel	Satisfaction (on a 100-point scale)	WoMI Score	NPS Score	NPS-Defined Detractors*	WoMI-Defined Detractors**	Average Overstatement of Detractors***
Top 17 Financial Services	Mobile	77	36	21	23%	8%	299%
Top 25 Travel	Mobile	77	36	22	20%	6%	270%
Top 7 Banks	Web	82	41	35	15%	10%	85%

*The NPS definition of detractors is anyone who rates their likelihood to recommend a company 6 or lower on a 10-point scale.

**WoMI defines detractors as anyone who rates their likelihood to detract from a company with a 9 or 10 on a 10-point scale. This group is also referred to as "True Detractors."

***Overstatement of detractors is calculated using the following formula: (% of NPS-defined detractors – % of WoMI-defined detractors)/% of WoMI-defined detractors. The average overstatement at the category level is an average of the company-level overstatements of detractors. The overall average overstatement is the average of the overstatements of each underlying category.

The Top 100 U.S. Brands

In April 2013, ForeSee measured satisfaction, WoMI, and NPS for Interbrands 2012 list of the top 100 brands (the actual list reflects 89 companies, as we were not able to collect sufficient sample sizes to calculate statistically significant scores for the remaining 11 brands). The research was reflects more than 21,000 surveys and utilized

Figure A.3   Apple WoMI Scores and NPS Overstatement of Detractors

Apple	Satisfaction	WoMI Score	NPS Score	Overstatement of Detractors
Apple: Overall Brand	83	56	47	225%
Apple: U.S. Website	80	49	45	67%
Apple: U.K. Website	77	47	33	700%
Apple: Stores	83	58	54	57%
Apple: Mobile Site and App	83	57	52	71%

a nationwide panel of consumer households who have agreed to participate in opt-in surveys. The full report can be downloaded at http://wordofmouthindex.com/.

The research is illuminating (see Figure A.4). On average, NPS overstates detractors for the biggest brands by 300 percent (overstatement of detractors varies somewhat by industry).

The Top 100 U.S. Online Retailers

ForeSee measured satisfaction, WoMI, and NPS for the top 100 retailers in the United States by sales volume, as determined by *Internet Retailer Magazine's 2012 Top 500 Guide*. The research was conducted in November and December 2012 and reflects more than 24,000 surveys from shoppers who had visited the top 100 retail websites within the previous two weeks. This study utilized a nationwide panel of consumer households who have agreed to participate in opt-in surveys. The full report can be downloaded at www.fore see.com.

ForeSee's measurement of the customer experience is based on a methodology founded in academia and proven to be a predictor of future financial success at both the macroeconomic and microeconomic levels.

Figure A.4   The Top 100 U.S. Brands

Industry Top 100 Brands (based on InterBrand list)	Satisfaction (on a 100-point scale)	WoMI Score	NPS Score	NPS-Defined Detractors*	WoMI-Defined Detractors**	Average Overstatement of Detractors***
Average Across Top 100 Brands	77	42	28	21%	7%	299%
Top Automotive Brands						
Automotive Brands: Average	79	44	38	17%	11%	85%
Audi	79	30	37	16%	23%	−30%
BMW	78	37	40	14%	17%	−18%
Ford	77	43	28	22%	7%	214%
Harley Davidson	81	54	52	10%	8%	25%
Honda	82	52	49	11%	8%	38%
Hyundai	79	52	39	19%	6%	217%
Kia	80	46	39	16%	9%	78%
Mercedes-Benz	80	43	39	18%	14%	29%
Nissan	77	44	35	16%	7%	129%
Toyota	78	42	33	18%	9%	100%
Volkswagen	78	42	28	23%	9%	156%
Top B2B Brands						
B2B Brands: Average	79	43	36	17%	11%	96%
3M	82	55	46	13%	4%	225%
Caterpillar	80	39	41	15%	17%	−12%
Cisco	80	39	38	16%	15%	7%

Industry Top 100 Brands (based on InterBrand list)	Satisfaction (on a 100-point scale)	WoMI Score	NPS Score	NPS-Defined Detractors*	WoMI-Defined Detractors**	Average Overstatement of Detractors***
General Electric	75	36	20	24%	8%	200%
John Deere	83	56	54	11%	9%	22%
Nokia	75	37	22	22%	7%	214%
Oracle	74	36	25	23%	12%	92%
Xerox	80	43	41	14%	12%	17%
Computer/Electronics Manufacturers						
Computer/Electronics Manufacturers: Category Average	78	45	33	18%	6%	264%
Adobe	75	39	25	20%	6%	233%
Apple	83	56	47	13%	4%	225%
BlackBerry(RIM)	74	36	21	25%	10%	150%
Canon	80	50	41	15%	6%	150%
Dell	77	42	28	21%	7%	200%
HP	76	43	29	18%	4%	350%
IBM	78	34	27	18%	11%	64%
Intel	79	42	35	17%	10%	70%
Microsoft	75	42	29	20%	7%	186%
Nintendo	80	51	43	12%	4%	200%
Panasonic	80	46	39	12%	5%	140%

(Continued)

Industry Top 100 Brands (based on InterBrand list)	Satisfaction (on a 100-point scale)	WoMI Score	NPS Score	NPS-Defined Detractors*	WoMI-Defined Detractors**	Average Overstatement of Detractors***
Philips	78	48	33	19%	4%	375%
Samsung	77	44	23	23%	2%	1,050%
Sony	80	55	43	16%	4%	300%
Consumer Packaged Goods (CPG)						
Consumer Packaged Goods (CPG): Category Average	78	44	31	19%	5%	399%
Avon	81	58	52	11%	5%	120%
Budweiser	77	41	29	18%	6%	200%
Coca-Cola	77	41	20	25%	4%	525%
Colgate	77	37	18	23%	4%	475%
Corona	77	39	18	25%	4%	525%
Danone	78	30	31	12%	13%	−8%
Gillette	78	44	28	20%	4%	400%
Heineken	78	43	34	16%	7%	129%
Heinz	80	48	31	18%	1%	1,700%
Jack Daniels	81	55	45	15%	5%	200%
Johnnie Walker	80	45	38	17%	10%	70%
Johnson & Johnson	80	48	40	12%	4%	200%
Kellogg	77	43	27	19%	3%	533%
Kleenex	79	50	31	21%	2%	950%

Industry Top 100 Brands (based on InterBrand list)	Satisfaction (on a 100-point scale)	WoMI Score	NPS Score	NPS-Defined Detractors*	WoMI-Defined Detractors**	Average Overstatement of Detractors***
L'Oréal	78	52	40	20%	8%	150%
Moet & Chandon	78	45	37	16%	8%	100%
Nescafé	79	47	33	18%	4%	350%
Nestlé	78	43	28	20%	5%	300%
Pampers	79	47	37	17%	7%	143%
Pepsi	78	41	20	26%	5%	420%
Smirnoff	78	41	24	20%	3%	567%
Sprite	75	39	17	25%	3%	733%
Financial Services Brands						
Financial Services: Category Average	70	28	1	35%	8%	527%
American Express	78	44	29	21%	6%	250%
Citi	69	24	−13	45%	8%	463%
Goldman Sachs	69	15	5	29%	19%	53%
HSBC	64	14	−24	49%	11%	345%
J.P.Morgan	73	33	8	33%	8%	313%
Mastercard	72	30	5	29%	4%	625%
Morgan Stanley	74	41	16	28%	3%	833%
Santander	61	16	−25	51%	10%	410%
Visa	74	37	8	31%	2%	1,450%

(Continued)

Industry Top 100 Brands (based on InterBrand list)	Satisfaction (on a 100-point scale)	WoMI Score	NPS Score	NPS-Defined Detractors*	WoMI-Defined Detractors**	Average Overstatement of Detractors***
Top Retail Brands						
Retail: Category Average	80	47	39	15%	6%	222%
Adidas	77	40	28	18%	6%	200%
Amazon	85	61	53	11%	3%	267%
Burberry	82	44	45	11%	3%	267%
eBay	80	52	39	17%	4%	325%
Gap	75	36	21	21%	6%	250%
Gucci	83	45	45	12%	12%	0%
H&M	73	37	21	19%	3%	533%
Ikea	80	53	46	10%	3%	233%
Louis Vuitton	79	46	40	15%	9%	67%
Nike	78	44	30	17%	3%	467%
Ralph Lauren	79	42	33	16%	7%	129%
Tiffany & Co.	83	57	51	11%	5%	120%
Walt Disney	83	59	50	12%	3%	300%
Other Top Brands						
Other: Category Average	73	33	10	30%	6%	499%
Allianz	74	27	8	30%	11%	173%
AXA	73	27	12	28%	13%	115%
Facebook	64	19	−21	46%	6%	667%

Industry Top 100 Brands (based on InterBrand list)	Satisfaction (on a 100-point scale)	WoMI Score	NPS Score	NPS-Defined Detractors*	WoMI-Defined Detractors**	Average Overstatement of Detractors***
Google	75	40	19	25%	4%	525%
KFC	74	36	14	27%	5%	440%
McDonald's	68	26	−8	38%	4%	850%
MTV	73	28	12	28%	12%	133%
Pizza Hut	75	39	22	22%	5%	340%
Shell	71	25	−15	44%	4%	1,000%
Starbucks	77	45	23	24%	2%	1,100%
UPS	79	51	39	18%	6%	200%
Yahoo!	73	31	9	27%	5%	440%

*NPS definition of detractors is anyone who rates their likelihood to recommend a company 6 or lower on a 10-point scale.

**WoMI defines detractors as anyone who rates their likelihood to detract from a company with a 9 or 10 on a 10-point scale. This group is also referred to as "True Detractors."

***Overstatement of detractors is calculated using the following formula: (% of NPS-defined detractors − % of WoMI-defined detractors)/% of WoMI-defined detractors. The average overstatement at the category level is an average of the company-level overstatements of detractors. The overall average overstatement is the average of the overstatements of each underlying category.

Figure A.5 shows that the top online retailers in America have a wide range of scores on all fronts:

- Satisfaction (on a 100-point scale) ranges from a high of 88 for Amazon.com to a low of 72 for Gilt and Fingerhut. Margin of error is +/−2 points.

- WoMI scores range from a high of 67 for Amazon.com to a low of 21 for Follett Higher Education Group.

- Net Promoter Scores range from a 64 for Amazon.com to a low of 4 for Fingerhut. Keep in mind these scores have a margin of error of +/−10 points.

- The overstatement of detractors calculation shows that for companies like Net-a-Porter, NPS actually understates detractors by 32 percent. On the other end of the range, NPS overstates detractors by more than 1,000 percent for companies like Fingerhut, Target, and Williams Sonoma. When we average the overstatement of detractors for all of the measured e-retailers, the average overstatement of detractors is 271 percent.

Top 40 U.K. Online Retailers

ForeSee measured satisfaction, WoMI, and NPS for the top 40 retailers in the United Kingdom, selected based on the IMRG Experian Hitwise Hot 100 Retailer list. More than 10,000 U.K. customers who visited one of the top 40 retail websites in the previous two weeks were surveyed via online panel in November and December 2012. The full report can be downloaded at www.foresee.com.

Figure A.6 shows that the top U.K. online retailers have a wide range of scores on all fronts:

- Satisfaction (on a 100-point scale) ranges from a high of 86 for Amazon.co.uk to a low of 61 for Ryanair.com. Margin of error is +/−2 points.

- WoMI scores range from a high of 64 for Amazon.co.uk to a low of 18 for Homebase.

Figure A.5   The Top 100 U.S. e-Retailers

Top 100* U.S. e-Retailers	Satisfaction**	WoMI Score***	NPS Score****	NPS Overstatement of Detractors*****
1-800 Contacts Inc.	82	49	47	22%
1-800-Flowers.com Inc.	80	40	30	125%
Abercrombie & Fitch Co.	75	35	15	667%
Amazon.com Inc.	88	67	64	75%
American Eagle Outfitters Inc.	76	36	19	340%
Amway Global	78	35	30	36%
Ann Inc. (formerly Ann Taylor Stores Corp.)	78	42	31	157%
Apple Inc.	80	49	45	67%
Avon Products Inc.	81	52	41	275%
BarnesandNoble.com Inc.	79	52	39	325%
Bass Pro Outdoor Online LC	76	36	19	243%
Best Buy Co.	77	41	26	375%
Blue Nile Inc.	76	30	26	27%
Buy.com Inc.	75	30	12	300%
Cabela's Inc.	81	53	40	260%
CDW	77	29	26	19%
Chico's FAS Inc.	80	45	36	129%
Costco Wholesale Corp.	78	56	50	200%
Crate and Barrel	73	28	8	333%

(Continued)

Top 100* U.S. e-Retailers	Satisfaction**	WoMI Score***	NPS Score****	NPS Overstatement of Detractors*****
CVS Caremark Corp.	76	32	12	250%
Dell·Inc.	77	43	28	250%
Disney Shopping Inc.	78	45	33	171%
Eddie Bauer LLC	77	41	29	171%
Edible Arrangements International	79	48	38	143%
Estée Lauder Companies, Inc.	83	49	44	50%
Fanatics Inc.	78	32	28	31%
Fingerhut	72	36	4	1,067%
Follett Higher Education Group	75	21	20	5%
Foot Locker Inc.	76	28	18	77%
Fresh Direct (Grocery)	80	29	30	−6%
FTD Group Inc.	74	35	16	271%
GameStop Corp.	77	39	29	111%
Gap Inc. Direct	77	37	19	450%
Gilt Groupe	72	31	7	480%
Hayneedle Inc.	76	38	22	145%
Home Depot Inc.	78	46	36	333%
HP Home & Home Office Store	80	48	32	320%
HSN Inc.	81	49	39	500%
Hudson Bay	77	42	24	300%
J. Crew Group Inc.	77	39	27	150%
J.C. Penney Co. Inc.	78	47	31	800%

Top 100* U.S. e-Retailers	Satisfaction**	WoMI Score***	NPS Score****	NPS Overstatement of Detractors*****
Keurig	82	57	52	83%
Kohl's Corp.	80	50	40	333%
L.L. Bean Inc.	85	66	56	500%
Liberty Media Corp. (QVC, Liberty E-Commerce)	84	61	51	250%
Lowe's Companies Inc.	75	33	9	400%
Macy's Inc.	77	42	23	475%
Microsoft Corp.	78	42	28	233%
Musician's Friend Inc.	80	48	46	22%
Neiman Marcus Group Inc.	77	41	24	243%
Net-a-Porter LLC	77	26	33	−32%
Netflix Inc.	80	56	48	200%
Newegg Inc.	81	54	43	275%
Nike Inc.	76	39	29	100%
Nordstrom Inc.	79	43	28	214%
Northern Tool + Equipment Co.	76	37	21	229%
Nutrisystem Inc.	73	31	8	256%
Office Depot Inc.	78	42	29	260%
OfficeMax Inc.	77	35	14	350%
Orchard Brands Corp.	80	47	31	400%
Oriental Trading Co. Inc.	80	51	42	150%

(Continued)

Top 100* U.S. e-Retailers	Satisfaction**	WoMI Score***	NPS Score****	NPS Overstatement of Detractors*****
Overstock.com Inc.	75	36	13	767%
PC Connection Inc.	74	28	11	142%
PC Mall Inc.	75	23	17	46%
Peapod LLC	77	36	28	62%
Ralph Lauren Media LLC	77	33	29	31%
Recreational Equipment Inc.	76	31	19	133%
RueLaLa.com	73	31	11	367%
Saks Direct	79	46	34	200%
Scholastic Inc.	82	53	49	57%
Sears Holdings Corp.	75	36	15	525%
Shoebuy.com Inc.	75	29	12	243%
Shop.com	74	26	5	300%
shopmyexchange.com	75	27	18	56%
ShopNBC.com	78	40	28	120%
Shutterfly Inc.	80	53	37	533%
Sierra Trading Post Inc.	78	40	29	183%
Sony Store, Online	79	37	30	58%
Sportsmans Guide	78	55	44	275%
Staples Inc.	77	38	19	633%
Symantek	77	32	21	79%
Target Corp.	79	54	40	1,400%
Tigers Direct	76	41	24	567%

Top 100* U.S. e-Retailers	Satisfaction**	WoMI Score***	NPS Score****	NPS Overstatement of Detractors*****
Toys 'R' Us Inc.	76	37	17	500%
U.S. Auto Parts Network	75	30	19	100%
Urban Outfitters Inc.	77	34	17	243%
"Victoria's Secret Direct & Bath and Body Works"	80	53	44	225%
Vistaprint Ltd.	83	55	49	86%
Vitacost.com Inc.	84	54	50	50%
W.W. Grainger Inc.	77	39	32	70%
Walgreen Co.	80	43	33	200%
Walmart.com	78	42	20	733%
Wayfair LLC	75	32	13	211%
Weight Watchers International Inc.	79	49	41	133%
Williams-Sonoma Inc.	79	47	33	1,400%

*The top 100 e-retailers were measured; only those with sufficient sample size to calculate a statistically significant score are reported here (95 retailers).

**NPS definition of detractors is anyone who rates their likelihood to recommend a company 6 or lower on a 10-point scale.

***WoMI defines detractors as anyone who rates their likelihood to detract from a company with a 9 or 10 on a 10-point scale. This group is also referred to as "True Detractors."

****Overstatement of detractors is calculated using the following formula: (% of NPS-defined detractors − % of WoMI-defined detractors)/% of WoMI-defined detractors. The average overstatement at the category level is an average of the company-level overstatements of detractors. The overall average overstatement is the average of the overstatements of each underlying category.

Figure A.6 The Top 40 U.K. e-Retailers

Top 40 U.K. E-Retailers*	Satisfaction**	WoMI Score***	NPS Score****	Average Overstatement of Detractors*****
Amazon.co.uk	86	64	57	350%
Amazon.com	84	55	43	240%
Apple	77	47	33	700%
Argos	75	34	15	475%
ASDA	76	39	24	300%
ASDA Direct	77	39	22	340%
ASOS	73	32	13	475%
B&Q	71	26	7	317%
Boots	74	32	10	733%
British Airways	72	30	10	333%
Cineworld Cinemas	74	27	10	213%
Currys	72	23	−4	450%
Debenhams	76	30	13	283%
Easyjet.com	73	33	13	500%
Expedia.co.uk	72	30	7	288%
Homebase	71	18	−9	450%
House of Fraser	73	24	1	460%
Ikea	73	31	15	267%
John Lewis	80	52	42	250%
Lastminute.com	70	23	−2	833%
Lovefilm.com	74	32	14	360%
Marks and Spencer	75	38	24	467%
Netflix.com	68	25	−5	429%
New Look	74	27	10	243%
Next	73	37	21	320%
Odeon Cinemas	72	30	5	625%
Piay.com	79	44	29	500%
River Island	72	23	1	314%

Top 40 U.K. E-Retailers*	Satisfaction**	WoMI Score***	NPS Score****	Average Overstatement of Detractors*****
Ryanair	61	19	−23	840%
Sainsbury's	74	36	17	950%
Sports Direct	74	32	11	350%
Tesco	76	33	13	500%
Tesco Direct	74	36	14	1,100%
Thetrainline.com	74	40	15	2,500%
Thomas Cook	71	22	−1	288%
Ticketmaster UK	69	30	0	600%
Topshop.com	71	24	7	189%
TravelRepublic.com	74	29	11	257%
Vary.co.uk	72	26	−5	1,033%

*Top 40 U.K. e-retailers were measured; only those with sufficient sample size to calculate a statistically significant score are reported here.

**NPS definition of detractors is anyone who rates their likelihood to recommend a company 6 or lower on a 10-point scale.

***WoMI defines detractors as anyone who rates their likelihood to detract from a company with a 9 or 10 on a 10-point scale. This group is also referred to as "True Detractors."

****Overstatement of detractors is calculated using the following formula: (% of NPS-defined detractors − % of WoMI-defined detractors)/% of WoMI-defined detractors. The average overstatement at the category level is an average of the company-level overstatements of detractors. The overall average overstatement is the average of the overstatements of each underlying category.

- Net Promoter Scores range from a 57 for Amazon.com to a low of −23 for RyanAir. Keep in mind these scores have a margin of error of +/−10 points.
- The overstatement of detractors calculation shows that Net Promoter is significantly overstating detractors for all of the

largest online retailers in the United Kingdom, ranging from an overstatement of 189 percent for TopShop to an overstatement of 2500 percent for thetrainline.com.

Seven Largest U.S. Banks

ForeSee measured satisfaction, WoMI, and NPS for the top seven banks in the United States. More than 3,000 online banking customers were surveyed in April 2011. The full report can be downloaded at www.foresee.com.

This survey was conducted among more than 3,000 respondents in April 2011. Survey respondents were online panelists who had used online services through their bank or credit union.

Figure A.7   The Top Seven American Banks

Largest American Banks	NPS Score*	WoMI Score**	Average Overstatement of Detractors***
Bank of America	38	33	428%
Citibank	26	37	157%
JPMorgan Chase Bank	33	42	100%
PNC Bank	36	41	50%
U.S. Bank	40	47	117%
Wells Fargo Bank	37	45	114%

*NPS definition of detractors is anyone who rates their likelihood to recommend a company 6 or lower on a 10-point scale.

**WoMI defines detractors as anyone who rates their likelihood to detract from a company with a 9 or 10 on a 10-point scale. This group is also referred to as "True Detractors."

***Overstatement of detractors is calculated using the following formula: (% of NPS-defined detractors − % of WoMI-defined detractors)/% of WoMI-defined detractors. The average overstatement at the category level is an average of the company-level overstatements of detractors. The overall average overstatement is the average of the overstatements of each underlying category.

Figure A.7 shows that the top American banks are fairly tightly grouped in terms of WoMI and NPS, suggesting that these metrics are of less value as a competitive advantage:

- WoMI scores range from a 33 for Bank of America to a 47 for U.S. Bank, a 14-point range.
- Net Promoter Scores range from 26 for Citibank to 40 for U.S. Bank.
- The overstatement of detractors calculation shows that for Bank of America, NPS actually underestimates detractors, while for Citibank, NPS overstates detractors by 157 percent.

The Top 29 U.S. Retail Stores

ForeSee measured satisfaction, WoMI, and NPS for the largest 29 retail stores in the United States by sales volume (see Figure A.8). The research was conducted in November and December 2012 and

Figure A.8 The Top 29 Retail Stores in the United States

Top 29 Stores	Satisfaction	NPS*	WoMI**	Average Overstatement of Detractors***
Ace Hardware	83	45	55	250%
Apple Stores	83	54	58	57%
Barnes & Noble	82	44	51	140%
Bed Bath & Beyond	80	42	54	600%
Best Buy	80	38	48	333%
Bj's Wholesale Club	79	40	50	250%
Costco	82	54	58	67%
CVS Caremark	76	21	42	525%
Dollar General	75	23	41	300%
J.C. Penney	75	26	44	450%

(Continued)

Top 29 Stores	Satisfaction	NPS*	WoMI**	Average Overstatement of Detractors***
Kohl's	81	42	55	650%
Lowe's	81	45	59	1,400%
Macy's	80	37	49	400%
Meijer	77	28	45	567%
Nordstrom	79	37	50	260%
Office Depot	79	26	42	267%
RiteAid	75	13	40	900%
Ross Stores	73	21	40	380%
Sears	74	14	35	350%
ShopRite	81	43	53	250%
Staples	79	34	49	375%
Target	81	44	54	333%
The Home Depot	79	38	50	240%
TJ Maxx	75	33	46	260%
Toys 'R' Us	72	17	35	300%
True Value	80	40	52	300%
Verinn Wireless	78	31	42	138%
Walgreen	78	23	44	2,100%
Walmart	75	17	41	600%

*NPS definition of detractors is anyone who rates their likelihood to recommend a company 6 or lower on a 10-point scale.

**WoMI defines detractors as anyone who rates their likelihood to detract from a company with a 9 or 10 on a 10-point scale. This group is also referred to as "True Detractors."

***Overstatement of detractors is calculated using the following formula: (% of NPS-defined detractors − % of WoMI-defined detractors)/% of WoMI-defined detractors. The average overstatement at the category level is an average of the company-level overstatements of detractors. The overall average overstatement is the average of the overstatements of each underlying category.

reflects more than 7,000 surveys from shoppers who had purchased from one of the stores on this list within the previous two weeks. This study utilized a nationwide panel of consumer households who agreed to participate in opt-in surveys.

ForeSee's measurement of the customer experience is based on a methodology founded in academia and proven to be a predictor of future financial success at both the macroeconomic and microeconomic levels.

The 25 Top Mobile Retail Sites and Apps

The ForeSee Mobile Satisfaction Index (available for free download at www.foresee.com) focused on the mobile experience by analyzing mobile satisfaction scores, impacts, future behaviors and other key findings through the eyes of the consumer. These scores reflect the customer experience with mobile sites and apps on phones and tablets (see Figure A.9). More than 4,500 surveys were collected in August 2012 for this research. There were 25 companies with widely

Figure A.9   The Top 25 Mobile Retail Sites and Apps

Retail Mobile Experience	Satisfaction	NPS	WoMI	Average Overstatement of Detractors***
Amazon.com	85	66	67	17%
Apple	83	52	57	71%
Barnes & Noble	79	40	47	140%
Best Buy	77	30	39	100%
Buy.com	77	22	33	110%
Costco	78	46	54	160%
Footlocker	79	40	47	88%
Gilt Groupe	74	15	31	145%
Hewlett Packard	78	40	48	133%

(Continued)

Retail Mobile Experience	Satisfaction	NPS	WoMI	Average Overstatement of Detractors***
HSN	79	35	47	240%
J.C. Penney	77	34	42	114%
Kohl's	78	45	52	117%
Macy's	77	37	45	114%
NewEgg	80	44	51	100%
One King's Lane	77	27	31	24%
Overstock	74	19	32	217%
QVC	83	63	64	25%
RueLaLa.com	74	15	31	160%
Sears	74	20	37	243%
Shop NBC	73	19	33	175%
Sportsmans Guide.com	78	30	35	36%
Staples	77	32	40	80%
Target	77	37	46	129%
Victoria's Secret	80	47	53	75%
Walmart	75	31	48	425%

*NPS definition of detractors is anyone who rates their likelihood to recommend a company 6 or lower on a 10-point scale.

**WoMI defines detractors as anyone who rates their likelihood to detract from a company with a 9 or 10 on a 10-point scale. This group is also referred to as "True Detractors."

***Overstatement of detractors is calculated using the following formula: (% of NPS-defined detractors − % of WoMI-defined detractors)/% of WoMI-defined detractors. The average overstatement at the category level is an average of the company-level overstatements of detractors. The overall average overstatement is the average of the overstatements of each underlying category.

used mobile sites and apps measured in the study, which was done using a consumer panel.

- Satisfaction (on a 100-point scale) ranges from a high of 85 for Amazon to a low of 73 for ShopNBC.
- WoMI scores range from a high of 61 for Amazon to a low of 31 for RueLaLa.
- Net Promoter Scores range from a high of 66 for Amazon to a low of 15 for Gilt Groupe and RueLaLa.
- The overstatement of detractors calculation shows that Net Promoter is overstating detractors by 425 percent for Walmart and by large margins for most of the other mobile retail experiences included in this study.

Seventeen Mobile Financial Services Sites and Apps

The ForeSee Mobile Satisfaction Index: Financial Services Edition (available at www.foresee.com) concentrates exclusively on financial services and serves as a great starting point for companies that want to benchmark their mobile performance against some of the best businesses in these categories.

More than 4,500 surveys were collected in October 2012 for the ForeSee Mobile Satisfaction Index: Financial Services Edition. There were 17 companies with widely used mobile sites and apps measured in the study, which was done using a consumer panel. The scores are on a 100-point scale and reflect customers' perceptions of the mobile experience overall, whether it be an m.site or an app, on a tablet or a phone. (See Figure A.10.)

- Satisfaction (on a 100-point scale) falls in a fairly narrow range: from a low of 73 for Visa to a high of 79 for American Express (bank and credit card), Charles Schwab, Discover, and Wells Fargo.
- WoMI scores range from a high of 44 for Wells Fargo to a low of 28 for Visa.

Figure A.10 Seventeen Mobile Financial Services Sites and Apps

Mobile Financial Services	Satisfaction	NPS	WoMI	Average Overstatement of Detractors***
American Express (bank)	79	24	31	54%
American Express (credit card)	79	29	41	150%
Bank of America (bank)	76	21	36	167%
Capital One (credit card)	76	12	34	1,100%
Charles Schwab	79	30	36	43%
Chase (bank)	78	22	43	525%
Citibank (bank)	76	25	36	122%
Citibank (credit card)	75	11	32	350%
Discover	79	22	39	283%
E*TRADE	77	29	35	50%
Fidelity	78	28	41	130%
Mastercard	75	6	32	520%
Scottrade	77	26	31	36%
TD Ameritrade	76	28	33	36%
U.S. Bank	78	17	41	480%
Visa	73	2	28	520%
Wells Fargo	79	23	44	525%

*NPS definition of detractors is anyone who rates their likelihood to recommend a company 6 or lower on a 10-point scale.

**WoMI defines detractors as anyone who rates their likelihood to detract from a company with a 9 or 10 on a 10-point scale. This group is also referred to as "True Detractors."

***Overstatement of detractors is calculated using the following formula: (% of NPS-defined detractors − % of WoMI-defined detractors)/% of WoMI-defined detractors. The average overstatement at the category level is an average of the company-level overstatements of detractors. The overall average overstatement is the average of the overstatements of each underlying category.

- Net Promoter Scores range from a high of 30 for Charles Schwab to a low of 2 for Visa.
- The overstatement of detractors calculation shows that Net Promoter is overstating detractors by 1,100 percent for Capital One.

Twenty-Five Mobile Travel Sites and Apps

Figure A.11 concentrates exclusively on the 25 largest U.S. mobile travel companies (by revenue). More than 6,000 surveys were collected from visitors to these 25 companies' mobile apps and sites on phones and tablets from February 4 to 12, 2013. The study was conducted using a consumer panel. All scores are on a 100-point scale.

Figure A.11   Twenty-Five Mobile Travel Sites and Apps

Mobile Travel Experiences	Satisfaction	NPS*	WoMI**	Average Overstatement of Detractors***
American Airlines	77	22	36	233%
Amtrak	76	25	39	200%
Avis Rent-a-Car	78	18	30	150%
Best Western International	76	18	34	200%
Budget	77	23	37	200%
Choice Hotels International	80	31	41	167%
Delta Airlines	77	17	35	300%
Dollar	75	16	29	163%
Enterprise Rent-a-Car	78	27	39	300%
Expedia Inc.	76	21	35	280%
Hertz	77	23	37	200%

(Continued)

199

Appendix A

Mobile Travel Experiences	Satisfaction	NPS*	WoMI**	Average Overstatement of Detractors***
Hilton Worldwide	77	23	35	200%
Hotels.com	75	16	31	250%
Hyatt Corp	78	22	32	125%
Intercontinental Hotels & Resorts	78	24	33	90%
Kayak	78	31	40	129%
Marriott International	79	28	39	275%
Orbitz LLC	75	18	35	340%
Priceline	76	23	40	425%
Southwest Airlines	82	40	48	160%
Starwood Hotels & Resorts Intl.	77	17	34	567%
Travelocity (Sabre Holdings)	78	27	41	350%
United Airlines	75	16	33	340%
US Airways	74	9	32	575%
Wyndham Hotels & Resorts	78	27	43	533%

*NPS definition of detractors is anyone who rates their likelihood to recommend a company 6 or lower on a 10-point scale.

**WoMI defines detractors as anyone who rates their likelihood to detract from a company with a 9 or 10 on a 10-point scale. This group is also referred to as "True Detractors."

***Overstatement of detractors is calculated using the following formula: (% of NPS-defined detractors − % of WoMI-defined detractors)/% of WoMI-defined detractors. The average overstatement at the category level is an average of the company-level overstatements of detractors. The overall average overstatement is the average of the overstatements of each underlying category.

Are Those Least Likely to Recommend Actually the Most Likely to Discourage?

As discussed in Chapter 2, Net Promoter suggests that anyone who rates their likelihood to recommend a six or below is a detrac tor (Figure B.1). This scale simply doesn't work, and as shown in Chapter 4 and Appendix A, this calculation overstates detractors by 260 percent to 270 percent on average.

However, over time, some companies have come up with their own definitions of detractors. Some companies consider only those who rate their likelihood to recommend a one a super detractor; some companies say that anyone who answers a one or two is a super detractor.

However, there is no way to use the single "how likely are you to recommend" question as a proxy for detractors. We ran analysis on every definition of NPS-defined detractors to see how many of them say they are actually likely to discourage people from doing business with the company.

We define *True Detractors* as those who rate their likelihood to discourage someone from doing business with a company at a 9 or 10 on our 10-point scale. The following analysis shows how many NPS-defined promoters are actually detracting from the company, and the data underscore that likelihood to recommend cannot be used as a proxy for detraction, no matter what scale we use.

The results follow.

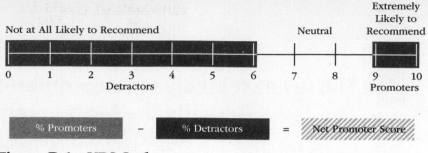

Figure B.1   NPS Scale

Least Likely to Recommend: 1s

When asked, "How likely are you to recommend?" a small percentage of people answered a 1 on a 10-point scale.

Of the respondents scoring likelihood to recommend as 1 on a scale from 1 to 10, 39 percent are defined as true detractors (answering 9 or 10). Therefore, 61 percent of people who rate their likelihood to recommend a 1 are not actively detracting from the business (see Figure B.2). Just because they are not likely to recommend does not necessarily mean they are likely to detract.

Least Likely to Recommend: 1s and 2s

Of the respondents scoring likelihood to recommend as 1 or 2 on a scale from 1 to 10, 21 percent stated that they were very likely to discourage, and only 29 percent meet the criteria for true detractors (see Figure B.3).

Moreover, the following chart shows that 20 percent of people who say they are very unlikely to recommend also say they are very unlikely to detract. Whether these are people who are just constitutionally unlikely to discourage someone from doing business with a company, whether they are using products or services that they wouldn't recommend or whether they are actually satisfied and potentially even loyal, it is clear that "likely to recommend" cannot be used as a proxy for detraction.

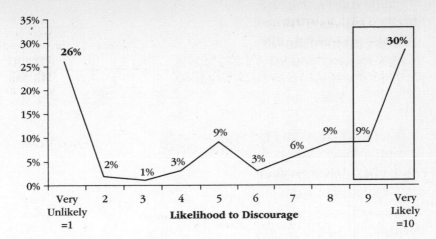

Figure B.2   Least Likely to Recommend: 1

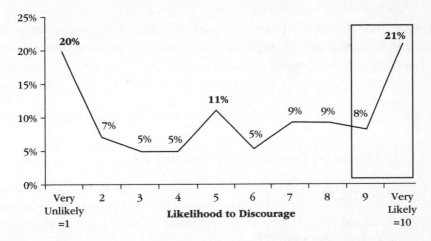

Figure B.3   Least Likely to Recommend: 1 or 2

Low Likelihood to Recommend: 1 to 3 on a 10-Point Least Likely Scale

Of the respondents scoring likelihood to recommend as 1 to 3 on a scale from 1 to 10, 15 percent stated that they were very likely to discourage, and only 21 percent meet the criteria for true detractors

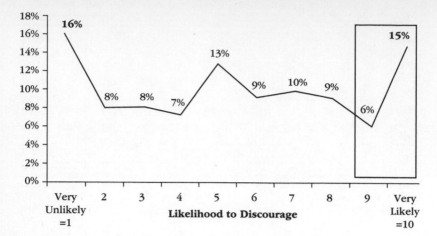

Figure B.4　Low Likelihood to Recommend: 1 to 3

(see Figure B.4). We still see the small portion of the entire population that would actively discourage someone from doing business with the company in question.

Low Likelihood to Recommend: 1 to 4 on a 10-Point Scale

Of the respondents scoring likelihood to recommend as 1 to 4 on a scale from 1 to 10, 10 percent stated that they were very likely to discourage and only 14 percent meet the criteria for true detractors (Figure B.5). We do see a higher percentage of respondents falling in the mid-range, with 18 percent choosing a 5 on the 1 to 10 scale for likelihood to discourage.

Low Likelihood to Recommend: 1 to 5 on a 10-Point Scale

This trend continues as we expand the definition in an effort to identify a proxy for likelihood to discourage. Almost half of the respondents fall into the midsection of the scale (Figure B.6), possibly expressing indifference to discouraging someone from doing business with the company in question.

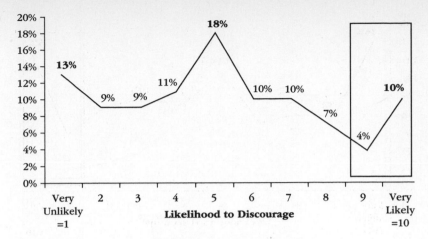

Figure B.5   Low Likelihood to Recommend: 1 to 4

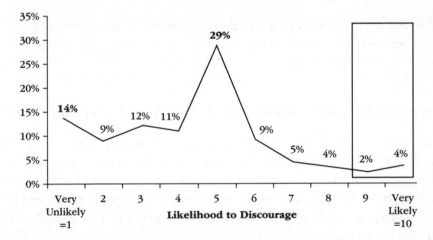

Figure B.6   Low Likelihood to Recommend: 1 to 5

Low Likelihood to Recommend: 1 to 6 on a 10-Point Scale

As likelihood to recommend increases, we see the likelihood to discourage decrease dramatically, but there is still a very mixed response

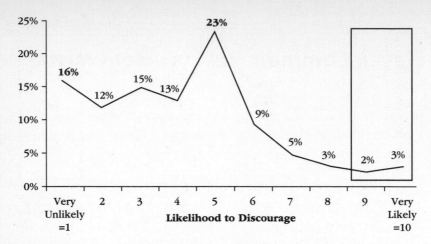

Figure B.7   Low Likelihood to Recommend: 1 to 6

for all respondents when asked their likelihood to discourage (see Figure B.7).

In short, there is no way to rely solely on the likelihood to recommend question to get an accurate representation of detractors.

Eleven Common Measurement Mistakes

All businesses need an accurate, precise, and reliable methodology to measure success. Inaccurate and imprecise methodologies lead to poor decisions and to a false sense of confidence in those decisions. Unfortunately, I see many companies making a series of mistakes in their measurements. A discussion of common mistakes follows.

Common Measurement Mistake #1: Drawing Conclusions from Incomplete Information

Every day your business generates a tremendous amount of data, but those data may not tell the full story. Your analytics show that visitors spend a relatively high amount of time on a particular page. Is that page great, or is it problematic? Visitors may love the content, or they may be getting stuck because of a problem on the page.

Your call center statistics show that your average call time has decreased. Is this good news or bad news? When calls end more quickly, costs go down, but have you actually satisfied callers, or have you left them disgruntled, dissatisfied, and on their way to your competition? Without additional information to better evaluate the data, you simply cannot know.

Never draw conclusions from any statistical analysis that does not tell the whole story.

Common Measurement Mistake #2: Failing to Look Forward

Every company seeks to look forward. Many analytics programs are dominated by behavioral data. Behavioral data tell us what has happened, not what will happen. We may have visited, purchased, downloaded, registered, or whatever else the company is looking for us to do. Will we do it again? That depends on if our needs were met and we had a high level of satisfaction with the experience. When consumers have freedom of choice, they will go where their experiences are satisfying them. By its very nature, satisfaction is predictive of what consumers will do in the future. The ForeSee model takes those predictive analytics to another level, identifying the causal impact between key drivers of the experience and the overall satisfaction with the experience. These predictive analytics provide us the ability to know which investments will pay the biggest dividends to us. When we combine the measurement of the customer experience with behavioral data, analysis is even more insightful.

Common Measurement Mistake #3: Assuming That a Lab Is a Reasonable Substitute

Usability groups and observation panels are certainly useful. The problem is that the sample sizes are small and the testing takes place in a controlled environment. If you bring people into a lab and tell them what you want them to do, does a group of eight participants represent your broader audience? Does measuring and observing them when they do what *we* tell them to do provide the same results as real users who do what *they* want to do? Observation is helpful, but applying science to the voices of customers and measuring the customer experience through the lens of customer satisfaction is critical to success. I have seen numerous companies prove out their theories with usability tests, only to find out later the problems they were identifying were not impacting consumers' choices on where to do business. A pharmaceutical company did a series of usability tests to help them narrow in on the problem it was facing: Not enough consumers were asking for more information and taking the path through the site that the company determined was most likely to get those consumers to ask their doctor about the drug being marketed. The usability tests seemed to work fine. When the company asked consumers to find certain information on the site, in the lab many of the users were not successful. The company made the improvements to the site and was expecting a big improvement. But the problem was that the company was fixing the wrong problem. In a lab environment, you give the testers a task and see how they perform. Then through the observation, you identify what things to change. The problem that is you are fixing what you think are the important things. You are not taking direction from the consumer in what they are trying to accomplish.

Common Measurement Mistake #4: Forgetting That the Real Experts Are Your Customers

Experts, like usability groups, have their place. But who knows customer intentions, customer needs, and customer attitudes better than actual customers? It takes more time and work, but the results are much more valuable. I cannot say how many times I have been in meetings with consultants, analysts, and experts who swear that a new site navigation system will solve every problem on a particular website. (Oddly enough, there often is money to be made if the consultants are hired to develop that new navigation system. Unfortunately, solutions are often based on what the expert can provide rather than what the customer needs.) Meanwhile, what customers want are more product varieties to choose from. Experts, analysts, and consultants certainly have their place, but their advice and recommendations must be driven by customer needs as much as, if not more than, by organizational needs and by their own opinions. ForeSee worked with a retailer's contact center a few years ago. The experts told the center that it was doing too much upsell on the call and it was alienating its customers and driving them away. As we got engaged and started measuring the customer experience, it was very clear from the analysis that customers were not put off by the thoughtful recommendations the agents were making. In fact, when agents didn't try to sell the consumer additional products, they were less likely to recommend the retailer. While experts opinions are important and helpful, the voice of our customer is more important.

Common Measurement Mistake #5: Confusing Causation and Correlation

Failing to understand the difference between correlation and causation, and how those concepts should be applied, is a major problem that often leads companies to make major strategic mistakes.

Let's say I plan to write a white paper on public safety. I conduct research and determine that the more firefighters who fight a fire, the more damage the fire causes.

I am surprised. That cannot make sense—possibly my sample size is too small? I research other towns and get the same results. I conduct sufficient research to ensure that my results are statistically valid. Even accounting for an appropriate margin of error, clearly more firefighters equals more fire damage.

If I take my results at face value, I might decide that dramatically reducing the number of firefighters will decrease the amount of damage caused by fires. That decision would also be a huge mistake.

Why? I mistook correlation for causation.

The number of firefighters fighting a fire does indeed *correlate* with the amount of damage caused by the fire. The reason is simple. The bigger the fire, the more firefighters needed to fight the fire. The bigger the fire, the more damage caused by the fire. Originally, we correlated two data points—more damage and more firefighters—when, in fact, both were caused by a third element, bigger fires.

While this is a simple example, it is often easy to use intuition, gut feel, or fuzzy logic to distinguish between causation and correlation. Confusion between correlation and causation often occurs in science, health, and even sports and is seen in virtually every media report regarding most new research findings. Now this confusion between correlation and causation is serious and can lead to many bad decisions, but it is a very common mistake. I admit that until I started working with Dr. Fornell and we were starting to form ForeSee, I made the same mistake between correlation and causation. And hardly a week goes by when I don't hear very intelligent people making the same mistake as I did. People are seeking correlations to help them make their decisions. And in many cases, that is all the information they have. But when you can find the causal relationships, the power in your hand can be game changing and give you that competitive advantage you are looking for.

In theory, causation and correlation are easy to distinguish. Correlation exists when there is a relationship between two variables (events or actions). Causation exists when one event is the direct result of another event. A prime example is that smoking can cause lung cancer.

The same action or occurrence can also *correlate* with another occurrence; smoking is correlated with alcohol abuse. One action that directly causes another action is causation. But simply because two actions *occur* together in no way indicates that one action *causes* the other action.

Here's another example. Towns with higher ice cream sales have higher drowning rates. Clearly, ice cream does not cause drowning. The two facts are correlated but not causal. The causal factor is weather. In towns with higher temperatures, more ice cream is sold, more people swim . . . and more people drown. A town that attempts to prevent drowning by restricting ice cream sales would obviously miss the mark.

Let's look at correlation and causation in business terms.

You are selling clothing off-line and online. One of the shirts you sell is available in a variety of colors. In an off-line environment, shoppers can easily see the different colors in person; online is a different story. You decide to add an application to your site allowing visitors to change the color of the image of a particular shirt instead of simply viewing a set of color swatches; that way, potential customers can see the difference on a virtual product. Sales go up, and conversion rates go up. (In fact, one of our clients enjoyed the same results when they made a similar change to their website.)

In this example, the change you made correlates to higher sales and conversions and also is a causal factor. If you made no other changes to your site, ran no promotions, and did not market differently, you can safely determine that your change was a direct—and positive—causal factor.

What if you made that change but also ran a special on the shirts? You would need to dig deeper to determine the relative effects of those two different actions on sales and conversion rates. Was it the new application on your website that increased sales, or did sales increase because of the special?

To generate truly meaningful data, you must know a lot more about your customers—where they came from, why they visited your site, what they did while on your site, and so on—before you can determine which actions correlate and which are truly causal factors.

Common Measurement Mistake #6: Confusing Feedback and Measurement

When people talk about voice of customer, they often confuse feedback with measurement. Measurement is a random sample of consumers that gives us data that are representative of the broader audience. Feedback is unsolicited by the company and either is direct from the consumer to the company or from the consumer via social networks. There is a big difference between feedback and measurement, and it is important that we don't confuse the two. When feedback is direct to the company, it is mostly extremely negative with a small portion extremely positive and very little in between. Social feedback is mostly very positive with some extremely negative and very little in between. The silent majority, those who don't raise a hand to give feedback or shout their opinions in social networks, are mostly ignored in feedback. In VOC measurement, when done right, we get a random sample representing the entire audience, including the silent majority. The problem with opt-in feedback is its inherent bias. People who like you seldom give you feedback. People who hate you often will. (I know *hate* is a strong word, but opt-in feedback is often delivered in very strong words.) We don't ever send an e-mail to the CEO saying the product and service they provide is okay. We don't ever post on a social network that we had a pretty decent meal and maybe would go there again. We say the service was horrible, the associate was incredibly helpful, or the product stinks and we will never buy it again.[1]

That being said, we still get value from feedback. The consumers with extreme opinions often help us identify some low-hanging fruit, easy things to be remedied, such as errors in our website, missing graphics, and bad links. You can use feedback to add context and color and possibly gain a deeper understanding of the insights you have gained from analysis of voice of customer measurement. Those with strong opinions often give you more details of the issues when they are providing their feedback. This can help you home in on that problem by using feedback to let you move from identifying an area of focus to identifying specific actions.

And most important, whenever a customer gives you feedback, you should always listen. In fact, the more open feedback paths you can create, the better. But simply receiving feedback via the opt-in approach is in no way sufficient. Examples of opt-in feedback include a customer who clicks a link and completes a feedback form, a customer who calls your 800-number to complain, a customer who writes a letter (does anyone still get letters?), a consumer who posts on a social network, or a customer who sends an e-mail to the CEO. In all these examples, the customer took the initiative to provide feedback.

You need to determine whether limited opinions obtained through feedback truly represent a larger group of customers. Absent other data, such feedback should not cause you to make wholesale product changes. On the other hand, some customers who love your

---

[1]You can see a chart representing typical curves for feedback and measurement in this article I wrote for the *Harvard Business Review* blog: http://blogs.hbr.org/cs/2013/04/are_you_listening_to_your_most.html.

products tend to share those feelings by using word of mouth either the old fashioned way, talking to others, or by posting to social networks. But many will not voice their feelings and simply keep buying. The quiet majority is often least likely to provide feedback.

So make it easy for customers to provide feedback, but never try to use opt-in feedback as a measurement or as a critical metric. Don't use opt-in feedback to help you set priorities. Opt-in feedback is only information, not intelligence. Opt-in feedback provides reactive information; measurement provides proactive intelligence.

Common Measurement Mistake #7: Gaming the System

Unfortunately, many feedback and measurement systems create bias and inaccuracy. How? Ask the wrong people, bias their decisions, ask them to rate you better, or give them incentives for participation. Measuring correctly means creating as little measurement bias as possible, while generating as little measurement noise as possible.

Try to avoid incenting people to complete surveys, especially when there is no need. Never ask for personal data; some customers will decline to participate for privacy or confidentiality concerns. And try to prevent your staff from asking or begging their customers to give them good scores. I know I have experienced that in a couple of places, the most common being from automotive dealers. This can also happen when you have staff follow up with everyone who gave a bad score. That conversation often turns into more of an effort to convince them to give you a good score next time instead of used as an intelligence tool identifying the faults and opportunities for improvement. We must devise a measurement system that tries to eliminate the chances for employees to game the system, resulting in less useful information.

Also never measure with the intent to prove a point. Unfortunately, research run by internal staff can often contain some amount of built-in bias. As employees, we may, however unintentionally, create customer measurements to prove that our opinions are correct or to support our theories, but to what end? Every time I return a car to a certain car rental company while on a business trip, the associate asks me, "would you say our customer service was excellent today? A 10 on a 10-point scale?" Most people will reply that yes, it was fine, and that associate marks themselves down for another 10. But what if I tell the associate that it was terrible, and I would rate them a 4. Is that employee taking as much care to record and report poor scores as good ones? Doubtful. Meanwhile, that company's executives are back at headquarters thinking, "Wow, we've really got this nailed. Our customer satisfaction scores are incredible!"

Customer measurements must measure from the customers' perspective and through the customers' eyes, not through a lens of preconceived views.

Common Measurement Mistake #8: Sampling Problems

Sampling works well when it is done correctly. Sample selection and sample size are critical to creating a credible, reliable, accurate, precise, and predictive methodology. Sampling is a science in and of itself. We need samples representative of the larger population that are randomly selected. Samples can be inadvertently biased or be a way for people to try to game the system, for example, a retailer highlighting the invitation to participate in a survey on the receipt only to those consumers you think had a great experience. A bad sample can lead to misleading results.

Common Measurement Mistake #9: Faulty Math

Taking a binary approach to measuring satisfaction—in effect, asking whether I *am* or *am not* satisfied—leads to a very simplistic and inaccurate measurement.

Intelligence is not binary. People are not just smart or stupid. People are not just tall or short. Customers are not just satisfied or dissatisfied. *Yes* and *no* do not accurately explain or define levels or nuances of customer satisfaction. The *degree* of satisfaction is what determines the customer's level of loyalty and positive word of mouth.

A top-box or top-two-box approach can create a simpler way to communicate success. However, we need to be careful to remember we can use a top-box approach to make it easier to communicate, but it is not a very precise way to use in analysis. Claiming that 97 percent of your customers are satisfied certainly makes for a catchy marketing slogan but is far from a metric you can use to manage your business going forward.

Why do the research if you cannot trust and use the results?

Common Measurement Mistake #10: Measurement by Proxy

Trying to measure customer satisfaction by measuring a behavior such as task completion is commonly referred to as *measurement by proxy*. When measuring by proxy, there may at times be a correlation between task completion and satisfaction, but all too often that is not the case.

The key is to identify causation. How many times have you completed a particular task but still left dissatisfied and vowing never to do business with the company again? It is important that you don't fall into the proxy trap because at an aggregate view of the data it looks like it works. We are likely to see that the higher the percentage of people who completed the task, the higher the satisfaction and loyalty. However, we may also see that 30 percent of the people who completed the task were very dissatisfied and likely to defect as customers and 25 percent of those who did not complete the task are satisfied and loyal. This is a real-world situation that I have seen many times before.

The same phenomenon occurs if you attempt to measure customer loyalty by evaluating customer recommendations or by examining the likelihood that customers will make a recommendation. Either way, the end result is measurement by proxy; you attempt to determine one attitude or intention by measuring another. Doing so can create significant measurement noise and render your measurements useless in the process.

To highlight the point, let's look more closely at task completion.

Some tools measure task completion as a proxy for customer satisfaction. The underlying theory assumes that when a customer completes a task, he or she must therefore be satisfied.

That theory falls apart if a software update takes 10 minutes to download and another 20 minutes of struggle and frustration to install. The customer may have completed the task but is far from satisfied and may never return. Worse, the customer may say negative things to others and generate negative word of mouth.

Here's another example. Say you visit a store to find a special tie for a party you will attend tonight. You find the tie, but locating an employee to ring up your purchase is a challenge. After 10 minutes of searching, you find a salesperson. He is less than friendly, bordering on rude. Do you still buy the tie? Yes, because you don't have time to go elsewhere, but as you leave the store, you vow never to return.

At the party you receive a nice compliment on the tie (your shopping experience was awful, but your fashion sense is impeccable), and you tell the story about the terrible service you received, compounding the impact of your bad experience by generating negative word of mouth.

Task completion measures only—no surprise—whether a task was completed; it does not measure satisfaction and does not measure future intentions. It is a poor stand-in for customer satisfaction, but since the data can be gathered fairly easily, many businesses and even experts yield to temptation and use it as a proxy for customer satisfaction.

Using proxies is easy. Measuring well is hard. The result of using proxies is measurement and management by inference rather than management based on real data, real intelligence, and real knowledge.

Some people may be likely to recommend Whole Foods, especially if they wish to be perceived as health and environment conscious. On the other hand, some may not be as likely to recommend the Walmart grocery department to their friends, even though they are incredibly loyal Walmart customers. A number of products—deodorants, toilet paper, dandruff shampoos—fall into this recommendation paradigm. We tend not to share our dirty laundry or our less-than-flattering secrets.

Personality can also play a major role in whether we recommend products or services. Many highly loyal customers simply do not recommend products or companies to others.

Perceived perception also can greatly influence whether you are likely to recommend, but perception does not have the same impact on customer loyalty. Say you find great clothing at a discount retailer. Some may recommend the discount retailer to others, but many will not because they prefer that others assume they buy their clothing from high-end retailers. The influence of perception affects not their level of loyalty but their likelihood to recommend.

Finding ways to get customers to recommend your business and measuring their likelihood to recommend your business is a smart approach and often generates substantial revenue. But never use recommendations as a proxy for satisfaction or loyalty, and never use satisfaction as a proxy for recommendations or loyalty. And while it should go without saying, never use loyalty as a proxy for satisfaction or recommendations.

If you decide to measure recommendations, then by all means measure recommendations, but never try to infer loyalty in the process. The relationship between recommendations and loyalty is not causal, even if at times it does show correlation.

Research from universities and corporations around the world consistently proves that satisfaction is causal and a key driver of recommendations and customer loyalty.

Common Measurement Mistake #11: Keep It Simple—Too Simple

The keep-it-simple approach does not work for measuring customer satisfaction (or, really, for measuring anything regarding customer attitudes and behaviors).

Customers are complex individuals who make decisions on the basis of a number of criteria—most rational, some less so. Asking three or four questions does not create a usable metric or help to develop actionable intelligence. Still, many companies take this approach and make major strategic decisions—and often compensate their executives—on the basis of a limited and therefore flawed approach to measurement.

Great managers do not make decisions on the basis of hunches or limited data; "directionally accurate" is simply not good enough when our companies and our customers are at stake. Great managers also pay attention.

An Overview of Measurement and Model Analysis Methods

A ForeSee Technical White Paper

Russ Merz, PhD, Research Director, ForeSee

We are providing this white paper on the methodology behind ForeSee's customer experience metrics for people (such as Alex, from Chapter 1) who are interested in a more in-depth understanding of how the modeling works.

Introduction

Background: The methodology behind ForeSee's customer experience models and technology has a proven relationship with customer spending,[1] shareholder value,[2,3] cash flows,[4] and business

---

[1] Claes Fornell, Roland T. Rust, and Marnik G Dekimpe, "The Effect of Customer Satisfaction on Consumer Spending Growth," Journal of Marketing Research 47, no. 1 (2010): 28.

[2] Claes Fornell, Sunil Mithas, Forrest Morgeson, and M. S. Krishnan, "Customer Satisfaction and Stock Prices: High Returns, Low Risk," *Journal of Marketing* 70, no. 1 (2006): 3.

[3] Eugene Anderson, Claes Fornell, and Sanal Maznancheryl, "Customer Satisfaction and Shareholder Value," *Journal of Marketing* 68, no. 4 (October 2004): 172.

[4] Thomas S. Gruca and Lopo L. Rego, "Customer Satisfaction, Cash Flow, and Shareholder Value," *Journal of Marketing* 69 (July 2005): 115–130.

performance.[5] The underlying theory and modeling approach supporting the index are backed by more than 80 years of rigorous scientific inquiry in the fields of consumer psychology and psychometrics, coupled with advanced analytic techniques from statistics and econometrics. While applicability of this methodology to the management of commercial product and service companies has been repeatedly demonstrated in the literature,[6,7] this paper provides a basic description of the underlying measurement and model analysis methods that are used by ForeSee in the design, development, and delivery of products.

The purpose of this paper is to provide the reader with an overview of how ForeSee uses measurement and analysis methods to meet the performance measurement requirements of the business community and improve the management and delivery of their products and services to customers. This is accomplished by:

- An examination of how ForeSee has incorporated the ACSI-derived technology into ForeSee's portfolio of products. This section focuses on highlighting the critical elements of the ForeSee measurement and analysis methods that provide highly diagnostic performance measurements coupled with sensitive improvement prescriptions and powerful prognostic capabilities.

- Summarizing the major components of ForeSee's measurement and model analysis methods and the benefits realized by managers.

[5]Neil Morgan and Lopo Rego, "The Value of Different Customer Satisfaction and Loyalty Metrics in Predicting Business Performance," *Marketing Science* 25, no. 5 (September–October 2006): 426.

[6]Claes Fornell, Michael D. Johnson, Eugene W. Anderson, Jaesung Cha, and Barbara Everitt Bryant, "The American Customer Satisfaction Index: Nature, Purpose, and Findings," *Journal of Marketing* 60 (October 1996): 7–18.

[7]Eugene W. Anderson, Claes Fornell, and Roland T. Rust, "Customer Satisfaction, Productivity and Profitability: Differences between Goods and Services," *Marketing Science* 16, no. 2 (Summer 1997): 129–145.

- Comparing ForeSee's methods with some of the more common alternative solutions offered by competing firms.

- Providing technical appendixes with in-depth discussions of various aspects of the ForeSee methods.

- Documenting the scientific basis of the ForeSee methods by numerous references to secondary literature throughout the paper and in the bibliography.

The Three Essential Questions for Managers

As discussed in Chapter 6, the management of customer experiences across multiple points of contact requires measurement systems that address three essential management questions:

"How are we doing?"

The system must measure all areas of the customer's experience and provide accurate and precise diagnostic measurement of performance in each area.

"What should we do?"

The system should provide managers the capability to prescribe two things: (1) what performance improvement targets are needed to enhance customer experiences and (2) how they should be prioritized.

"Why should we do it?"

Managers need a system with the predictive power for assessing how resources allocated to improvement targets will affect future business outcomes and ROIs before they make the investment.

The measurement-based models built and delivered by ForeSee help managers answer these questions and provide support for their decisions. The design and development of ForeSee's products are based on:

- Validated cause-and-effect theoretical frameworks.

- Voice-of-the-customer (VOC) input from surveys.

- Leading-edge analysis using the latest *structural equations modeling* algorithm.

The Theoretical Framework

The essence of ForeSee's methodology can be addressed in three parts: consumer behavior theory, psychometrics, and statistics. The basic framework is derived from consumer behavior theory backed by knowledge and empirical findings from 80 years of social psychology research, along with an additional 20 years of econometric research by the American Customer Satisfaction Index (ACSI), developed by Dr. Claes Fornell at the University of Michigan.

Consistent with these findings, ForeSee's measurement systems are based on models that *measure and statistically link* the three levels of a customer's thought processes that occur as a result of an experience with a product or service (illustrated in Figure D.1):

- *Perceptions of the performance* delivered by the various facets of the product and/or service experience.

- Overall *attitudinal evaluation* of the experience (such as customer satisfaction).

- *Future behavioral intentions* toward the product or service in question.

These measures are embedded in a *model of cause-and-effect linkages* that allow for three distinct benefits, each of which addresses one of the previous managerial questions (see Figure D.2 for a summary):

1. Performance scores for measures at each level of the model (product or service performance, satisfaction, and intentions) provide the *diagnostic* capability of the system.

Figure D.1 Cause-and-Effect Network of Measures

**Figure D.2   The Benefits Received from ForeSee's
Measurement Products**

Managerial Needs $\longrightarrow$ ForeSee Benefits Delivered	
Three Strategic Questions: DSSs for managing customer experiences should address:	**Powerful Diagnostic Capability** Use of valid, reliable, and sensitive scientific measurement ensures *highly accurate performance metrics* that managers can use confidently to assess customer experiences.
1. "How are we doing?" Can it provide accurate and meaningful performance measures at any point in time and across time?	
2. "What should we do?" Can it provide improvement priorities and targets for investments?	**Prescriptive Guidance** Advanced modeling algorithms result in *prioritized improvement guidelines that optimize resource allocations.*
3. "Why should we do it?" Can it make predictions of financially relevant future outcomes and assist in the calculation of ROI before the investment is made?	**Prognosis of Future Outcomes** The combined cause-and-effect framework provides *tools for the prediction of future outcomes that yield realistic ROI calculations.*

2. Quantification of the linkages between the perceived experiences and attitudinal evaluation. These are *prescriptive* linkages that quantify the changes that are necessary at the experience level to affect the greatest amount of change in the subsequent evaluation level.

3. Quantification of the linkages between the attitudinal evaluation and future intentions provides users with the tools for making *prognoses* about future financially relevant outcomes from improvement investments before the investments are made.

For any customer point of contact, this set of metrics, with their cause-and-effect linkages, gives decision makers an unequaled ability to manage the economic or relationship value of the customer base by providing marginal resource allocation guidance for product and service quality.[8] In the following sections, each of these facets (diagnostic capability, prescriptive guidance, and prognosis of future outcomes) is described in detail.

What Are the Technology Platforms Used by ForeSee?

The products and services delivered by ForeSee are produced from a combination of technology platforms that are unique in their combination in ForeSee. In Figure D.3, the five groups of technology platforms are organized around three sets of processes: data capturing, data refining, and knowledge sharing.

1. Data capturing is concerned with using technologies to collect data about customers, either through the use of surveying techniques (questionnaires) or through observation (recording website travel patterns).

2. Data refining uses advanced statistical technologies to build models of customer satisfaction or other constructs, while usability analysis uses clinical techniques to analyze the construction and functioning of websites that customers experience.

---

[8]The *marginal resource allocation* concept is sometimes called derived importance. In the cause and effect measurement networks executed by ForeSee, all experience facets are fundamentally important to the customer/citizen. However, from a prescriptive perspective, the concern centers on how to achieve the greatest amount of change in a desired outcome (e.g., satisfaction), so the issue is most efficient marginal allocation of resources—not the reallocation of resources. An efficient allocation of resources is an allocation that satisfies the rule marginal benefit = marginal cost for each area of investment.

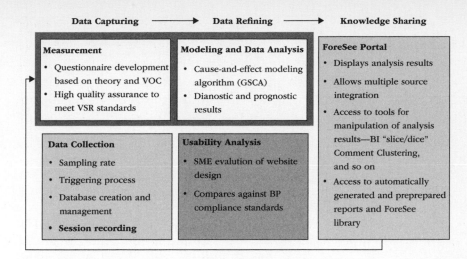

Figure D.3   The ForeSee Technology Platforms

3. Knowledge sharing is accomplished through the application of technologies that focus on the presentation and manipulation of the knowledge collected and refined in the first two stages. This paper addresses two of these platforms: measurement and modeling and data analysis.

Measurement

Superior performance measurement requires *reliability* and *validity* for statistical precision, and it also requires *sensitivity* for statistical power (see Figure D.4 for a summary of the characteristics).

- **Reliability:** Reliability is the quality of a measurement tool that allows it to obtain similar results over time and across situations. (This is also referred to as the *internal consistency* of a measure.) It is the degree to which measures are free from random error and therefore yield consistent results.
  - Example: A rifle that is fired at a target the same way each time by the same rifleman should result in the same pattern

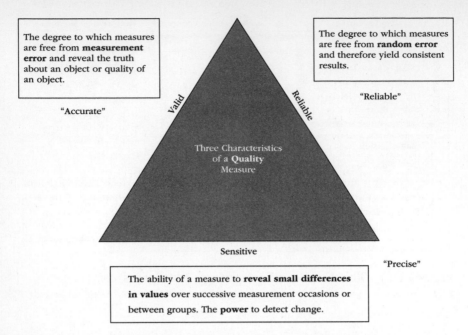

The degree to which measures are free from **measurement error** and reveal the truth about an object or quality of an object.

"Accurate"

Valid

Reliable

The degree to which measures are free from **random error** and therefore yield consistent results.

"Reliable"

Three Characteristics of a **Quality** Measure

Sensitive

"Precise"

The ability of a measure to **reveal small differences in values** over successive measurement occasions or between groups. The **power** to detect change.

Figure D.4 The Characteristics of a Quality Measure

of hits each time it is fired. If it does, then the rifle is considered to be reliable. If it doesn't, then there may be a flaw in the construction of the rifle (the sights are loose) that prevents it from being consistent. (See Figure D.5 for an illustration of this concept.)

- **Validity:** Validity is the quality of a measurement tool to measure what we intend it to measure. In other words, extending the rifle analogy, does the rifleman hit the bull's-eye of the target? It is the degree to which measures are free from measurement error and reveal the truth about an object or a quality of an object.

  - For example, in measuring intention to buy, if a question is not worded correctly, there could be a systematic bias to identify brands "I wish I could afford" rather than the brand usually purchased.

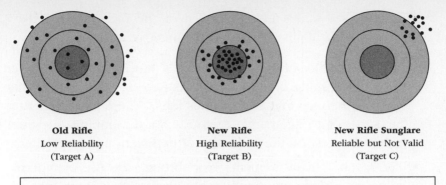

Old Rifle
Low Reliability
(Target A)

New Rifle
High Reliability
(Target B)

New Rifle Sunglare
Reliable but Not Valid
(Target C)

Reliability versus Validity: Reliability, although necessary for validity, is not in itself sufficient. Target A illsutrates low reliability (shots are ungrouped) and low validity (very few hit the target—high error). Target C illustrates high reliability (tightly grouped) with no validity (none hitting the intended target). Target B shows high reliability (tight grouping) and validity (most hitting the intended target—low error).

Figure D.5 A Comparison of Two Measurement Quality Characteristics: Reliability and Validity

- **Sensitivity:** The sensitivity of a measurement tool is important, particularly when changes in attitude or other hypothetical constructs are under investigation. Sensitivity refers to the ability of an instrument to identify variability in stimuli or responses over successive measurement occasions or between groups (*power to detect change*).

  - Adding additional questions or items can increase the sensitivity of a single-question or single-item scale.

  - In other words, because index measures allow for a greater range of possible scores, they are more sensitive than single-item scales.

ForeSee uses an advanced measurement and analysis system that combines best practices from psychometric science with an advanced structural equation-modeling algorithm that ensures potent levels of *precision* (validity combined with reliability) and *power* (sensitivity—ability to detect change).

What are the salient characteristics of the measures, used by ForeSee, that make them superior to competitive approaches?

- The use of voice-of-the-customer (VOC) techniques to discover the true meaning of a customer's experience and convert the customer's voice into survey questions.[9] These techniques are far superior to alternative methods for developing questionnaires that rely on the judgment or experience of researchers.

- Reduction of measurement error through the use of multiple measures of important experience factors (see Figure D.6 for an illustration) and satisfaction levels. It is a well-documented scientific fact that the use of multiple-item measures is far superior to single items for capturing the underlying truth of customer experiences and satisfaction. Multiple-item measures are the best way to measure intangible psychological concepts such as performance perceptions and attitudes, since a single measure has a very high probability of missing the target. Why this is so is addressed in this section.

- The derivation of optimal measure weights based on the cause-and-effect relationships between experiences, evaluations, and intentions for combining the multiple measures into a single index.

The measurement method used by ForeSee relies on advanced psychometric measurement theory as the basis for developing valid and reliable multiple-item measures. In general, there are three reasons for using multi-item measures.[10]

1. The first issue relates to the *specificity* of individual items with respect to a particular trait. Single-item measures usually have lower correlations with the particular phenomena being investigated and may also be correlated with other characteristics or phenomena at the same time. For example, on a spelling test,

[9]Abbie Griffin and John Hauser, "The Voice of the Customer," *Marketing Science* 12, no. 1 (Winter 1993): 1.

[10]Jum C. Nunnally, *Psychometric Theory*, 2nd ed. (New York: McGraw-Hill, 1978), 66–67.

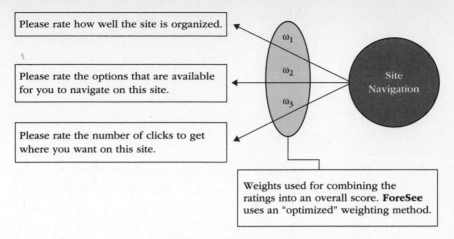

Figure D.6   An Example of a Multiple-Item Measure

the correct spelling of the word *umpire* may reflect the spelling ability of the test taker, but it also may reflect the speller's interest in baseball. A child who spent much time reading baseball stories might spell the word correctly even though he or she was a poor speller in general. This lack of specificity is a serious problem that can be remedied by the use of multiple measures, assuming that the measures are well designed.

2. A second issue in measurement is the ability of the measure to make fine *distinctions* between individuals. The greater the ability of a measure to make fine distinctions between individual respondents, the more sensitive the measure for detecting changes. Dichotomous measures (e.g., yes/no or top-box) categorize respondents into two categories at most. A five-point or seven-point scale increases the number of distinctions to five or seven. In most measurement situations, it is desirable to make as many fine distinctions among respondents as possible, and this can seldom be done with a one-item measure. Foresee's index approach uses three 10-point items that can make very fine distinctions between respondents because an individual's score is the average of the three ratings. This allows a wide range of possible groupings from one group (if everyone in the sample answered all questions the same—an unlikely scenario) to an upper limit of n groups, where n = number of respondents.

3. The third issue is that individual items have considerable random *measurement error*; this is because any single item is basically unreliable in its ability to accurately measure a psychological phenomenon. This can be demonstrated by asking respondents to repeat a test procedure after a period of time. They may give a rating of 3 on one measurement occasion and then indicate a 5 on the next repetition of the rating. This randomness in the ratings means that a single item cannot be trusted to give a reliable measurement of a psychological construct such as intelligence. This unreliability averages out when scores on numerous items are combined to obtain a total score, which is then highly reliable.

Fundamentally, the main focus in measurement should be on ensuring measure validity. Although there are different types of validity, the most important is *construct validity*—whether the measure specifically measures what it purports to measure.

- Traditional survey providers often violate construct validity. For example, while there are a number of ways to measure satisfaction, most firms make the mistake of treating satisfaction as a simple binary concept—simple in the sense that only one question is used, binary in the sense that customers are categorized as either satisfied or dissatisfied (a so-called top-box approach), often in percentage terms (e.g., we have 80 percent satisfied customers) or frequency counts. This approach is flawed because it violates the three rules and consequently does not provide sufficiently valid information in a reliable manner[11] (this is because there is more measurement error in top-box measures and a

---

[11]Binary or dichotomous measures (also known as *nominal scales*) have two to three times the amount of error around the estimated population parameter (which is a proportion) than measures based on 10-point interval-scaled measures (usually means) at the same confidence level.

lower likelihood of detecting a change in customer satisfaction). Given the low quality of the resulting metric, it is not surprising that many firms fail to find any relationship between quality and satisfaction or between satisfaction and profit.

- As an illustration, compare satisfaction, as a concept, to intelligence. Both are multidimensional (i.e., they possess many different aspects), and they are not directly observable (i.e., one cannot see intelligence or satisfaction by observing somebody). Any attempt to measure intelligence by a simple question (are you dumb or smart?) is not likely to yield useful information. It is not reasonable to think that one can assess a person's intelligence by a single question (or by a single test question). Likewise, it is not reasonable to assume that one can capture the concept of satisfaction by a single overall question. (What if the target is missed? There is no perfect measure.)

- The same logic also applies to the many different experiences that customers have with products or services. Each experience is multifaceted. To get a true unbiased picture of what customers are experiencing requires a number of questions (three to five is usually sufficient) to triangulate on the essence or truth of the experience. This is essential to have a valid measurement tool. As illustrated in Figure D.7, the more overlapped (and highly correlated) the individual measures are, the more valid (or true) the resulting combined measure is likely to be—the greater the likelihood of hitting the target.[12]

---

[12]Note that just because a measure uses multiple indicators does not ipso facto result in a valid measure. It depends on how the indicators were developed. Questionnaire items that are based on the judgment or guesswork of the researcher may be completely unrelated to the concept being measured. The result will be a flawed multi-item measure that may give reliable results—but it is important to note that just because a measure uses multiple indicators does not ipso facto result in a "valid" measure. It depends on how the indicators were developed. Questionnaire items that are based on the judgment or guess work of the researcher may be completely unrelated to the concept being measured. The result will be a flawed multi-item measure that may give reliable results but completely "miss" the target. Only by using VOC qualitative methods can one be reasonably confident that the customer measures are valid.

Observed Score = True Score + Measurement Error

66%   34%

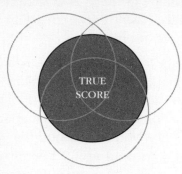

The more overlapped (and highly correlated) the individual measures are the more valid (or true) the resulting combined measure is likely to be—that is, the greater the likelihood of hitting the target.

Figure D.7   Measurement Error for Single-Item Measures Is High Compared to Multiple-Item Measures

Clearly, all measurement involves some degree of error. Ryan, Buzas, and Ramaswamy (1995) found that the measurement approach used by ForeSee leads to an increase in precision (expressed as confidence intervals) over traditional methods by 20 to 30 percent. This can lead to a direct reduction in sample size requirements on the average by 22 percent and still obtain the same precision as conventional methods. Also, the explanatory power with respect to the consequences of satisfaction (e.g., behavioral intentions) is 56 percent better than with conventional methods. This is a result of using multiple measures for overall satisfaction.[13,14] The increase in measurement precision implies that smaller samples can be used with the same measurement precision as traditional methods, which results in cost savings for the client (or, alternatively, in higher precision with the same sample size).

---

[13]Claes Fornell, Byong-Duk Rhee, and Youjae Yi, "Direct Regression, Reverse Regression, and Covariance Structure Analysis," *Marketing Letters* 2, no. 3 (1991): 309–320.

[14]Michael J. Ryan, Thomas Buzas, and Venkatram Ramaswamy, "Making Customer Satisfaction Measurement a Power Tool," *Marketing Research* 7, no. 3 (Summer 1995): 11–16.

Without enough precision in a measure, it is almost impossible to know whether a desired outcome has been achieved.[15] The reason is that lack of precision shows up as random variation in the measure. As a result, it will be much more difficult to identify how satisfaction (or other targeted metric) levels change as management institutes quality improvements. Overall, the importance of the gain in precision that a multiple-item measurement system offers can hardly be understated.

Exhibit 1: Difference between Precision and Power

After good measures have been identified, a major issue in measurement is how best to combine the multiple measures into their respective indexes—the formation of what is known as a *measurement model* (see Figure D.8). The method chosen can have important

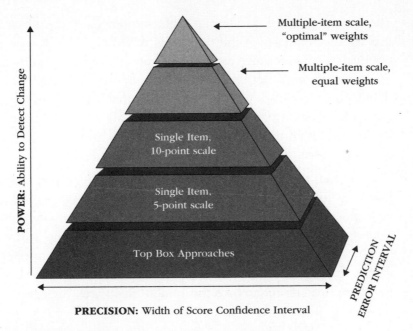

Figure D.8   Measurement Power and Precision

[15]John R. Hauser, Duncan I. Simester, and Birger Wernerfelt, "Internal Customers and Internal Suppliers," *Journal of Marketing Research* 33, no. 3 (August 1996): 268.

effects on the analysis results, especially if the results will be used for dispensing prescriptive guidance and making prognoses of future outcomes.

The typical ForeSee measurement system is based on a network of multiple-measure concepts that are linked together in a cause-and-effect framework. The scores of the various experience indexes, the customer satisfaction index, and the future intention outcomes are a function of the simultaneous optimization of the entire framework (see Figure D.9). This empirical process is superior to any other method for ensuring prescriptive and prognostic power.

For example, in developing a satisfaction index, some firms use relative weights derived from the factor analysis[16] of a number of questions about different aspects of product or service on quality.

- The resulting index is simply a consequence of the shared aspects (correlation) of the questions without regard to some optimizing criterion such as a dependent variable like customer retention or other desired behavioral outcome. A particularly debilitating drawback of this approach is that if there are more questions about a particular attribute, that attribute will have a disproportionate representation in the index and can bias the resulting score.

- The fact that quality aspects correlate among themselves often has little to do with customers' satisfaction levels, yet some firms persist in using this confounded measure by mixing customers' experiences with their satisfaction levels—the causes are lumped together with the effects. Since the weights applied to the variables to create the satisfaction index are based on the intercorrelations among the quality measures themselves,

---

[16]The purpose of factor analysis is to discover simple patterns in relationships among the variables. In particular, it seeks to discover whether the observed variables can be explained largely or entirely in terms of a much smaller number of variables called *factors*.

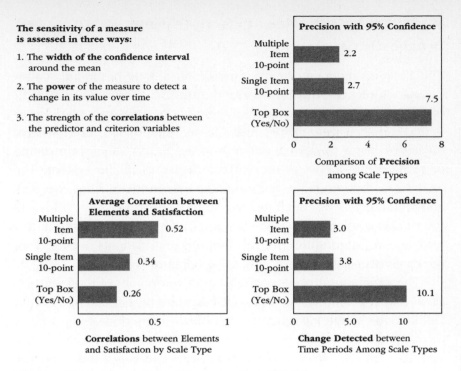

The sensitivity of a measure is assessed in three ways:

1. The **width of the confidence interval** around the mean

2. The **power** of the measure to detect a change in its value over time

3. The strength of the **correlations** between the predictor and criterion variables

Precision with 95% Confidence

Multiple Item 10-point: 2.2

Single Item 10-point: 2.7

Top Box (Yes/No): 7.5

Comparison of **Precision** among Scale Types

Average Correlation between Elements and Satisfaction

Multiple Item 10-point: 0.52

Single Item 10-point: 0.34

Top Box (Yes/No): 0.26

Correlations between Elements and Satisfaction by Scale Type

Precision with 95% Confidence

Multiple Item 10-point: 3.0

Single Item 10-point: 3.8

Top Box (Yes/No): 10.1

Change Detected between Time Periods Among Scale Types

Figure D.9   Assessing Measure Sensitivity

there is little reason to expect that the resulting indexes have any relationship with performance outcomes such as customer retention.

- Thus, this weighting scheme is based on an irrelevant criterion (intercorrelations as opposed to optimizing on an objective criterion). To be useful, a performance index or a satisfaction index must be based on a more relevant criterion (e.g., repurchase or willingness to pay).[17]

---

[17]Other firms use even less sophisticated methods for combining individual items into a satisfaction index by relying on summing or averaging the ratings on the various questionnaire items.

Model Analysis Provides Prescriptive and Prognostic Capabilities

The ForeSee modeling analysis relies on a state-of-the-art statistical algorithm known as generalized structure components analysis (GSCA) to empirically produce a system of optimally weighted scores or indexes. It is *optimal* because the weights for the multiple-item measures in the model are derived on the basis of the optimization of relationships between the various measures in the system. The analysis method estimates the missing parameters (loadings, weights, and path coefficients) such that the sum of squares of all residuals in the model is minimized across all respondents using an alternating least squares algorithm. The resulting optimal weights are used for the calculation of scores or indices (see Figure D.10).[18]

The weighting process used in the development of the measurement model is a critical first part of ForeSee's measurement systems. Unlike other weighting schemes, an objective criterion of importance to managers (minimization of error) is used to optimally weight the various measures in the product or service quality and customer satisfaction indexes. Since the weights are determined on the basis of the performance-satisfaction-behavior relationships in the model, this minimizes the common problem (experienced by competitors using less sophisticated weighting schemes) that an increase in a precursor index (e.g., service quality) does not lead to an increase in a successor index (e.g., customer satisfaction).

Prescriptive Guidance: Impacts versus Importance

The connective pathways between the experience indexes, customer satisfaction, and behavioral intentions play an important role in the determination of the weights used for score calculation. But

---

[18]For a detailed description of the optimization procedure, see Heungsun Hwang and Yoshio Takane, "Generalized Structured Component Analysis," *Psychometrika* 69 (2004): 81–99.

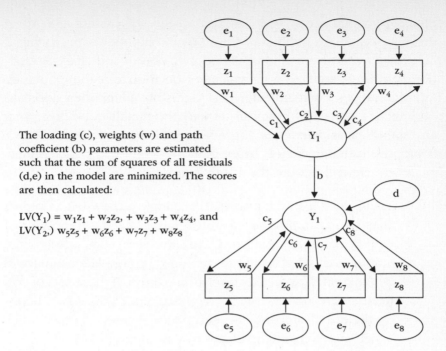

The loading (c), weights (w) and path coefficient (b) parameters are estimated such that the sum of squares of all residuals (d,e) in the model are minimized. The scores are then calculated:

$$LV(Y_1) = w_1z_1 + w_2z_2, + w_3z_3 + w_4z_4, \text{ and}$$
$$LV(Y_2,) \ w_5z_5 + w_6z_6 + w_7z_7 + w_8z_8$$

Figure D.10   A Generalized Structured Component Analysis Schematic

these paths also provide the backbone for the second key feature of ForeSee's measurement system—impacts.

The most fundamental task of any organization (commercial or government) is the efficient allocation of scarce resources needed to accomplish desired performance outcomes. The ForeSee analysis technology quantifies the impact of experience changes on satisfaction and, in turn, the impact of satisfaction on future behavior. Managers can then use this information for efficient resource allocation. What are the properties of the ForeSee modeling analysis that make this possible?

The ForeSee modeling analysis is a cause-and-effect system that isolates the effects of a change in an experience on the change in customer satisfaction (and the subsequent change in desired behavioral outcomes). It is also characterized by a simultaneous treatment of all its components (i.e., quality, satisfaction, intentions). All of these aspects make it different from other competitive approaches.

It is generally not well understood, but a cause-and-effect assumption is made every time a management decision is made ("if we do x, y will happen"). Unfortunately, managers often base their decisions on hunches, cross tabs, or correlation coefficients that do not support any sort of causal inferences. ForeSee's modeling analysis is different. It supports causal inferences based on considerable scientific backing.

There are two reasons for this difference:

1. The first is somewhat technical. The logic is the same as in path analysis and covariance structure analysis: the decomposition of correlations into causal paths. This involves a comparison of the empirical correlations in the data and the correlations imposed by the model (expected correlation matrix). If those sets of correlations are identical (within sampling error), there is evidence for the causal structure imposed by the theoretical model (e.g., experience component x leads to customer satisfaction).

2. The second important point concerns what is meant by effect. The ForeSee system defines this as the marginal effect of component x on y when other components are held constant—that is, the effect of a *change* in x on y. If we graph x on the horizontal axis and y on the vertical axis, it is represented by the *slope* of the function, as illustrated in Figure D.11.

It is critical to understand this concept because it is different from what most other competitors provide, and the results may be different from what seems intuitive to the client. Market research firms, for example, often talk about importance and use correlation coefficients as measures of importance. But a high correlation does not imply that a change in x will cause a change in y.

Other firms use "stated" importance measures, but these are equally flawed for the measurement of customer satisfaction. For example,

- Allen and Rao (2000) state that "few, if any, consultants advocate the stated importance framework today. Its shortcomings

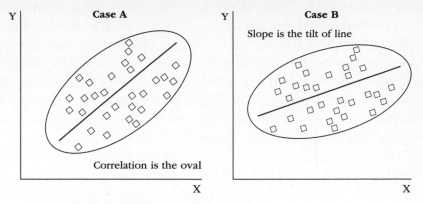

Same Correlation but Different Slopes

Y | Case A Y | Case B
Slope is the tilt of line

Correlation is the oval

X   X

X has the same correlation with Y in both cases,
but in Case A, a change in X will have a larger effect
on Y than in Case B (Slope = ΔY/ΔX).

Figure D.11   Correlation and Slope

have been illustrated with the airline safety example in which stated and derived importance metrics lead to disparate conclusions."[19]

- In addition, such methods increase the length of the questionnaire by requiring shadow importance measures for every perceived performance or experience item included on the questionnaire.

- If ranking or constant sum scaling methods are used instead, then some kind of reduction of measures needs to be performed since respondents are psychically unable to rank or allocate points over more than five to seven measures in a meaningful way. Plus, this approach is not based on the sound psychometric principles of multiple measures and error reduction described previously.

---

[19]Derek Allen and Tanniru Rao, *Analysis of Customer Satisfaction Data* (Milwaukee, WI: ASQ Quality Press, 2000), 70.

Thus, practitioners advocating stated importance methods are basically offering measures that have high levels or unknown levels of error in them, which are then exacerbated when the perceived performance or importance pairs are manipulated by either multiplying or subtracting the measures to arrive at some confounded indication of effect or focus. Resource allocations targeted for the management of customer satisfaction and retention based on measures of this nature are akin to using a dartboard for decision making and are ultimately doomed to failure.[20]

For management to efficiently allocate resources, they need to know what will happen if there are changes (usually improvements) in a certain aspect of the customers' experiences; this is what ForeSee's measurement and analysis system provides. It also means that the use of the term *important* in this context refers to what will happen as a result of a change in something, not what is important per se. For example, both price and quality can be highly correlated to satisfaction, but a change in one of them may produce a greater effect than the other in terms of changing satisfaction.

Standardized versus Unstandardized Impacts

The proper use of analysis tools is critical when quantifying effects. Other satisfaction analysts usually miss this point. For example, some firms in Europe use some of the same theoretical foundations as ForeSee but do not understand that the core structural

---

[20]One customer-perceived value (CVP) practitioner advocates the misguided use of a perceived performance/stated importance measurement framework for the management of customer loyalty for all customers regardless of whether they are current customers or new customers. Why the concept of loyalty is germane to new customers is in itself puzzling. That aside, it is well known that retention strategies are quite different from acquisition strategies in terms of both content and costs. Consequently, the guidance dispensed from this confused measurement approach will certainly result in a misallocation of scarce resources for those who have unfortunately bought into this method.

equation-modeling program is unsuitable without certain modifications to the impacts. Basically, the problem is this:

- To solve the unknowns in equations with latent variables, some restrictions have to be put on the system; otherwise, there would be too many unknowns.

- One set of restrictions quite common in psychology involves setting all variances to unity and all means to zero, that is, to *standardize* all variables.

- However, in terms of *quantifying effects*, standardization renders the results useless and destroys comparability between samples.

- What is then interpreted as importance is the impact of quality x on the spread (standard deviation) of satisfaction. This makes no sense and is, of course, very different from ForeSee measurement and analysis systems (which do not rely on standardization). In practice, it turns out that the results provided by ForeSee are quite different from what the generic structural equation-modeling program provides. The modifications to the analysis algorithm are proprietary and highly technical. They involve a solution to the multicollinearity[21] problem and a rescaling method to ensure comparability of results.

Figure D.12 illustrates the problem with using standardized measures. The example shows two models for two different business units in the same company. The bolded quantities are the unstandardized measures (component means and impacts), and the italicized quantities are the standardized measures (means and impacts). Using unstandardized measures is straightforward—for business unit 1, a one-unit (point) change in the *Autonomy* score yields a 0.22 change in the *JobAtt* score. Using the standardized measures is less

---

[21]For an explanation of multicollinearity, see http://en.wikipedia.org/wiki/Multicollinearity.

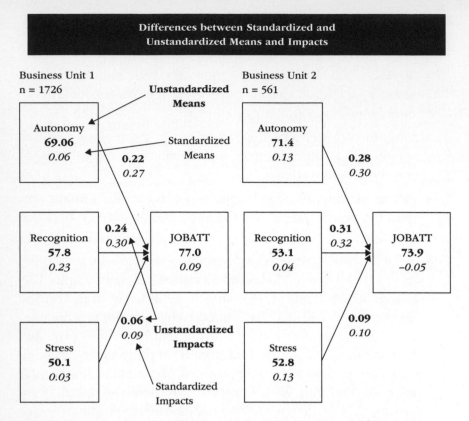

Figure D.12   Standardized and Unstandardized Measures

intuitive—for business unit 1, a one-unit (standard deviation) change in *Autonomy* yields a 0.27 standard deviation change in *JobAtt*.

Notice also the rather large differences in the standardized scores (*Autonomy* has a standardized score of 0.06 and *Recognition* is 0.23) of the variables both within each business unit model (reflecting the different variances for each component) and across business units (*Recognition* in unit 1 is 0.23, and in unit 2 it is 0.04).

This illustrates that because standardized measures are dependent on the variation (or spread) in the data, which can differ from sample to sample, comparability is lost. For this reason, it is best not to compare groups using standardized means or impacts.

The Multicollinearity Problem

A very difficult problem in impact estimation is the isolation of the individual effect of each experience component from other components. This is because respondents tend to see many components as interrelated to some extent. This halo effect can contribute to high correlations between the components, resulting in what is known as multicollinearity. No statistical technique is equipped to handle such multicollinearity, and the result is misleading diagnosis. Some structural equation-modeling techniques can help in reducing multicollinearity but not enough to overcome the problem. The ForeSee modeling incorporates a regularization GSCA computation[22] method to adjust path coefficients for extreme intercorrelations among predictors.

Other consulting firms either ignore the problem, at worst, or conduct a factor analysis of the experience components (thus grouping them together) and then conduct a regression analysis with customer satisfaction or some other dependent variable, using the factor analysis groups. The problems with this approach are so serious that it is virtually impossible to make sense of the results.

- First, it destroys the meaning of the variables as they were originally conceived and measured; the resulting factors must be interpreted post hoc by the analyst, raising questions of validity.

- Second, the imposed correlational structure among the factors is highly artificial and far removed from how the respondents perceived things. The most common way is to force all the factors to be independent from each other (i.e., constrain the factors to have zero correlations with one another). This is most certainly wrong and very different from how the respondents perceived them—the halo effect.

- Third, usually the first factor extracted in a factor analysis solution will be totally overwhelming in terms of information (variance) content, which makes it necessary to use some sort of

---

[22]For details, see H. Hwang, "Regularized Generalized Structured Component Analysis," *Psychometrika* 74 (2009), 517–530.

rotation scheme (introducing yet another artificial device) so the results can be interpreted by the analyst.

- Fourth, factor analysis plus regression represents a piecemeal two-step approach. Any errors existing in the first step are magnified by the second step; an optimal index cannot be constructed under this scenario. The post hoc–interpreted factors may not resemble those quality components that have maximal impact on satisfaction (and subsequent behaviors).

Two other approaches that are often used by firms to analyze satisfaction are stepwise regression and conjoint analysis. Stepwise regression assumes that absolutely nothing is known beforehand and everything is left to a sample of data points. In other words, the solution is an artifact of the data. As the name implies, stepwise regression is a technique for including so-called important variables in a regression in a stepwise manner. The limitations of stepwise regression are:

- Notoriously unstable results.
- High likelihood of omitting a key variable.
- An inferior technology if any theory exists.
- Results of stepwise regression not being evaluated by statistical significance testing.
- Biased regression coefficients.

Stepwise regression will almost never be used in articles published by respectable scientific journals (for the reasons just given).

Conjoint analysis is a different matter. In contrast to stepwise regression, conjoint analysis is a useful scientific method. The problem is that it is not well suited to the measurement and diagnosis of customer satisfaction. The basic problems are that it cannot handle many attributes and that there has to be a level of each quality attribute that the respondent is asked to evaluate. Conjoint analysis is more suitable for new product (or service) development, in which respondents are asked to evaluate different prototypes (on paper) that have different levels of each attribute. For companies using ForeSee's measurement, conjoint analysis or A/B testing can be used to find out what customer satisfaction would be if certain attributes were added to the product (or service) and what the importance of each attribute would be. A nice benefit of conjoint analysis in this context is that it can be done on a single customer.

The Prognosis of Future Outcomes

The ultimate proof of a good measurement system is its ability to make accurate predictions. The models built on the principles described here provide managers with measurement-based tools for better management of intangible assets (such as customers). With the patent-pending process[23] used in the development of the ForeSee measurement and modeling systems, managers in commercial and public service organizations alike can be assured that they are getting valid, reliable, and sensitive measures within a cause-and-effect framework that allows them to evaluate their decisions *before* they make them.

Once an initial model is built, the resultant component scores and impacts provide managers with high-powered metrics for determining the best courses of action (i.e., prescriptive guidance) they can take for accomplishing desired outcomes. Competing measurement systems statically compare self-reported importance measures against current performance measures. The ForeSee measurement and modeling analysis provides a dynamic tool that prescribes for managers the changes that are important in affecting desired customer relationship outcomes (e.g., increases in customer satisfaction). This distinction is a critical one for the success of resource allocation decisions that managers make daily. Without the knowledge of what to expect when executing a plan, decision making devolves to a mere guessing game.

Beyond the prescriptive guidance provided by the impacts onto a target such as customer satisfaction, the ForeSee approach gives

---

[23]U.S. patent application no. 12820650; visit www.uspto.gov for more information.

managers the ability to make prognoses about financially relevant future outcomes. For instance, ForeSee has shown the predictive power of its measurement and analysis approach by demonstrating the effect of the Customer Satisfaction Index Score on revenue change among firms in its Top 40 e-Retail Satisfaction Index study (see Figure D.13). In addition, ForeSee has demonstrated that website Customer Satisfaction Score can be used to forecast in-store purchase probabilities up to two weeks after the website visit (see Figure D.14).

Most traditional approaches to market research confuse comparison of levels (e.g., current performance and levels of importance as provided by customers) with marginal contributions (e.g., what should be changed), fail to make the connections to desired performance outcomes (such as economic returns), or both. As discussed

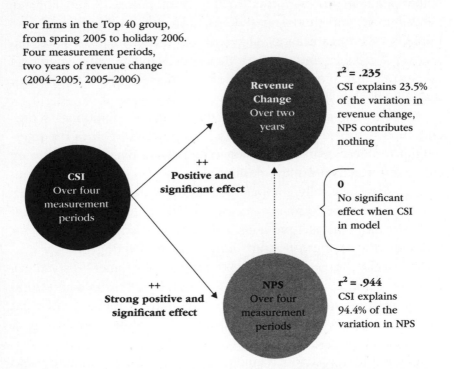

For firms in the Top 40 group, from spring 2005 to holiday 2006. Four measurement periods, two years of revenue change (2004–2005, 2005–2006)

Revenue Change Over two years

$r^2 = .235$
CSI explains 23.5% of the variation in revenue change, NPS contributes nothing

CSI Over four measurement periods

++
Positive and significant effect

0
No significant effect when CSI in model

++
Strong positive and significant effect

NPS Over four measurement periods

$r^2 = .944$
CSI explains 94.4% of the variation in NPS

Figure D.13 The Prognostic Power of Customer Satisfaction on Future Revenue

CSI = Customer Satisfaction Index score, NPS = Net Promoter Score

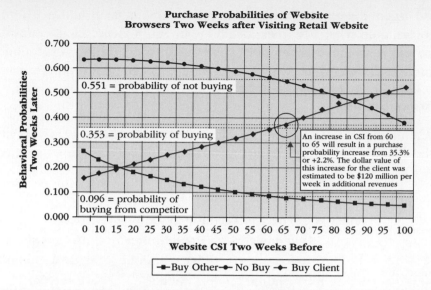

Purchase Probabilities of Website Browsers Two Weeks after Visiting Retail Website

0.551 = probability of not buying

0.353 = probability of buying

0.096 = probability of buying from competitor

An increase in CSI from 60 to 65 will result in a purchase probability increase from 35.3% or +2.2%. The dollar value of this increase for the client was estimated to be $120 million per week in additional revenues

Y-axis: Behavioral Probabilities Two Weeks Later

X-axis: Website CSI Two Weeks Before

0 10 15 20 25 30 35 40 45 50 55 60 65 70 75 80 85 90 95 100

Legend: —■— Buy Other —●— No Buy —◆— Buy Client

Figure D.14   The Prognostic Power of Website CSI to Forecast In-Store Purchase Probabilities

previously, ForeSee's measurement and modeling analysis allows all of these features:

- The perceived performance comparisons for *diagnosing* performance problems.

- The impact of quality components on satisfaction for *prescriptive* guidance about what to fix in a way that makes the most efficient allocation of resources.

- The impact of satisfaction on future behaviors for *prognoses* about what to expect.

The ForeSee system provides specific and quantifiable information about the levels of service and quality and the marginal contribution to both customer satisfaction and profits that will result from a change in a process, service, aspect of quality, or other feature. Unlike other approaches used by consulting firms, ForeSee utilizes a cause-and-effect system that isolates the effects of a change in a quality component on the change in customer satisfaction and the subsequent change in economic returns. This is very different from focusing on what customers deem important. It is also characterized by a systems treatment of all its components (i.e., quality, satisfaction, profit). All of these aspects make it different from other approaches.

Summary Table

A summary of the key points made in the foregoing discussion about the characteristics of ForeSee's technology and the resulting benefits is found in Figure D.15.

Elements of ForeSee Technology Implementation

	Diagnosis "How are we performing?"	Prescription "What should we do?"	Prognosis "What happens if we do?"
Benefits	• Accurate • Meaningful—tied directly to customer experience • Comprehensive—incorporates all aspects of customer experiences • Understandable—simple scoring method • Comparable—by using unstandardized scores	• Prioritizes improvement efforts • Provides impacts that are additive in nature and comparable across groups • Allows for more efficient allocation of resources based on the economic concept of marginality	• Focuses on the dynamic/quantification of change • Increased ability to envision future change in key financial performance outcomes before investing • Enables fact-based ROI calculation

Figure D.15 How the Three Managerial Questions Are Answered

Elements of ForeSee Technology Implementation

	Diagnosis "How are we performing?"	Prescription "What should we do?"	Prognosis "What happens if we do?"
Objective	• Reliable (precision) • Valid • Sensitive (power to detect change)	•Impact or key driver analysis ("What changes are needed to improve customer satisfaction, and what matters the most?")	•Future outcomes prediction ("If changes in experiences occur, what is the financial payoff?")
Characteristics	• "Voice of the customer" (VOC) based • Multiple measures optimally weighted on the basis of strength of relationships in measurement network • Reduced measurement error • Reduced confidence intervals • Uses unstandardized performance scores	• Calculated within the context of a complex cause-and-effect network • Based on unstandardized slopes, not correlation • Optimized with regard to key management objectives (i.e., CS or behaviors) • Control of multicollinearity provides more reliable impact estimation	• "What if" predictive tool • Quantifies the effects of changes across multiple nodes (experience to evaluation to intention) • Future effects are comparative across time, location, or segment given planned investment levels

Figure D.15 *(Continued)*

The Use of 10-Point Scales

ForeSee's use of 10-point scales over commonly used 5-point scales is based on a number of statistical and managerial criteria.

A common basis for recommending five-point scales often rests on the assumed inability of people to reliably discriminate more than five levels on a scale, where offering more than five levels would introduce error into the measurement and offer weaker correlations and lower explanatory power. Research has clearly shown that people can handle more than five pieces of information at one time, particularly depending on their experience in a given area and ability. A 10-point scale is within capabilities of most people with little experience, and in areas of professional expertise, people are able to and will make much finer distinctions.

Because customer satisfaction data are negatively skewed (where customers less frequently use the lower ends of scales), a 5-point scale is really closer to a 3-point scale, and a 10-point scale behaves more like a 7-point scale. Since most customers don't really use the lower ends of scales (values 1 and 2 on a 5-point scale) and mostly use values 3, 4, and 5, a 5-point scale offers little opportunity to differentiate positive responses. This negative skew introduces error into the measurement process and loss of critical, meaningful information compared with a 10-point scale.

Societal norms and the fact that customers typically like companies they do business with tend to limit the number of customers who use the very low ends of response scales. In most cases, if customers are so completely dissatisfied as to use the lower ends of the scale, they will leave and stop doing business with the company. As a result, the 5-point scale effectively turns into a 2- or 3-point scale due to limited response at values 1 and 2.

This compression effect also militates against the common assumption that 5-point scales offer a midpoint that can be considered as the average response, a characteristic not present in 10-point scales. The midpoint argument is valid only if respondents use, or at least contemplate, all points of the scale, and as just discussed, they do not, and responses are consequently negatively skewed.

The use of 10-point scales significantly enhances the information that is transmitted in the surveying process. The increased information content yields:

- Greater precision of results, thereby providing opportunity to reduce sampling costs while maintaining the same precision obtained using five-point scales, or ability to reduce the number of questions on the questionnaire (which also reduces sampling costs as a result of reduced questionnaire length) while maintaining the same measurement reliability offered while using five-point scales.

- Greater ability to link satisfaction results to internal performance measures or measures of employee satisfaction due to the gains in reliability and precision.

Another critical benefit of the use of 10-point scales is in the increase explanatory (as measured by R^2) power gained.

- The gain in R^2 from using the 10-point scale is an important component of accurately identifying the drivers of satisfaction and predicting the economic returns associated with improving satisfaction. In addition, for businesses that have inherently small populations, use of 10-point scales may make the difference in being able to discern these linkages.

Further, the gain is valuable within the context of linking employee compensation to CSI. Higher correlation (R^2) within the model ensures that targeted employee actions will be reflected in the CSI measure and will provide less error within the compensation system (i.e., reducing Type I and Type II errors, where employees are not rewarded when CSI really did change or when employees are rewarded and CSI did not really change). There is one area in which 10-point scales are not appropriate relative to 5-point scales: when there is a desire to label each response point within the scale (e.g., 1 = poor, 2 = not so good, 3 = satisfactory, 4 = good, 5 = outstanding). There are several arguments for not attaching labels to response categories, most notably, (1) added error due to violation of the interval/ratio data assumption, where it can no longer be assumed that the distance between 1 and 2 is the same as the distance between 2 and 3, and so forth, and (2) respondent burden and increased questionnaire length.

Criteria for Evaluating Scales and Supporting Evidence

Cox[24] has reported the statistical benefits of 10- versus 5-point scales.

Information Content

As Figure D.16 illustrates, more information is transmitted in 10- versus 5-point scales—approximately 2.4 bits on a 5-point scale versus 3.4 bits on a 10-point scale.

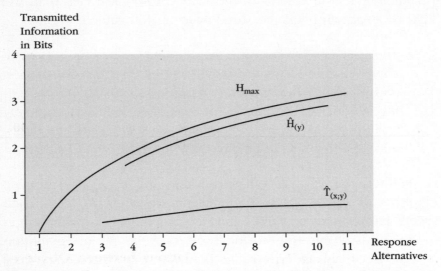

Figure D.16   Relationship between the Number of Response Alternatives and Transmitted Information Found by Bendig and Hughes (1953)

---

[24]Eli P. Cox, "The Optimal Number of Response Alternatives for a Scale: A Review," *Journal of Marketing Research* 17 (November 1980): 407–422.

- Explainability and predictability (R^2).
- Figure D.16 illustrates the significant added benefit of increasing R^2, which we have defined as explainability (ability of the quality components to explain changes in satisfaction) and predictability (ability of satisfaction to explain changes in performance measures).

The largest increased returns are achieved when employing 4- or 5-point scales, but 10-point scales continue to strengthen and tighten the relationships of the entire model.

Mean Squared Correlations

Figure D.17 provides strong evidence that the use of 10-point scales increases the reliability and accuracy of measures over 5-point scales. Specifically, using correlations as the benchmark level (where higher

	Categories						
	2	3	5	7	9	10	14
Items							
2	.551	.657	.718	.736	.744	.747	.752
3	.604	.702	.759	.776	.783	.785	.790
5	.680	.766	.813	.827	.833	.835	.839
7	.725	.804	.845	.857	.863	.865	.868
9	.756	.828	.865	.876	.880	.882	.885
10	.769	.839	.874	.885	.889	.890	.893
14	.810	.868	.899	.907	.911	.912	.915

Figure D.17   Mean Squared Correlations between Observed and True Composites by the Number of Items and Response Alternatives Found by Jenkins and Taber (1977)[25]

[25]C. Douglas Jenkins Jr. and Thomas Taber, "A Monte Carlo Study of Factors Affecting Three Indices of Composite Scale Reliability," *Journal of Applied Psychology* 62, no. 4 (August 1977): 392.

correlations are better, indicating greater reliability), three items on a 10-point scale provide comparable reliability (0.785) to four items on a 5-point scale (taking the average of 0.759 and 0.813, which is 0.785).

More recently, in a study using ratings of service quality in restaurants and stores, Preston and Colman[26] found:

- The rating scales that yielded the least reliable scores turned out to be those with the fewest response categories.

- According to the indexes of validity and discriminating power examined, the scales with relatively few response categories performed worst.

- No corroboration with the contention that reliability and validity of scores are independent of the number of response categories and that nothing is gained by using scales with more than two or three response categories.

- Statistically, scales with small numbers of response categories yield scores that are generally less valid and less discriminating than those with six or more response categories.

- Scales with 5, 7, and 10 response categories were rated as relatively easy to use. Shorter scales with two, three, or four response categories were rated as relatively quick to use, but they were rated extremely unfavorably on the extent to which they allowed the respondents to express their feelings adequately; according to this criterion, scales with 10, 11, and 101 response categories were much preferred.

- On the whole, taking all three respondent preference ratings into account, scales with 2, 3, or 4 response categories were least preferred, and scales with 10, 9, and 7 were most preferred.

- From the multiple indexes of reliability, validity, discriminating power, and respondent preferences used in the study, a remarkably consistent set of conclusions emerged.

---

[26]Carolyn C. Preston and Andrew M. Colman, "Optimal Number of Response Categories in Rating Scales: Reliability, Validity, Discriminating Power, and Respondent Preferences," *Acta Psychologica* 104 (2000): 1.

In general, it was found that scales with two, three, or four response categories yielded scores that were clearly and unambiguously the least reliable, valid, and discriminating. The most reliable scores were those from scales with between 7 and 10 response categories; the most valid and discriminating were from those with 9 or more. The results regarding respondent preferences showed that scales with 2, 3, or 4 response categories once again generally performed worst and those with 10, 9, or 7 performed best. Taken together, the results suggest that rating scales with 7, 9, or 10 response categories are generally to be preferred.

Why Does ForeSee Use Three Indicators of Customer Satisfaction?

Managers must carefully evaluate the multitude of measurement options offered in the marketplace to ensure they use the most accurate, reliable, and valid measurements of customer satisfaction. To squarely address these concerns, ForeSee uses measures of satisfaction that blend state-of-the-art customer satisfaction research theory from leading universities with leading-edge statistical technologies. As Fornell (1992) stated:

The literature on customer satisfaction/dissatisfaction suggests that satisfaction is an overall post-purchase evaluation. There is no consensus on how to measure it, however. Hausknecht (1990) identifies more than 30 different measures that have been used in previous research. Among them, three different facets of satisfaction can be identified—CSB attempts to capture the degree of (1) general satisfaction (as in the studies by Moore and Shuptrine 1984; Oliver and Bearden 1983; Oliver and Westbrook 1982; Westbrook 1980, 1981), (2) confirmation of expectations (as in the studies by Oliver 1977; Swan, Trawick, and Carroll 1981), and (3) the distance from the customer's hypothetical ideal product (similar to the work of Tse and Wilton 1988; Sirgy 1984).

In other words, customer satisfaction is defined as a function of three indicators that are allowed to be measured with error. An advantage over traditional approaches to satisfaction measurement is that causes of satisfaction are not confounded with the phenomenon itself. Other advantages are that the fallibility of measures is acknowledged and taken into account and that the indicators defining customer satisfaction can be weighted such that their composite has maximal impact on loyalty and customer retention.[27]

Specifically, ForeSee uses three concepts to measure customer satisfaction (see Figure D.18) and to explicitly assess the distinct dimensions of customer satisfaction. These concepts also correspond to the levels of satisfaction expressed by Kano. The Kano model is an oft-cited and well-accepted conceptual model of customer satisfaction (see Figure D.19).[28]

- *Overall satisfaction*—This dimension assesses a customer's overall evaluation, quantifying what the Kano model characterizes

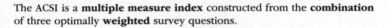

The ACSI is a **multiple measure index** constructed from the **combination** of three optimally **weighted** survey questions.

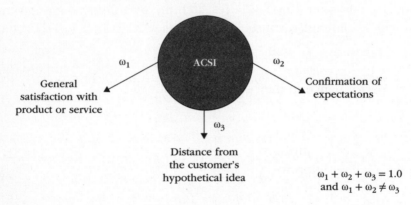

Figure D.18   The American Customer Satisfaction Index

Source: Claes Fornell, "A National Customer Satisfaction Barometer: The Swedish Experience," *Journal of Marketing* 56, no. 1 (1992): 6–21.

---

[27]Claes Fornell, "A National Customer Satisfaction Barometer: The Swedish Experience," *Journal of Marketing* 56, no. 1 (1992): 6–21.

[28]For details about the Kano model, see http://en.wikipedia.org/wiki/Kano_model.

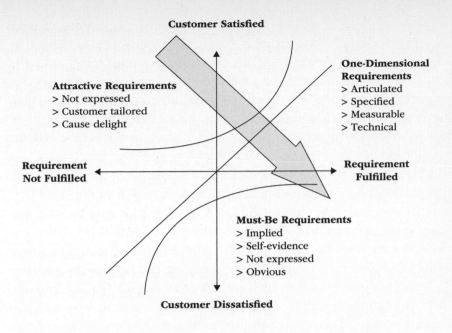

Customer Satisfied

One-Dimensional
Requirements
> Articulated
> Specified
> Measurable
> Technical

Attractive Requirements
> Not expressed
> Customer tailored
> Cause delight

Requirement
Not Fulfilled

Requirement
Fulfilled

Must-Be Requirements
> Implied
> Self-evidence
> Not expressed
> Obvious

Customer Dissatisfied

Figure D.19   The Kano Model of Customer Satisfaction

as evaluation of "performance" or "spoken" attributes. (This dimension of satisfaction encompasses those attributes for which customers reward high performance and punish low performance in their satisfaction ratings.)

- *Meeting expectations*—This dimension provides specific evaluation of what the Kano model characterizes as "basic" or "expected" attributes (i.e., those attributes that *must* be present as a condition for a person to be satisfied; a good example is safety on airplanes). It addresses the disconfirmation theory of customer satisfaction, which states that an individual's satisfaction level with a product or service is strongly related to how well his or her experience either confirms or disconfirms what the customer thought he or she would experience. (The expectations dimension of satisfaction concerns those attributes where customers punish low performance with lower ratings but do not necessarily reward performance beyond their minimum requirements for satisfaction.)

Being ideal—This question provides specific evaluation of what the Kano model characterizes as "surprise" or "delight" attributes (i.e., those aspects of the product or service that are unexpected and add value for the customer). The ideal measure accounts for the fact that customers likely refer to a benchmark or standard when evaluating their experiences with a company's product or service. The ideal measure provides a more absolute evaluation of satisfaction and is based on the collection of experiences an individual has had over time and across industries. Of particular importance is that the ideal dimension complements expectations and helps explain loyalty. For example, *ideal* is why individuals don't always eat fast food. Fast food may be satisfying and meet expectations but may not always be ideal. (This dimension of satisfaction encompasses people's attitudes toward attributes where low or absent performance is not punished but high performance is greatly rewarded through high satisfaction ratings.) Questions based on these three concepts are used to build a composite or multiple-item measure of customer satisfaction that, in addition to its conceptual rigor, offers superior reliability (freedom from measurement error), validity, and precision (of score estimates) over other traditional measures (especially single-item overall measures).[29] Three questions are necessary to achieve these benefits because, as discussed elsewhere, satisfaction is made up of multiple dimensions. Asking only one question severely limits measurement coverage of customer satisfaction and subjects the measurement to bias and measurement error.

Another important point is that by consistently employing these three questions, valid and reliable comparisons can be made across different individuals, market segments, companies, and even industries. This ability is invaluable to clients seeking a valid and relevant basis on which to benchmark their customer satisfaction scores.

Single- versus Multiple-Item Measures

How should customer satisfaction and its causes and effects be measured? Is it sufficient to simply ask customers to rate their satisfaction

---

[29]Michael Ryan, Tom Buzas, and Venkatram Ramaswamy, "Making CSM a Power Tool," *Marketing Research* 7, no. 3 (1995): 11–16.

with a recent experience by checking a yes or no box? If the objective is to simply screen respondents for some further activity, then perhaps a dichotomous or other categorical response is acceptable. But if the intention is to gather data for analysis, then serious problems will ensue. Single-item measures, especially those with limited response categories, possess severe measurement deficiencies that limit their usefulness in advanced statistical analyses of the type usually encountered in consumer satisfaction research.

Differences between Single- and Multiple-Item Measures

In addition to their ubiquitous and common use as screeners in many survey research designs, single-item measures are often used in two additional ways:

1. Those measuring self-reported facts that allow for the *classification* of respondents, such as years of education, age, and number of previous jobs.

2. Those purporting to measure attitudinal and behavioral *psychological constructs*, such as satisfaction, recommendation, or purchase intentions.[30]

Measuring the former with a single item is a commonly accepted practice. Errors from this usage occur largely because of response biases; that is, respondents may not be totally honest about their income level or age. However, the use of single-item measures for psychological constructs is typically discouraged, primarily because they are presumed to have questionable validity and low levels of reliability. This problem stems from the multifaceted and complex nature of most psychological constructs, making it extremely difficult to adequately capture meaning with a single item. There are exceptions to the norm of using only scales to measure psychological constructs. If the construct being measured is sufficiently narrow or is

---

[30]John P. Wanous, Arnon E. Reichers, and Michael J. Hudy, "Overall Job Satisfaction: How Good Are Single-Item Measures?" *Journal of Applied Psychology* 82, no. 2 (1997): 247–252.

unambiguous to the respondent (e.g., the measurement of subjective probabilities, such as future behaviors), a single-item measure may suffice. But for more complex psychological constructs (especially those based on attitudes), it is usually recommended that scales with multiple items be used.

Nunnally and Bernstein (1994), McIver and Carmines (1981), and Spector (1992) discussed the reasons for using multi-item measures instead of a single item for measuring psychological attributes. They identified the following issues:

- First, individual items have considerable random measurement error, that is, are unreliable. In recommending multiple-item scales, Nunnally and Bernstein (1994) state, "Measurement error averages out when individual scores are summed to obtain a total score" (p. 67).

- Second, an individual item can categorize people only into a relatively small number of groups. An individual item cannot discriminate among fine degrees of an attribute. For example, with a dichotomously scored item, one can distinguish between only two levels of the attribute; that is, they lack precision.

- Third, individual items lack scope. McIver and Carmines (1981) say, "It is very unlikely that a single item can fully represent a complex theoretical concept or any specific attribute for that matter" (p. 15). They go on to say, "The most fundamental problem with single item measures is not merely that they tend to be less valid, less accurate, and less reliable than their multi-item equivalents. It is rather, that the social scientist rarely has sufficient information to estimate their measurement properties."

- Thus, their degree of validity, accuracy, and reliability is often unknowable (p. 15). Blalock (1970) has observed, "With a single measure of each variable, one can remain blissfully unaware of the possibility of measurement [error], but in no sense will this make his inferences more valid" (p. 111).

In summary, classic measurement theory holds that single items are at a relative disadvantage to multi-item measures because more items produce replies that are more consistent and less prone to distortion from sociopsychological biases, and this enables the random error of the measure to be canceled out. Hence they are more stable over time, more reliable, and more precise than single-item measures (see Figure D.20 for a point-by-point comparison of the two types of measures).

How Individuals Respond to Questions in a Survey

Many things can influence how individuals respond to survey questions (e.g., mood, events they encountered that day). They may choose yes to a question one day and say no the next day. It is also possible that people give a wrong answer or interpret the question differently over time. Using multiple-item measures mitigates the tendency for individuals to be inconsistent. This is because, as noted before, a multi-item measure has several questions targeting the same issue, and the final composite score is based on all questions. People are less likely to make such mistakes to multiple items, and thus the resulting composite score is more consistent over time.

Many measured social characteristics are broad in scope and simply cannot be assessed with a single question. Multi-item measures are necessary to cover more content of the measured characteristic and to fully and completely reflect the construct domain. These issues are best illustrated with an example. To assess people's job satisfaction, a single-item measure could be as follows: I'm not satisfied with my work (1 = disagree, 2 = slightly disagree, 3 = uncertain, 4 = slightly agree, 5 = agree). To this single question, people's responses can be inconsistent over time. Depending on their mood or specific things they encountered at work that day, they might respond very differently to this single question. Also, people may make mistakes when reading or responding. For example, they might not notice the word *not* and agree when they really disagree. Thus, this single-item measure about job satisfaction can be notoriously unreliable. Another problem is that people's feelings toward their jobs may not be simple. Job satisfaction is a very broad issue, and it includes many aspects (e.g., satisfaction with the supervisor, satisfaction with coworkers,

Points of Comparison	Single-Item Measures	Multiple-Item Measures
Validity—ability to capture the true value of construct	Varies—can be acceptable if correlated with another validated measure of the construct. Without evidence of such convergent validity, it is impossible to assess.	Moderate to high potential for a valid measure. Has a greater likelihood of capturing multiple facets of psychological constructs.
Reliability—ability to be free of random variation; consistency of measurement	Usually low—internal consistency cannot be evaluated, is best assessed by repetitive measures with the same respondent.	Moderate to high potential for measures to be reliable. Coefficient alpha (the basic reliability metric) can be easily computed.
Information content	Relatively low—because of limited number of scale points typically used (e.g., 1–3, 1–5, etc.).	Relatively high because of multifaceted nature. Greater specificity is possible due to multiplier effect.
Statistical power (sensitivity)—ability to accurately detect changes in its value over time	Low if scale is dichotomized (e.g., top-box or NPS), acceptable if 7- to 10-point intervals are used (e.g., behavioral intention—type measures).	Highest levels of sensitivity possible because the number of distinctions between individuals is higher.
Simplicity of administration, analysis, and managerial use	High in all areas.	Low because of the need for more questionnaire items and multivariate analytic techniques. Managerial understanding is often stretched.

Figure D.20 Comparison of Single- and Multiple-Item Measures

Points of Comparison	Single-Item Measures	Multiple-Item Measures
Summary of strengths	• Easy to administer. • Can be collected quickly. • Suitable for very large samples or census studies. • Useful for screening respondents. • Good for collecting factual information (e.g., age, income, etc.). • Useful for low-level descriptive and comparative analyses).	• Greater sensitivity to variations between respondents, allowing finer distinctions among them. • Allows for greater coverage of the different aspects of an unobservable construct (e,g., beliefs, attitudes, and intentions). • Measure reliability can be readily assessed. • Higher levels of potential construct validity. • Best for advanced statistical analyses.
Summary of weaknesses	• Unsuitable for measuring multifaceted attitudinal constructs. • Require calibration with multi-item scales to establish validity. • Reliability can be established only with repeated measures. • Low sensitivity to variation between respondents.	• Require longer questionnaires and more time to collect. • May require larger sample sizes to meet degrees of freedom requirements and to adequately assess validity. • Potential for common methods bias. • Meaning is often difficult for practitioners and managerial users to understand.

Figure D.20 *(Continued)*

satisfaction with work content, satisfaction with pay). Subjects may like certain aspects of their jobs but not others. The single-item measure will oversimplify people's feelings toward their jobs.

A multi-item measure can reduce these problems. The results from a multi-item measure should be more consistent over time. As mentioned earlier, with multiple items, random errors tend to average out. That is, with 10 items, if a respondent makes an error on one item, the impact on the overall score is quite minimal. More important, a multi-item measure allows subjects to describe their feelings about different aspects of their experiences. This greatly improves the precision and validity of the measure. Therefore, multi-item measures are one of the most important and frequently used tools in social science.

Research Evidence

A lengthy stream of research findings in various fields explore the points just articulated, for example:

- In a series of related studies, Nagy (2002); Wanous, Reichers, and Hudy (1997); Wanous and Hudy (2001); and Dolbier, Webster, McCalister, Mallon, and Steinhardt (2005) examined the usefulness of a single-item measure of employee satisfaction. They found support of the use of a single-item scale as a substitute for multi-item measures of the same construct. Loo (2002) challenged these findings by arguing for the use of single-item measures as surrogates for previously validated multiple-item scales.

- Gardner, Cummings, Dunham, and Pierce (1989, 1998) examined the performance of single- versus multiple-item measures of focus of attention at work. They found little difference between the two in terms of validity and common methods bias.

- Desalvo, Fan, McDonell, and Fihn (2005) and Desalvo, Fisher, Tran, Bloser, Merrill, and Peabody (2006) compared single- and multi-item measures of self-rated health to predict mortality and clinical events. They found that the single-item measure of general self-rated health demonstrated good reproducibility, reliability, and strong concurrent and discriminant scale performance with an established multi-item health status measure. In a similar way, Sloan, Aaronson, Cappelleri, Fairclough, and Varricchio (2002) described the strengths and weaknesses of single items and summated scores (from multiple items) as quality of life (QOL) measures. They concluded that no gold standard QOL measure can be recommended because there is no one size fits all. Single items have the advantage of simplicity at the cost of detail. Multiple-item indexes have the advantage of providing a complete profile of QOL component constructs at the cost of increased burden and of asking potentially irrelevant questions. The two types of indexes are not mutually exclusive and can be used together in a single research study or in the clinical setting.

- Wirtz and Lee (2003) found that a single-item customer satisfaction measure was less reliable and explained less variance than competing six-item and four-item satisfaction measures. Gliem and Gliem (2003) reported similar findings for course evaluations made by students.

- In survey research with customers, Drolet and Morrison (2001) advocate trading off the higher reliability of fewer multi-item scales against the greater information content of many single-item measures. Shamir and Kark (2004) suggest the use of single-item measures as a way to control common methods bias.

Overall, these examples from the literature provide a taste for the research examining the use of single-item measures. Figure D.20 provides a summary of the key research findings regarding the characteristics, advantages, disadvantages, and best uses for each type of scale.

Bibliography

Allen, Derek, and Tanniru Rao. *Analysis of Customer Satisfaction Data*. Milwaukee, WI: ASQ Quality Press, 2000.

Anderson, Eugene W., and Claes Fornell. "Foundations of the American Customer Satisfaction Index." *Journal of Total Quality Management* 11, no. 7 (2000).

Anderson, Eugene, Claes Fornell, and Sanal Maznancheryl. "Customer Satisfaction and Shareholder Value." *Journal of Marketing* 68, no. 4 (October 2004): 172.

Anderson, Eugene W., Claes Fornell, and Roland T. Rust. "Customer Satisfaction, Productivity and Profitability: Differences between Goods and Services." *Marketing Science* 16, no. 2 (Summer 1997): 129–145.

Andrews, Frank M. "Construct Validity and Error Components of Survey Measures: A Statistical Modeling Approach." *Public Opinion Quarterly* (1984): 404–442.

Blalock, H. M., Jr. "Estimating Measurement Error Using Multiple Indicators and Several Points in Time." *American Sociological Review 35,* no. 1 (1970): 101–111.

Carmines, E. G., and R. A. Zeller. *Reliability and Validity Assessment*. Thousand Oaks, CA: Sage, 1979.

Cox, E. P. "The Optimal Number of Response Alternatives for a Scale: A Review." *Journal of Marketing Research* 17 (1980): 407.

DeSalvo, Karen B., Vincent S. Fan, Mary B. McDonell, and Stephan D. Fihn. "Predicting Mortality and Healthcare Utilization with a Single Question." *Health Research and Educational Trust* 40, no. 4 (August 2005): 1234–1246.

DeSalvo, K. B., W. P. Fisher, K. Tran, N. Bloser, W. Merrill, and J. Peabody. "Assessing Measurement Properties of Two Single-Item General Health Measures." *Quality of Life Research* 15, no. 2 (March 2006): 191–201.

Dolbier, C. L., J. A. Webster, K. T. McCalister, M. W. Mallon, and M. A. Steinhard. "Reliability and Validity of a Single-Item Measure of Job Satisfaction." *American Journal of Health Promotion* 19, no. 3 (January–February 2005): 194–198.

Drolet, Aimee L., and Donald G. Morrison. "Do We Really Need Multiple-Item Measures in Service Research?" *Journal of Service Research* 3, no. 3 (2001): 196–204.

Falk, R. Frank, and Nancy B. Miller. *A Primer for Soft Modeling*. Akron, OH: University of Akron Press, 1992.

Fornell, Claes. "A National Customer Satisfaction Barometer: The Swedish Experience." *Journal of Marketing* 56, no. 1 (1992): 6–21.

Fornell, Claes, and Jaesung Cha. "Partial Least Squares." In *Advanced Methods of Marketing*, edited by Richard Bagozzi, 52–78. Hoboken, NJ: John Wiley & Sons, 1994.

Fornell, Claes, Michael D. Johnson, Eugene W. Anderson, Jaesung Cha, and Barbara Everitt Bryant. "The American Customer Satisfaction Index: Nature, Purpose and Findings." *Journal of Marketing* 60 (October 1996): 7–18.

Fornell, Claes, and David F. Larcker. "Evaluating Structural Equation Models with Unobserved Variables and Measurement Error." *Journal of Marketing Research* 18, no. 1 (February 1981): 39.

Fornell, Claes, and David F. Larcker. "Structural Equation Models with Unobserved Variables and Measurement Error: Algebra and Statistics." *Journal of Marketing Research* 18, no. 3 (August 1981): 382.

Fornell, Claes, Sunil Mithas, and Forrest V Morgeson III. "The Economic and Statistical Significance of Stock Returns on Customer Satisfaction." *Marketing Science* 28, no. 5 (2009): 820.

Fornell, Claes, Sunil Mithas, Forrest Morgeson, and M. S. Krishnan. "Customer Satisfaction and Stock Prices: High Returns, Low Risk." *Journal of Marketing* 70, no. 1 (2006): 3.

Fornell, Claes, B. D. Rhee, and Y. Yi. "Direct Regression, Reverse Regression, and Covariance Structure Analysis." *Marketing Letters* 20, no. 3 (1991): 309.

Fornell, Claes, Roland T. Rust, and Marnik G Dekimpe. "The Effect of Customer Satisfaction on Consumer Spending Growth." *Journal of Marketing Research* 47, no. 1 (2010): 28.

Gardner, Donald G., L. L. Cummings, Randall B. Dunham, and Jon L. Pierce. "Single-Item versus Multiple-Item Measurement Scales:

An Empirical Comparison." *Educational and Psychological Measurement* 58, no. 6 (1998): 898–915.

Gardner, Donald G., Randall B. Dunham, L. L. Cummings, and Jon L. Pierce. "Focus of Attention at Work: Construct Definition and Empirical Validation." *Journal of Occupational Psychology* 62 (1989): 61–77.

Gliem, Joseph A., and Rosemary R. Gliem. "Calculating, Interpreting, and Reporting Cronbach's Alpha Reliability Coefficient for Likert-Type Scales." 2003 Midwest Research to Practice Conference in Adult, Continuing and Community Education, 82–88.

Gruca, Thomas S., and Lopo L. Rego. "Customer Satisfaction, Cash Flow, and Shareholder Value." *Journal of Marketing* 69 (July 2005): 115–130.

Haladyna, T. M. *Developing and Validating Multiple-Choice Test Items*. Hillsdale, NJ: Lawrence Erlbaum, 1994.

Hauser, John R., Duncan I. Simester, and Birger Wernerfelt. "Internal Customers and Internal Suppliers." *Journal of Marketing Research* 33, no. 3 (August 1996): 268.

Hwang, Heungsun. "Regularized Generalized Structured Component Analysis." *Psychometrika* 74 (2009): 517–530.

Hwang, Heungsun, Naresh K. Malhotra, Youngchan Kim, Marc A. Tomiuk, and Sungjin Hong. "A Comparative Study on Parameter Recovery of Three Approaches to Structural Equation Modeling." *Journal of Marketing Research* 47, no. 4 (August 2010): 699–712.

Hwang, Heungsun, and Yoshio Takane. "Generalized Structured Component Analysis." *Psychometrika* 69 (2004): 81–99.

Lohmoeller, Jan-Bernd. *Latent Variable Path Modeling with Partial Least Squares*. New York: Springer, 1989.

Loo, Robert. "A Caveat on Using Single-Item versus Multiple-Item Scales." *Journal of Managerial Psychology* 17, no. 1 (2002): 68–75.

Louviere, Jordan J., and Towhidul Islam. "A Comparison of Importance Weights/Measures Derived from Choice-Based Conjoint, Constant Sum Scales and Best-Worst Scaling." *Centre for the Study of Choice (CenSoC)*, University of Technology, Sydney, Working Paper No. 04-003 (2004).

McIver, J. P., and E. G. Carmines. *Unidimensional Scaling*. Thousand Oaks, CA: Sage, 1981.

Morgan, Neil, and Lopo Rego. "The Value of Different Customer Satisfaction and Loyalty Metrics in Predicting Business Performance." *Marketing Science* 25, no. 5 (September–October 2006): 426.

Nagy, Mark S. "Using a Single-Item Approach to Measure Facet Job Satisfaction." *Journal of Occupational and Organizational Psychology* 75 (2002): 77–86.

Nunnally, J. C. *Psychometric Theory*. 2nd ed. New York: McGraw-Hill, 1978.

Nunnally, J. C., and I. H. Bernstein. *Psychometric Theory*. 3rd ed. New York: McGraw-Hill, 1994.

Peterson, Robert A., and William R. Wilson. "Measuring Customer Satisfaction: Fact and Artifact." *Journal of Academy of Marketing Science* 20 (Winter 1992): 61–71.

Preston, Carolyn C., and Andrew M. Colman. "Optimal Number of Response Categories in Rating Scales: Reliability, Validity, Discriminating Power, and Respondent Preferences." *Acta Psychologica* 104 (2000): 1.

Ryan, Michael J., Thomas Buzas, and Venkatram Ramaswamy. "Making Customer Satisfaction Measurement a Power Tool." *Marketing Research* 7, no. 3 (Summer 1995): 11–16.

Schott, G. R., and W. Bellin. "An Examination of the Validity of Positive and Negative Items on a Single-Scale Instrument." *Evaluation and Research in Education* 15, no. 2 (2001): 84–94.

Shamir, Boas, and Ronit Kark. "A Single-Item Graphic Scale for the Measurement of Organizational Identity." *Journal of Occupational and Organizational Psychology* 77 (2004): 115–123.

Sloan, Jeff A., Neil Aaronson, Joseph Cappelleri, Dioane Fairclough, and Claudette Varricchio. "Assessing the Clinical Significance of Single Items Relative to Summated Scores." Symposium on Quality of Life in Cancer Patients. *Mayo Clinic Proceedings* 77 (2002): 479–487.

Spector, P. *Summated Rating Scale Construction*. Thousand Oaks, CA: Sage, 1992.

Verlegh, Peeter, W. J. Hendrik, N. J. Schifferstein, and Dick R. Wittink. "Range and Number-of-Levels Effects in Derived and Stated Measures of Attribute Importance." *Marketing Letters* 13 (February 2002).

Wanous, John P., and Michael J. Hudy. "Single-Item Reliability: A Replication and Extension." *Organizational Research Methods* 4, no. 4 (October 2001): 361–375.

Wanous, John P., Arnon E. Reichers, and Michael J. Hudy. "Overall Job Satisfaction: How Good Are Single-Item Measures?" *Journal of Applied Psychology* 82, no. 2 (1997): 247–252.

Wirtz, Jochen, and Meng Chung Lee. "An Examination of the Quality and Context-Specific Applicability of Commonly Used Customer Satisfaction Measures." *Journal of Service Research* 5, no. 4 (2003): 345–355.

Wold, H. "Soft Modelling by Latent Variables: The Nonlinear Iterative Partial Least Squares Approach." In *Perspectives in Probability and Statistics: Papers in Honour of M. S. Bartlett*, edited by J. Gani. London: Academic Press, 1975.

Acknowledgments

Book number two was no easy task and would not have been possible without the help, support, inspiration, and knowledge of many. They all deserve thanks and gratitude. Thanking everyone would take too long, but some cannot be ignored.

It always starts with family. Growing a business is more than a full-time job. Without the support provided by my wife, Laini, none of this would be possible. Her understanding of the many business trips and late-work nights, along with her constant support and encouragement, makes it all possible. I do not have enough words to describe my love for her and my appreciation for all her support.

My three sons—I am not talking about the 1960s sitcom but my three sons, Josh, Danny, and Jake. When ForeSee started in 2001, they were small kids. Now, as the second book is being finished, they are young men. As the company grew, as I grew as a CEO, they grew, too. As they have grown, I have enjoyed seeing their interests broaden, and now we talk about not only Michigan football and basketball but also technology, business, and metrics. That is inspiring. (But we also still talk about Michigan!)

"The team, the team, the team." Without the team from ForeSee, there would be no ForeSee and no book. It is the team that wins, not the individuals, both in sports and in business. There are too many to list, but every individual has contributed to both my individual growth and the growth and success of ForeSee. Every team needs great leaders, and our executive team members at ForeSee are exactly that.

The idea that led to this book came out of a board meeting, and I thank Dr. Claes Fornell, Barry Goldsmith, Noah Walley, and Phil Dur for not only their help in spawning the idea of WoMI and the next generation of Net Promoter but also their support over the years as our business has flourished.

The three most important words in most business used to be "location, location, location." Now they are "customer, customer, customer." I want to thank our clients, whom I consider to be some of our greatest teachers and the ones who will not let us stand still but drive us to keep pushing the envelope and keep innovating.

Without Sarah Allen-Short's hard work, great insights, taskmaster skills, and encouragement, this book would not exist. Larry Rothstein's skill and expertise helped bring it all together. Both Sarah and Larry were instrumental in helping turn the ideas and stories into a book.

My acknowledgments started with family and end with family. I learned many lessons from my father, Jack, that are central to my approach to business and to life. The wisdom he had, learned, and honed over many years of owning and growing a business cannot be found in business books or MBA classes. While I have not mastered it all, every bit I have learned is irreplaceable. Unfortunately, my father is no longer alive, but I hope that, in some way, I carry his wisdom and can pass some of his legacy along to my sons.

Index

277

Index

280

Index